A Knight at the Opera

Heine, Wagner, Herzl, Peretz, and the Legacy of Der Tannhäuser

Shofar Supplements in Jewish Studies

A Knight at the Opera

Heine, Wagner, Herzl, Peretz, and the Legacy of Der Tannhäuser

Leah Garrett

Purdue University Press / West Lafayette, Indiana

Library of Congress Cataloging-in-Publication Data

Garrett, Leah, 1966-
   A Knight at the opera : Heine, Wagner, Herzl, Peretz, and the legacy of der Tannhäuser
/ Leah Garrett.
      p. cm. -- (Shofar supplements in Jewish studies)
   Includes bibliographical references and index.
   ISBN 978-1-55753-601-3 (pbk.) -- ISBN 978-1-61249-153-0 (epdf) -- ISBN 978-1-
61249-152-3 (epub) 1. Wagner, Richard, 1813-1883. Tannhäuser. 2. Tannhäuser. 3.
Heine, Heinrich, 1797-1856. 4. Herzl, Theodor, 1860-1904. 5. Peretz, Isaac Leib, 1851 or
2-1915. I. Title.
   ML410.W1A2943 2012
   830.9'351--dc23
                          2011023379

Cover image: Detail from Tannhäuser by Aubrey Beardsley. From the Rosenwald
Collection, National Gallery of Art, Washington. Image courtesy National Gallery of
Art, Washington.

Dedication

This book is dedicated to my mother Susan Vladeck, who, like Tannhäuser's Jewish mother in I. L. Peretz's *Mesires-nefesh*, always believes that her children are geniuses who can do no wrong. I am very thankful for her constant faith and support.

Contents

Acknowledgments

The legacy of Tannhäuser in my own life has taken almost as many twists and turns as the story I discuss in this book. This book grew out of an essay I published in the journal *Jewish Social Studies* that sought to account for the influence of Tannhäuser on Heinrich Heine, Theodor Herzl and I. L. Peretz. Writing the essay merely piqued my interest in the story, and a few years later I returned to the project to try and fill in some of the missing pieces. In the first version of the manuscript I chose only to write about the legacy in Jewish life and to skip over a full consideration of Richard Wagner's opera. However, in due time I realized that like it or not, Wagner was a central figure in the evolution of the Tannhäuser meme, and in order to do full justice to the story, he needed to be included.

In the years it has taken to write this book I have pestered many of the most important scholars working in Heine, Wagner, Herzl, and Peretz studies. Profound thanks to Jeffrey Sammons, Dieter Borchmeyer, and Jacques Kornberg. I also am grateful for suggestions I received from Ken Frieden, Paul Lawrence Rose, Daniel Jütte, and Michael Hau over aspects of this book. Needless to say, I am completely responsible for any and all flaws. I also wish to give my deepest thanks to Richard Libowitz for his careful and considered line reading of the manuscript, and to the editor of the Shofar Supplements in Jewish Studies, Zev Garber, for his enthusiasm for the project. I also wish to thank Rebecca Corbin, Dianna Gilroy, and Charles Watkinson of Purdue University Press, who have made me feel that my book is in extremely capable hands.

I began the manuscript while still a member of the English and Judaic Studies departments at the University of Denver, where I was the recipient of an Academy of Learned Sciences Junior Research Fellowship that enabled me to spend a sabbatical year researching the book. Thank you to all the support and guidance I received from my friends and colleagues at the University of Denver. I completed the book while at Monash University, where I have found an exceptionally welcoming and congenial academic home. Thank you here to my friends and colleagues in the Australian Centre for Jewish Civilisation and the School of Historical Studies.

My daughters, Sophie and Arwynn, have been raised under the shadow of Tannhäuser, and to them I am deeply grateful for always reminding me to have fun. And to Adrian, thank you for reading and rereading the manuscript, and for being my best friend and best partner in crime.

Introduction

In July 2001, the well-known Jewish conductor, Daniel Barenboim, leading the Berlin Staatskapelle orchestra, asked his audience at the Israeli Music Festival in Jerusalem if they would like to hear some of Richard Wagner's music during the encore. Wagner had been unofficially banned in Palestine since 1938 in response to Kristallnacht. His music was condemned for two reasons: first, because he was one of the most outspoken and prominent anti-Semites of the nineteenth century, and second, because Hitler was obsessed with Wagner and many Israelis believed that Hitler played his music at the death camps.[1] At the 2001 performance, Barenboim decided to jump headlong into the fire by raising the issue in a public forum. After a heated debate, during which many walked out of the audience in protest, the orchestra played a piece from Wagner's *Tristan und Isolde*. The performance was followed by a standing ovation.

Few in the audience that night knew that the founder of political Zionism, Theodor Herzl, was deeply inspired by Wagner's music, and that in fact Herzl wrote the central Zionist manifesto, *Der Judenstaat* or *The Jewish State*, while attending nightly performances of Wagner's opera *Tannhäuser* in Paris. Moreover, two other major Jewish figures, Heinrich Heine and I. L. Peretz, also found the Tannhäuser legend an important inspiration for their reconstituted visions of Jewish culture.

This hidden story of Tannhäuser has never been told before in book form. *A Knight at the Opera* examines the relationship between the German ballad and these men. Heine, Herzl, and Peretz all turned to Tannhäuser at a moment in their lives when they were reconsidering their relationship to both Jewish and non-Jewish society, and each found in the German tale of self-sacrifice and redemption a tool to explore a number of questions about their identity and world view. *A Knight at the Opera* analyzes the evolution of the Tannhäuser legend as it came into contact with each of the Jewish thinkers, and explores how they changed it into a tool to foster Jewish identity and subvert anti-Semitism.

1

In the original medieval myth, a Christian knight, Tannhäuser, lives in sin with the seductive pagan goddess, Venus, in the Venusberg. He escapes her clutches and makes his way to Rome to seek absolution from the Pope. The Pope does not pardon Tannhäuser, who returns to the Venusberg to spend the rest of his days with the goddess.

This book traces Tannhäuser's evolution from medieval knight to Heinrich Heine's German scoundrel in early modern Europe to Wagner's idealized German male and finally to Peretz's pious Jewish scholar in the Land of Israel. Venus will also undergo major changes from pagan goddess to lusty housewife to overbearing Jewish mother.

A Knight at the Opera examines Tannhäuser as a useful meme to demarcate the relationship between Jewish culture and the broader society during the rise of the modern era. A meme is any cultural entity, such as an idea, a piece of art, or a popular notion such as democracy, that evolves as it moves through culture. By examining the evolution of a meme over time, theorists gain an insight into how a society creates, responds to, and adapts to its cultural environment. Heine's, Herzl's, and Peretz's interactions with Tannhäuser, which ranged from assimilation to rejection, were largely affected by the significant variations in Jewish culture between East and West. The relationship of Heine, Herzl, and Peretz to the Tannhäuser meme is one lens through which we can view the struggles and pressures that prominent Jewish thinkers faced as they sought to construct a viable Jewish culture in Europe. This meme is particularly interesting because it also played a large role in German culture through Wagner's opera.

The book examines the chronological evolution of the meme over time: chapter 2 provides an overview of the ballad's history; chapter 3 considers Heinrich Heine's 1837 poem, "Der Tannhäuser"; chapter 4 analyzes Richard Wagner's 1845 opera, *Tannhäuser und der Sängerkrieg auf der Wartburg* (Tannhäuser and the Singers' Contest at Wartburg); chapter 4 discusses the influence of Wagner's opera on Theodor Herzl's 1896 Zionist work *Der Judenstaat* (The Jewish State); and chapter 6 focuses on I. L. Peretz's 1904 Yiddish novella *Mesires-nefesh* (Self-Sacrifice). Whereas Heine rewrote the 1515 German ballad, and Wagner's opera was based on Heine's work, Herzl and Peretz were both responding to a meme "corrupted" by a prominent anti-Semite, Richard Wagner.

Each section begins with a biographical discussion. The aim is threefold. First, it will provide access to the backgrounds of these significant cultural figures. Second, it will fill in the larger story of how and why each man decided to rework the folktale. Third, it will set the stage for our understanding of why and how Eastern and Western Jewish upbringings led to different styles of appropriating folk material. We will see that the assimilation-minded German Jews, Heine and Herzl, sought to use the folktale in such a way that the original remained largely intact, although adapted to their needs. In contrast, Peretz had no interest in salvaging aspects of the original German folktale, instead creating an utterly new version of it in which the original is only a trace. The Polish Jew Peretz, a proud cultural nationalist who was becoming increasingly uncomfortable with Jewish assimilation into the broader society, evinced no desire to have his Jewish version be seen as a rewrite, or assimilation, of Wagner's version, rejecting the original and replacing it with a completely Jewish version.

The analysis then turns to what Heine, Wagner, Herzl, and Peretz did with the Tannhäuser legend and how their versions illuminate their understandings of their relationship with the broader world. The chapters conclude with a discussion of how their reworked versions of the folktale were introduced into, and influenced, the broader culture. As the meme develops we will see it change and transform in multiple ways while also deeply affecting those with whom it comes into contact. The story of Tannhäuser is a tale of prominent Jewish figures interacting with and subverting the German culture in which the folktale is rooted, and by so doing, making the meme into a tool with which they can express the uncertainties of Jewish life in the modern era.

Contested Origins

Heine, Wagner, and Peretz all sought to distance their versions of the ballad from the edition that had inspired its creation. Heine pretended that his poem was written by a German anonymous poet (although his readers would have likely recognized the fake authorship). He did this in order to create the illusion that the unnamed German author was merely presenting a simple rewrite of the 1515 original. In reality, however, Heine's version was a subversive adaptation that portrayed Germany as a backwater locale represented by the appropriately named Tannhäuser (backwoods man). For Wagner, his intention was to show that his opera was rooted in Germany's land and its folk creations, rather than being heavily indebted to the writings of a Jew. And Peretz so completely obfuscated the fact that his Yiddish novella was based on Wagner's opera that it takes a great deal of unpacking to see the connections between the two. This was likely done to downplay the fact that its inspiration was the opera of an anti-Semite. Instead, using an oral narrative voice, Peretz sought to give the impression that his novella grew out of the tradition of Jewish folktales. However, as with Heine, Peretz likely knew that his astute readership would recognize that the real inspiration was Wagner's opera.

This tendency to obfuscate and recreate the origins of the ballad is a long established tradition in uses of Tannhäuser. The story of the knight has appealed in different ways depending on the standpoint, time period, and geographical location of those who have worked with it.

Jewish Appropriations

A Knight at the Opera analyzes how three of the greatest Jewish thinkers of the modern era, Heine, Herzl, and Peretz, appropriated a central myth of nationalistic Germans and then transformed it to strengthen Jewish culture and to attack anti-Semitism, while in contrast, Wagner created his opera to perpetuate the values of German volk consciousness. Turning to Tannhäuser at moments of profound intellectual, spiritual, and artistic crises, they used it as an instrument to reassert their rejection of the broader world and to reinforce their Jewish identity. Located in different parts of Europe and in time periods spanning the nineteenth century, they experienced different forms of anti-Semitism and large variations in Jewish life. Nevertheless, each found in Tannhäuser a soil in which to plant a proud Jewish culture.

Heine, Herzl, and Peretz were not afraid to make use of a myth popular with German nationalists. Furthermore, the ways in which they utilized the Tannhäuser meme reflected their burgeoning views about how Jewish life should be conducted in the modern era. For Heine, his "Der Tannhäuser" poem demonstrated his problems with Germany. In the poem, Germany has a stagnating culture that is constantly focused on the past. Herzl found in Tannhäuser clues to help him sort out his Zionist vision. For Peretz, his Yiddish novella based on Tannhäuser expressed his version of cultural nationalism that called for a return to Jewish values and a rejection of assimilation. Heine's, Herzl's, and Peretz's use of Tannhäuser demonstrate how Jewish concepts of redemption, self-improvement, and transformation contrast with those of Christians such as Wagner.

This creative repositioning, where the work of an anti-Semite is transformed to engender a positive impact, is typical of many Jewish thinkers who have used the products of the broader society to strengthen and refashion the Jewish milieu. Before the Holocaust, the Yiddish speaking world played a critical role in the transmission of culture from East to West and West to East, lying as it did in the Pale of Settlement between Russia and Western Europe. Jewish writers and thinkers continually turned to the non-Jewish world to find the seeds for their art. Jewish authors rewrote *A Thousand and One Nights*, *Don Quixote*, *Aesop's Fables*, *King Lear* and many other works and transformed them into uniquely hybrid productions with Jewish and European characteristics. There are countless examples of Jewish writers and thinkers standing at the crossroads and rewriting, subverting, and Judaizing European cultural tropes.

A typical example of this tradition was the 1820 Yiddish novella that appeared in Galicia entitled "Robinzon di geshikhte fun Alter Leb" (Robinson, the history of Reb Alter Leb).[2] The novella, a rewrite of Daniel Defoe's *Robinson Crusoe*, was popular among the Yiddish reading public of Eastern Europe. In the Yiddish version, Robinson is a traditional Jew named Alter Leb from Hamburg. His fellow islander Friday, the escaped "savage" as Defoe called him, is renamed Shabes (or Sabbath) and becomes a practicing Jew. Their life on the island revolves around gathering food, praying to God, and following the Jewish holiday calendar. Alter Leb and Sabbath's diet remains kosher, of course, with herring replacing Robinson Crusoe's shell fish. As in Defoe's original, Alter Leb spends his time domesticating the llamas he finds on the island.

The Yiddish version of *Robinson Crusoe* marked an intersection between the two dominant hemispheres for central European literature in the nineteenth century, Germany and Russia. The author, a Russian speaking Jew, based his adaptation of *Robinson Crusoe* not on Defoe's work, but on the 1779 version by the famous German pedagogue Joachim Campe. In the process of adapting the work for a Jewish public, the text was transformed in a way that questioned many basic notions of European identity.[3]

Like Robinson Crusoe, many European Jews viewed themselves as stranded in a hostile land, albeit one where they were in a unique position in relation to established ideas of nationhood. Thus at a time when nation building and empire defined much of European identity, Jewish populations challenged the rhetoric of nationalism by being perceived to be diasporic outsiders. Alter Leb's author Joseph Vitlin, like other Jewish writers, dealt with his uncertain position in European society by taking a canonical text and rewriting its basic tropes. By so doing, he challenged the increasing European emphasis on belonging to the nation and its national culture. Alter Leb responds to the loss of identity he experiences on the island by seeking to become more "Jewish" than he was previously.

This hybrid tradition, as we will see documented in the evolution of the Tannhäuser meme, challenges the basic precepts of how culture works.[4] The Yiddish poet Mani Leyb writes of this in his poem "To the Gentile Poet":

> Heir of Shakespeare, shepherds and cavaliers
> Bard of gentiles, lucky you are indeed
> The earth is yours: it gives your fat hog feed
> Where e'er it walks, your Muse grazes on hers . . . .
> But I, a poet of the Jews—who needs it
> A folk of wild grass grown on foreign earth
> Dust-bearded nomads, grandfathers of dearth
> The dust of fairs and texts is all that feeds it
> I chant, amid the alien corn, the tears
> Of desert wanderers under alien stars.[5]

In other words, the political status of the Christian, European poet enables him to see the world as his own landscape that he can re-create in his poetry. His sovereign identity inspires him to write without having to question how his status is tied to his artistic creation. The Jewish predicament challenges outright the romantic notion of the muse and the individual poet who creates transcendent art. Jewish author's like Mani Leyb show that literature is only a solitary and transcendent endeavor for those who have certain political rights. For the disenfranchised, such as the Jews of Europe, their literature is tied to their location and "the dust of fairs and texts is all that feeds it."

In each instance of Jewish transformations of European tropes, ideas of nation, home, and selfhood as found in the original are challenged overtly or subtly as being falsely based on the assumption that all groups have basic freedoms. Thus studying Jewish uses of mainstream tropes such as Tannhäuser not only traces the subversive history of Jewish appropriations, but also illuminates Jewish writers' literary strategies in challenging canonical Western symbols. This array of subversive rewrites, from *Sinbad the Sailor* to *Tannhäuser*, suggests that Jewish culture was emphatically in conversation with European literature, rather than being parochial.

Jewish writing in Europe challenged the foundations of European literature and national identity. Yet we know little of the history or meaning of the long tradition of Jewish authors reworking canonical texts. This book uncovers and analyzes one story in the complex history of Jewish and European interchange in an era where "nationhood" was being used as a means to distinguish Europeans from non-Europeans. In each case, the Jewish thinker subverted nationalistic aspects of the German myth of Tannhäuser by transforming the meme into a tool to promote Jewish cohesiveness. The Judaizing of the Tannhäuser ballad, in turn, challenged the idea that there was an intrinsic "Germanic" folk culture that could be a basis for nation building. The relationship between the Jewish and German uses of the Tannhäuser myth show how cultural definitions of nationhood are fluid rather than static, even when nationalists such as Wagner assert that they are not.

☆ This book will consider the ways in which Jewish authors appropriated a European cultural symbol, re-imaged it to represent "Jewish" ideas, and reintroduced it back into the world.

The Jews who brought European tropes to the Jewish masses were frequently members of the educated elite who had access to European languages such as German. They were in Europe, but not totally of Europe, and literature became a tool to introduce the West to the Jew. By so doing, the dominant culture of Europe was transferred "home" and Judaized, as we will see in Peretz's remarkable appropriation of Wagner's opera. It may be troubling for some to see how these Jewish intellectuals were inspired by a preeminent paradigm of German nationalism, but rather than being infected by the anti-Semitism of Wagner, they changed the meme and the game.

The manner in which Heine, Herzl, and Peretz each reworked the meme will give us insights into the time, place, and viewpoint of each artist. Each moment of the meme can be understood as one guidepost among many on the path to modern Jewish life. As we watch Tannhäuser weave through the lives of three of the most central intellectuals in modern Jewish life, the story of its legacy will be analyzed as a valuable tool for understanding the relationship between Jewish intellectual life and the broader world during the advent of the modern era.

Notes

1. For a full overview of the true relationship between Wagner and Hitler that challenges many ideas about the role of Wagner's music in Nazi Germany and the death camps, see Pamela M. Potter's essay, "Wagner and the Third Reich: Myths and Realities," in

The Cambridge Companion to Wagner, ed. Thomas S. Grey (Cambridge: Cambridge University Press, 2008), 235-45.

2.   See Yoysef Vitlin's *Robinzon di geshikhte fun Alter-Leb* (Vilna: Chapbook, 1894).

3.   For an analysis of the manner in which Vitlin's story rewrote European concepts see my essay, "The Jewish Robinson Crusoe," *Comparative Literature* 54, no. 3 (2002), 215-28.

4.   Another interesting example of this hybrid tradition, similar to the use made of the Tannhäuser ballad by I. L. Peretz, is the 1878 Hebrew and Yiddish version of *Don Quixote* by Mendele Moycher Sforim, where the Jewish Don Quixote must travel around Poland, where he faces constant danger simply for being a Jew. In contrast, in Cervantes' original, Spain is a territory in which Don Quixote can freely reinvent himself. In the Jewish version, the repression of the Jews' political rights is dealt with by attempts at personal reinvention. For instance, the Jewish Sancho Panza becomes the cross-dressing wife of Don Quixote, after Don Quixote woos him with biblical and medieval love poetry. For an analysis of the differences between Cervantes's and Mendele Moycher Sforim's versions of *Don Quixote* see my book, *Journeys beyond the Pale: Yiddish Travel Writing in the Modern World* (Madison: University of Wisconsin Press, 2003), 38-56. For the Yiddish version, see Sholem Abramovitsh, *Kitser masoes Binyomin hashlishi*, in *Ale Verk fun Mendele-Moykher Sforim*, ed. N. Mayzl (Warsaw: Farlag Mendele, 1928), 9:3-118. For the English translation, see "The Brief Travels of Benjamin the Third," in *Tales of Mendele the Book Peddler*, ed. Ken Frieden and Dan Miron, trans. Hillel Halkin (New York: Schocken Books, 1996), 299-393.

5.   The English translation along with the Yiddish original of Mani Leyb's poem, "To the Gentile Poet" can be found in Irving Howe, Ruth R. Wisse, and Khone Shmeruk, eds., *The Penguin Book of Modern Yiddish Verse*, trans. John Hollander (New York: Penguin Books, 1987), 138-39.

Chapter One

The Original Tannhäuser Ballad

The Tannhäuser legend that influenced Heinrich Heine and Richard Wagner (and therein Theodor Herzl and I. L. Peretz), is a 1515 version from Nuremberg.[1] There is much disagreement about whether the knight discussed in the ballad was a historical thirteenth-century *Minnesänger* who is only known by the poems he created, a knight who partook in the crusades, or was a wholly invented figure.

The 1515 version of the legend does not give any background information on Tannhäuser (called Danuser in some versions), perhaps assuming that since there were so many copies of the ballad circulating at the time the audience would already be familiar with the knight. The ballad also does not explain how he made his way to the abode of Venus, the Venusberg. Instead, it begins with the plot fully underway as the pagan goddess Venus asserts her love to Tannhäuser and reminds him that he has made an oath to stay with her. It is implied that Tannhäuser entered the Venusberg because he was curious to explore its wonders, yet after being there a year he realized that he was ready to depart.

In order to entice Tannhäuser to stay, Venus offers him a companion to keep as his wife. In response, Tannhäuser states that he will burn in hell if he takes "another wife than she I have in mind." The wife to whom Tannhäuser seeks to remain true is, it is implied, Mary, the mother of Jesus. In other words, Tannhäuser will not give in to the seductions of paganism as embodied by Venus, instead preferring to return to the virtuous Catholic path represented by Mary.

They argue back and forth, with Venus pleading that he should remain, and Tannhäuser asserting that he must go. Eventually Tannhäuser departs "the mountain in sorrow and repentance," proclaiming that he "will go to the city of Rome, trusting in a Pope."

Tannhäuser heads there, wondering if Pope Urban "can save" him. He laments his sins and tells the Pope that he spent a year with Venus. From the Pope he seeks to "receive confession and penance, to find if [he] may look on God." The Pope responds by pointing to the small, dry, wooden Pilgrim's staff that he is holding. He tells Tannhäuser that it is as unlikely that he will find God's favor as it is that the Pope's staff of dry wood will blossom with leaves. To this, Tannhäuser pleads that he just needs one year to "receive confession and penance, and win the consolation of God."

Tannhäuser leaves the city in "sorrow and distress," bidding a sad goodbye to the home of his betrothed, Mother Mary. He returns to the Venusberg to live permanently with the pagan goddess, since this is God's judgment for him. Venus is jubilant to see him. On the third day of his stay with Venus, in Rome the Pope's staff mysteriously begins to bud.

Seeing the unexpected blossoming of the staff, the Pope sends "out in all lands (to see) where Tannhäuser had gone. But he was back in the mountain and had found his love. Therefore Pope Urban IV was also lost for ever." The Pope, it is implied, is as lost as Tannhäuser because he mistakenly refused to redeem the knight.

The legend showed up again in 1614 in Heinrich Kornmann's collection about Venus entitled, *Mons Veneris*, after which the ballad remained fairly static until the late eighteenth century, when Germany began to create its own nationalist myths as the builders of culture sought out stories and traditions that were "German" and that could be the basis for a unified society. The Tannhäuser legend thus became extremely fashionable with German Romantics, who were delving into medieval history to seek out stories of a proud German past and to find tropes to inspire their contemporaries to break free of the confines of traditional religion.[2] Tannhäuser was one of numerous folktales, myths, and legends that were used for culture building by the nascent nation, and it was extremely popular, as was shown by its many variations, from simple songs to high poetry.

The 1515 ballad was rewritten as a short story in 1799 by the popular German Romantic writer Ludwig Tieck. His "Der getreue Eckart und der Tannenhäuser" (Faithful Eckart and Tannhäuser) mutated the knight into a disaffected Romantic who seeks a more fulfilling life beyond the easy pleasures of the Venusberg. In 1806, the 1515 version was also reprinted in the extremely popular collection of folksongs, *Des Knaben Wunderhorn* (The Boy's Magic Horn), although Tannhäuser's plea to Mother Mary to help him break free from Venus was dropped from the tale.

Since its "rediscovery" by German Romantics in the eighteenth century, the roots of the ballad have been hotly contested. German historians, philologists, and Romantic writers have sought to show that the original ballad was imported in a protean form from Italy into Germany by German travelers. It was only when the ballad made its way onto German land that it transformed into the legend of the knight. In order to strengthen the argument that Tannhäuser was formed in Germany, some historians insist that the protagonist of the ballad is a version of an historical minstrel singer and German knight. However, this as well is open to debate.[3] There were nevertheless numerous prototypes of the ballad circulating before the 1515 version, which was the first to have a date stamped on it. These pre-1515 editions, some of which have only a scant resemblance to the 1515 ballad, are given more or less weight depending on the bias of the interpreter.

Whether or not the ballad has German origins, what is important is that many historians sought to claim it as a foundation myth of medieval Germany. Thus they dissected every aspect of the legend to seek its ties to Germany, be it in the figure of Venus, the use of a staff, the name of Tannhäuser, or the role of the Pope. As this study shows, it is not only Germans who contested the tale's origins when they sought to appropriate it for their own use: Heine, Herzl, and Peretz all formed ties to the original. And with Peretz we have such a remarkable Judaization of the text that Tannhäuser takes on seemingly authentic Jewish origins.

The early versions of the ballad were simple and crude forms of entertainment for the reading masses, and even the 1515 version that so inspired Heine and other German Romantics was written in very unpolished language. What was inspirational, rather than the style, was the content: a man's search for redemption after a fall. This universal theme transcended the simplistic composition and impelled the Tannhäuser legend to be revived in multiple forms from the eighteenth century onward, even playing a surprisingly central role in Jewish culture building.

Notes

1. A full English translation of the ballad along with the German original can be found in J. M. Clifton-Everest, *The Tragedy of Knighthood: Origins of the Tannhäuser-Legend* (Oxford: Society for the Study of Mediaeval Languages and Literature, 1979), 150-57. For bibliographies of sources on the legend, see Clifton-Everest; also see J. W. Thomas, *Tannhäuser: Poet and Legend* (Chapel Hill: University of North Carolina Press, 1974), 79-81.
2. For a discussion of the use made of Tannhäuser by the Young German movement, see Dieter Borchmeyer, *Drama and the World of Richard Wagner*, trans. Daphne Ellis (Princeton: Princeton University Press, 2003), 124-33.
3. See J. M. Clifton-Everest's very convincing challenge to the notion that the ballad is directly linked to the real historical figure in *The Tragedy of Knighthood: Origins of the Tannhäuser-Legend* (Oxford: Society for the Study of Mediaeval Languages and Literature, 1979), 111-16.

Chapter Two

Heinrich Heine

A Walk in Montmartre

In the November 5, 1981 edition of *The New York Review of Books*, the American literary critic, Alfred Kazin, told the troubling story of how "Hitler, flushed with triumph when he occupied Paris, ordered that Heine's grave in Montmartre be destroyed." Heinrich Heine (1797 or 1798-1856), whose poem, "Der Tannhäuser" would in large part inspire Richard Wagner to create his opera, was a writer whose poetry was seen as so subversive to the ideals of Germanic culture that apparently Hitler made it his top priority upon invading Paris to have his troops smash to rubble his final resting spot.[1]

I had come in the middle of the day during one of the worst heat waves in recent history to search Montmartre cemetery for a plaque or sculpture to show where the grave had once stood. The cemetery, usually crowded with tourists, was all but empty. The lone graveyard worker busily watering the grass so that it would not dry out, was at a loss to locate where Heine had lain, and instead offered to show me the tombs of Edgar Degas and Alexander Dumas. Politely refusing, I continued on my quest, yet after a fruitless hour I realized with sadness that Montmartre held nothing to mark the great poet except his name on their tourist maps. I decided to give the general area one more search before heading to a café to hydrate.

Imagine my surprise, then, when I nearly bumped into Heine's grave. Not the commemorative plaque I had been looking for, but the grave marker itself that the Vienna Boys Choir had erected in 1901. It is a huge gray obelisk with a harp-like gate on the front adorned with a circle of roses and the words *Heinrich Heine*. Atop sits the bust of a middle-aged Heine with a bushy goatee.[2] Kazin's information was completely false: the grave had not been vandalized. I do not know how the myth arose that the Nazis had smashed the grave. Perhaps it was because Heine was still seen as a danger or maybe it seemed likely that Hitler would send Wehrmacht troops to Montmartre in order to get revenge for Heine's many insults to the Reich.

Heinrich Heine was a troublemaker who frequently challenged and subverted many basic ideas of German nationalists. Where Wagner's creations were deadly serious, Heine's were often humorous and made fun of popular ideas. Not merely a satiric poet, during his lifetime Heine also produced eloquent prose, literary essays, philosophical works, and political commentaries. His writings covered the gamut and were noteworthy not only for their artistry, but also for how they challenged many accepted notions of the times.

Jewish by birth, Heine converted to Christianity in 1826, although many of his readers continued to view him as a Jew. His writings were considered by some to be an anti-German force because they were a special type of Jewish humor that challenged many of the more conservative values of German society. They were at times perceived to be "treacherously anti-German," and the fact that a Jewish writer (though a convert) created them gave fuel to antisemitic attacks.[3] This type of humor was pejoratively called by some *Judenwitz,* and could be viewed as tawdry, illegitimate, exotic, and sensational—in other words, as writing from marginal outsiders that threatened to break down mainstream society.[4] Nevertheless, Heine received acclaim from many of his famous contemporaries, including Frederick Nietzsche, Karl Marx and, as we will see, Richard Wagner. He was the favorite German poet for an array of intellectuals and artists.

Heine's 1836 poem, "Der Tannhäuser" was one of many examples of works he created in his role as a figure challenging the repressive reactionary waves in Germany in general, and in Prussia in particular, following the clampdown on revolutionary tendencies in the 1820s and 1830s. Heine's decision to write his poem was in part generated by his frustration with the efforts of the Prussian government to silence him and his art. His "Der Tannhäuser" can thus be seen as a model of how subversive humor can be used by those in a marginal position to oppose and break down mainstream dogmas. "Der Tannhäuser" marked a moment of intellectual and artistic crisis for Heine, as did the works discussed by all the thinkers considered in this book. The poem became a means for him to work through his relationship with a country that he both nostalgically longed for and despised because it offered no place for a rebel such as himself.

Early Life and Work

Heine's life unfolded at a time of rapid political, social, and economic change for Germans and Jews alike.[5] Germany in 1780 consisted of more than three hundred loosely affiliated states, most with a rural-based economy, which would, by 1871, be transformed into a single Empire.[6] In many respects, Heine's background would seem to point him toward a comfortable assimilated life rather than toward rebellion. Sketches of Heine portray him as a vulnerable-looking, handsome youth with an angular face, an aquiline nose with a bump in the middle, deep penetrating eyes, and a full stock of curly, light brown hair. In his middle years, he affected an artist's goatee. In portraits, he resembled the sensitive artist-poet in the style of Lord Byron, after whom Heine modeled himself.

The early critical perception of Heine has viewed him through one of two extreme lenses either as "an hedonistic dandy" or as a "champion of progress."[7] Certainly Heine's many quirks do not help us to pin down his personality. He was an intense man with an acerbic wit, who frequently offended others but was easily offended himself. A mass of contradictions, Heine was beloved and hated in equal measure. While his tongue was sharp, he had a shy bearing that made him seem a lonely figure. Devotedly loyal to his parents, he nevertheless had regular falling outs with his extended family. Able to create anguished poetry about love, in his own life his relationships were few and far between, and his sexual life all but nonexistent. In ill health and bedridden for nearly the final decade of his life, his mind nevertheless was always overly active; always thinking and responding, he wore his emotions on his sleeve. Heine was thus the type of person whom intellectuals often love to be around, but whom they would have hated to live with. Yet while his emotions were in many ways childlike—as were his love affairs—his writings showed extremely sophisticated perspectives on the world. Heine gave the impression that he was never quite comfortable in his own skin—whether because he was Jewish, or a writer, or later, sickly—and this influenced how he treated others and how they treated him.

Heine was born in the city of Düsseldorf. Later he would joke that in the future, Düsseldorf would be known because Heine was from there, but during his lifetime it was most famous for an equestrian statue. (He was partially prophetic, as Düsseldorf's university is now named after him).[8] Germany in the middle of the eighteenth century was undergoing changes that could move it in one of two directions—either toward an increasingly conservative culture or toward a liberal and open society based on Enlightenment principles. Jewish life in Germany had always been difficult, with numerous anti-Jewish edicts that sought to restrict all aspects of life for the small population. When Germany had been composed of independent states ruled by local nobles, the majority of the Jewish population had been extremely poor. The exception were the tiny number of court Jews—elite members of Jewish society who mediated between the nobility and the local population yet who were not full members of either. From the small number of court Jews, educated and urbane, there developed a liberal and reformist movement spearheaded by the Jewish philosopher Moses Mendelssohn, seeking a middle ground between Judaism and modernization.

The Jewish enlightenment, or Haskalah, modeled on the broader Enlightenment, offered the hope that if the Jews became less orthodox, different, and "backwards," they would receive civil emancipation. They thus began to act, speak, dress, and behave like members of German bourgeois society while working to transform Judaism from a "premodern" to a "modern" religion. Jewish children began to learn secular subjects along with Jewish ones; to speak, read, and write in Western languages; and to stop asserting that they were the "chosen people," embracing instead the brotherhood of man. Judaism itself was reworked along a Lutheran model. Asserting that Judaism continually evolved and was not stuck in the rigid model of a traditional legalistic religion, the enlighteners took a pick-and-choose stance towards many rules. Watered down or thrown out were laws such as following a strict kosher diet and doing no work on the Sabbath. Synagogue rituals were reworked with prayer books in German rather than Hebrew, the addition of choirs, and a focus on order and decorum. The reform movement was a means to make Jewishness more palatable in "enlightened, rational" society. One can view the Jewish enlightenment as devoted to reducing Judaism to a non-Christian Protestantism; alternatively, it can be seen as a movement seeking a way to have some aspects of Jewishness survive the strong outside pressures on it, or it can be understood as a combination of the two.

Where in the past Judaism had dictated every aspect of how one lived, the reformers sought to differentiate between how one should be Jewish in the public and private realms. In the world at large they would be German (or French or English), and dress, speak, eat, and interact with others like non-Jews. In the private world of the synagogue or home, they would be "Jewish" in their religious observances. Out of this trend arose large numbers of Jews who proudly embraced German culture because they believed that the Western enlightened world would accept them on equal terms. The vast number of Jewish conversions to Christianity in the mid-1700s were thus done as a practical means to fully enter German society.[9]

Heinrich was originally named Harry after an English business partner of his father's, and this was what he was called by his family throughout his life.[10] Heine's family were solidly middle class and both parents descended from court Jews. They believed, as did many in their social milieu, that the Jews could enter mainstream Germany and create a good life. As for being non-Christian, this could be downplayed by keeping fairly quiet about it and practicing one's religion in the home-centered observances of Jewish holidays. Parents imbued in their children a reformist version of Judaism while at the same time embracing German culture. Heine's mother Betty was born Peira van Geldern (1771-1859). She was raised in Düsseldorf by a liberal-minded physician father (her mother died when she was young) who trained her to be well read in a variety of languages, so much so that she was conversant with most of the major European literature of the day.

Throughout his life, Heine viewed his mother with "love and respect" and she remained a bewitching figure for him.[11] His sonnet to his mother shows her as an intimidating yet "lofty spirit that see all things right" who remains the constant love of his life:

And ever did I search for love-yes, ever
Pursued the quest of love, but found it never
And came back home, dejected and downcast
But there you came to welcome me again
And oh! within your eyes I saw it then
There was the sweet, the long-sought love at last.[12]

Interestingly, Heine and later Peretz both shared extremely intense and close relationships with mothers who often dominated them. The bewitching motherlike
figure for both would be explored in their Tannhäuser renditions.

Heinrich's father Samson (1764-1828) was the opposite of his wife. He was
a dreamer who had an artistic bent. He was raised in a middle-class family of
merchants in Hanover and became engaged to Betty one month after first meeting her in Düsseldorf in 1796. They married in February 1797 and Samson was
set up as a fabric merchant with the money from Betty's dowry, although business was not suited to his temperament. Heine always described his father with
the greatest affection, as a gentle, sensitive man who loved him unconditionally,
and he noted that "in all the world there was no one I loved as much as him."[13]
Heinrich seems to have thus grown up in a happy home with loving parents and
siblings who ended up living successful middle-class lives. For them, the carrot
and stick of the Jewish enlightenment seemed to bear fruit: they acted as respectable members of society and were rewarded with good careers.

As a child, Heine's family had enjoyed full equality with Christians as a result of the changes brought about by the Franco-Prussian wars. As Napoleon had
done for the Jews of France, he introduced civil emancipation in the conquered
territories. In fact, Heine's father was allegedly the first Jew since the Middle
Ages to gain a position in the civil guard.[14] Heine described how overwhelmed
he was to see his hero Napoleon as a child: "And those lips smiled and the eyes
smiled, too. Eyes as clear as the heavens; eyes which could read men's hearts,
which at a glance embraced everything in the world—while we see things only
one by one, and only as painted shadows."[15]

The arrival of the French meant the demise of the strong Austrian Empire
and a complete redrawing of Germany along new lines. France was able to exploit
the numerous divisions in the Holy Roman Empire, and by so doing it became
the dominant power in the region. Moreover, the arrival of the French into the
battered economy brought about modernization to Germany, both economically
and socially. This for the Jewish population was largely positive. For instance, the
education system was remodeled and a new one was instituted based on merit
rather than family heritage. For the Jewish population this meant that they would
be rewarded for their performance rather than hindered because of their religion, and they began to enter German schools in large numbers.

In the 1815 Congress of Vienna following the defeat of Napoleon, Heine's
hometown of Düsseldorf was fully established as part of Prussia, and Prussia

became the major power of the North of Germany. Reforms that had been introduced by Napoleon were now rescinded. When the Jews lost the rights that
they had briefly enjoyed under the French and realized how deeply anti-Jewish
sentiment ran, their disappointment was profound. However, the brief promise
of emancipation had stimulated the dreams of Jews who continued to embrace
the French traditions, and students such as Heine began learning French in their
schools.

For Germany, the long mapping and remapping of borders led (as it did
throughout much of Europe) to the monarchs seeking to construct a cohesive
national culture that would inspire loyalty from the general population and imbue them with the sense that they were all subjects of the nation. Many of the
monarchs thus began to turn to glorious images from the past, to folktales, stories of heroism, or long-forgotten rituals, and to propagate them to the broader
culture as a way to create a proud, noble, and unified Germany. A decade later
Romantic nationalists would revisit the medieval ballad, *Tannhäuser* and use it
as a tool to build Germanic consciousness.

Heine's relationship with his Jewishness is hotly disputed, with some
claiming that he was raised learning Hebrew and Yiddish and observing the Jewish holidays, and others asserting that Judaism was of little importance in his
home.[16] In fact, the truth lies somewhere in the middle. For instance, he did
briefly attend a Hebrew school as a child, although he soon transferred to a local
Christian one. Heine may have known a smattering of Hebrew from religious
services and was likely familiar with some Judeo-German terms, but he lived
and worked in German. In Heine's memoirs, his Jewishness inspired hatred and
many derogatory remarks: one of the most moving excerpts recalls his being
teased for having a grandfather who was "a little Jew with a long beard." Later in
life, he asserted, "whenever I hear of little Jews with long beards, a weird chill of
recollection creeps up and down my spine."[17]

While his Jewishness was pretty much downplayed throughout his childhood, nevertheless it did make him different from his German counterparts and
was something that would eventually become a central focus in his work and
life. As a young man, it made him uncomfortable because it marked him as a
member of an archaic, unmodern tribe. Later in life, however, he began to long
for the rituals of his childhood and sought information on Jewish history and
culture. As he grew older, it thus became a means to root himself in the world of
his parents, and his father in particular, whom he loved deeply.[18]

Popular myth has it that Heine's first great loves and poetic inspirations were
his cousins, Amalie (1799 or 1800-1838) and Therese (1807-1880). They were
the dark-haired, refined, beautiful daughters of his father's brother, the extremely
wealthy uncle Salomon. Some critics transformed the brief love affair into a major
force in Heine's poetry, often locating the unnamed lover as one of the cousins. His
cousins were his main crushes until Heine fell in love in Paris at the age of thirty-six
or thirty-seven with Mathilde, with whom he would spend the remainder of his life.

Uncle Salomon would play a prominent role in Heine's life because he was the person to whom Heinrich turned for financial support as a writer. Heine's development as an artist was closely related to his lifelong concerns with money. Unlike I. L. Peretz, who held a bureaucratic job but managed to be extremely prolific, Heine sought to be a full-time creative writer. His family, and in particular his mother, hoped that this was just a phase and instead pushed him towards business with the hopes that he would emulate his extremely successful uncle. After a try at business school, followed by a failed apprenticeship with Salomon in Hamburg, his family set him up in the trade business of *Harry Heine and Co.*, which quickly folded. In 1819, at his mother's suggestion, he decided to pursue a legal career and entered the University of Bonn.

1819 was the year of the anti-Semitic Hep-Hep riots in Bonn. Two people were killed and numerous homes and businesses were destroyed. Soon the riots spread to other German cities and towns, where university students and faculty began to join in. The shock to the Jewish population, in particular its bourgeois members, was tremendous; many had believed that this type of brutal, anti-Jewish mob action was a thing of the past and something enlightened Germans would not tolerate. Moreover, the riots were being instigated by many members of the educated classes. The promise of education as a means to divest Germany of its anti-Semitism was showing itself to be a lie. The 1820s in Germany was proving to be a "reactionary decade" with rising anti-Semitism, extensive press censorship, and police monitoring of those viewed to be subversive to the state.[19] Heine would soon be deemed a danger whose movements needed to be monitored and his works censored.

In response to the riots, Heine wrote his verse tragedy, *Almansor*, which can be read as a parable of recent events in Germany. In *Almansor*, Moors are tortured to convert to Christianity in Spain and the Koran is burned. In response to the riots, Heine also began to reconsider his relationship with German culture. Although a reluctant Jew, he had been forced to confront anti-Semitism firsthand, as a child and now as a witness to the Hep-Hep riots. A few months after the disturbances Heine asserted that "his true fatherland was the German language." Heine was now seeking to retain his artistic medium, the German language, while removing himself as much as possible from the culture that created it.

When Heine moved from the University of Bonn to Berlin in 1820, he became briefly a student of the great philosopher Frederick Hegel, while also joining the thriving Berlin salon society. The salons, often run by German Jewish bourgeois women, were where educated, assimilated Jews mingled and discussed art and literature with liberal-minded Germans. Heine developed a strong intellectual and social relationship with one of the leading hostesses, Rachel Varnhagen, and for a time he found it a social milieu that welcomed him on his own terms. In Berlin, Heine also found a local publisher for a book of his poems. The Jewish salon society was delighted with his writings, while the German critics lauded his poetry but criticized his political works as being the unpatriotic scribbling of a Jew. This view of Heine's work would occur regularly in Germany—acclaiming him as a writer while deriding him as a Jew.

In response to the Hep-Hep riots, a group of young, German Jewish bourgeois students formed the *Verein für Kultur und Wissenschaft des Juden* (Society for the Culture and Science of the Jews) better known as the *Wissenschaft* movement. Heine joined in 1822, in part as a reaction to the new anti-Semitic policies in the restrengthened Prussian government, including the one that would have the most direct impact on him, the ban on Jews entering academic careers. The *Wissenschaft* was dedicated to bringing the study of Jewish culture under the microscope of modern academic rigor. By so doing, the founding members believed that Judaism would show itself to be as worthy of scholarly respect as other disciplines. This they hoped would lift Jewish life from the ghetto into the hallowed halls of the university and in turn would encourage the German public not to exclude Jews for being premodern. Moreover, the Jewish population would gain a more sophisticated take on their heritage.

Heine's work with the group led him to serve as its secretary for a time and teach briefly at a *Wissenschaft* school and in 1824 he even began a "Jewish" novel entitled *The Rabbi of Bacharech*. However, his embrace of the *Wissenschaft's* ideology was never going to be wholehearted, since the lifelong cynic realized that the grand claim of the movement, to save Jewish life in Germany, was not likely to be met with grand results. Heine remained only a few years before moving on, yet he remained in close contact with some of the group and for many years explored questions about his Jewish identity in letters with one of the founding members, Moses Moser.[20] When reading the letters to Moser, one gets the feeling that Heine put a great deal of stock into the relationship and found it very important that Moser saw him as solidly Jewish. It is hard to tell if the author of the letters, serious and soul searching about being Jewish, is the authentic Heine, or someone who wanted to be seen in a positive light by a man he saw as authentically Jewish.

Whatever the case, on June 28, 1826, one year after beginning his "Jewish" novel and just a few years after being so involved with the *Wissenschaft* group, Heine, like the founding *Wissenschaft* member and leader Edward Gans, converted to Protestantism and changed his name from Harry to the more Germanic sounding Christian Johann Heinrich Heine. One can perhaps view ironically Heine's decision to rename himself Christian. The baptism and conversion were performed in great secrecy, which perhaps was evidence of his embarrassment towards the act. Thus "in a mixed mood of cynicism and passive, unheroic fortitude, he travelled in a rainstorm across the nearby Hanover-Prussian border to Heiligenstadt, where nobody except the parson knew who he was. (At the border he was asked the usual "What do you have to declare?" and answered [with the pre-Wildean epigram] "Nothing but thoughts and debts!")[21]

All evidence points towards Heine's conversion being done as a pragmatic way to maintain an academic career in the face of the Prussian edict excluding Jews. The nearness in time of his conversion to his *Wissenschaft* membership also suggests that the movement did not offer Heine the tools he was searching for to successfully navigate public German life as a Jew. In no way was the conversion an embrace of Christianity, although it was clearly an embrace of non-Jewish life. He wrote later that for him, "a baptismal certificate is a ticket of admission to European culture."[22] For the rest of his days, Heine regretted the decision, particularly when he realized he was despised even more so by Christians after he had converted. His family, however, did not seem unduly troubled, perhaps because many middle-class Jews were then converting for similar practical reasons.

Heine's conversion brings up the question of whether or not we should even consider him to be a Jewish artist. This has plagued his critics and become a central question in recent years. Some, such as Jeffrey Sammons, find Heine's "lack of solidarity with fellow Jews" significant, showing that it was not a large concern for him and instead was something that he was increasingly ashamed of, generally hiding it once he had emigrated to France, and even being known to make anti-Semitic remarks.[23] Others feel that the question of his Jewishness dogged Heine throughout his life and played a central role in his literary output.[24] Because he converted, the issue becomes even more complicated. Whether Heine saw his Jewishness in a positive or a negative light, it was an issue that he was forced to confront. When the Jews were under overt, public attack he tended to view himself as Jewish. When things were not in a crisis mode, he downplayed his Jewishness.

Heine became a poet of note with the 1827 publication of his *Buch der Lieder* (Book of Songs). The volume contains an incredible range of poems, many of which had been previously published in smaller volumes, including first-person verses that examine the poet's soul with a great deal of anguish, tragedies, and travel pictures. Rather like Walt Whitman's *Leaves of Grass*, over the course of Heine's life five more editions were published of the *Buch der Lieder*, with alterations, additions, and revised introductions by the author.

The poems focus heavily on relationships and often display a boiling rage at the lover:

> My songs are filled with poison
> Why shouldn't that be true
> Into my budding manhood
> You poured your poison through."[25]

The collection shows Heine to be completely at home in a broad range of poetic forms, from the sonnet to the ballad. Overall, they give a sense of Heine as a young man searching for the meaning of love and life, while being far too cynical to fall for any easy answers. They also display Heine's biting humor, as he attacks the German elite that beckons but never accepts him:

> Black frock coats and silken stockings
> Frilled with all the tailor's arts

Smooth-tongued talk and suave embraces
Oh, if only they had hearts.
Fare you well, you polished salons
Polished sirs and dames, adieu
I will climb up on the mountains
And laugh down on all of you."[26]

The writings also introduce a perspective that later arises throughout Heine's work: a self-critical awareness of the literary scene and his role in it and poetic productions. In other words, the poems overtly gauge their relationship to German poetry. For Heine, who sought to liberate himself from the constraints of a personal biography, it is noteworthy that his poems are so grounded in cultural contexts. They are not cut off from the world at large as if they were created in a vacuum of inspiration. In them, Heine was inventing the ironic poetic stance. It is understandable why this would be so dangerous to German culture, as he was undermining the poet as the inspired prophet and bringing German art down to a totally human level.

Heine's second major volume of poems was his 1844 *Neue Gedichte* (New poems), written during his time in Paris, while his third major collection of poems, *Romanzero* (Romancero, 1851), comes from the time of his "Mattress Grave"—his final decline in health—from 1848 until his death in 1856. Over the years his poetry became funnier, his vision darker, and his authorial stance increasingly ironic. Besides these important collections, Heine also wrote books of essays, journalistic accounts, and philosophical ruminations that converse with many of the major trends of the day: Romanticism in Germany, art in France, the role of religion, and Judaism. He also wrote a series of memoirs about his childhood in Düsseldorf.

As was typical of writers of his generation, Heine's literary idol was Johann Wolfgang von Goethe. As a young law student and aspiring writer he sent Goethe some poems and the note: "There are a hundred reasons why I should send Your Excellency my poems. I will name only one: I love you . . . I kiss your sacred hand, which has shown me and the whole German people the way to heaven."[27] A few years later, Heine even made a pilgrimage to see his idol:

He arrived in his stained travel clothes and in a cocky mood. After some small talk, Goethe asked politely, "What are you working on now?"
"On a *Faust*."
"Do you have other business in Weimar, Herr Heine?"
"Having crossed your Excellency's threshold, all my business in Weimar is done," Heine answered and took his leave.[28]

Even though Heine held Goethe in high esteem, their poetry could not be more different. Unlike Heine's ironic stance, Goethe's works at times expressed a positive embrace of life in all its beauty, such as is his 1774 poem *Ganymed* (Ganymede):

How in the morning gleam
All around you glow at me
Springtime, beloved
With joy of love a thousandfold
Rushes to my heart
Of your eternal warmth
A holy feeling
Infinite beauty![29]

Where Goethe's Romantic writings offer a world in harmony, and his role as a poet is to integrate himself into the natural rhythms of life, Heine speaks of dissonance, loss, and a world of fracture. As Heine grew as a writer, his infatuation with Goethe lessened, as is seen in his version of Tannhäuser, where he derides the cult of the sage of Weimar.

Heine, who would become one of the most important German poets during his lifetime, nevertheless was shunned by the major poetic press, J. G. Cotta, which published Goethe, Schiller, and other luminaries of German writing. The press that Heine ended up with was run by Julius Campe, and Heine made such a name for it that it survives to this day as Hoffman and Campe, still making money from his poems. Heine first met Campe in a Hamburg bookstore in 1826, five years after his *Buch der Lieder* had come out with a Berlin publisher. Besides the volatile relationship with uncle Salomon, the love affair with Mathilde, and his intense ties to his parents, the fourth relationship that had a massive influence on Heine was Julius. It was a tempestuous friendship that would help to define him as a man and as a poet and in many ways mimicked a stormy yet passionate marriage.

Where Heine liked to see himself as a free spirit, Campe was a pragmatist who helped keep Heine directed and fought his more radical impulses. Where Campe tried to keep him on a timeline, the ever-revising Heine was never one to meet a deadline. Campe had a warm broad face, penetrating eyes, and in later years, a full head of gray hair. He was an intellectual from a family that had played a prominent role in the Jewish enlightenment. A liberal willing to promote nonmainstream authors at a time when reactionary trends were on the rise, Campe continued to publish his star author even when their relationship became contentious over money and their dealings with censors.

Heine met Campe during a low point in his life when his father's business was going under and he was feeling so undirected and depressed that he even contemplated suicide. In 1827, Campe reissued the *Buch der Lieder*, which eventually would become "the most world-famous book of poetry in the German language."[30] In 1827, Campe also published Heine's *Ideas: The Book of Le Grand*. The collection also contained *Travel Pictures II*, which offered numerous witty and angry attacks on Germany. Again the critics were mixed: some were amused by his prose; others were apoplectic.

Paris

In 1827, Heine returned to Germany after a trip to England and briefly found work as an editor at the Cotta publishing house. Even though they were not open to publishing his works, they were willing to employ him. Heine followed this with a trip to Italy, finally returning to Germany where he learned of his beloved father's death. This profoundly increased his depressive state. After two-and-a-half years of drifting, the 1830 anti-Semitic riots in Hamburg only solidified Heine's belief that revolutions could transform into mob hatred directed against the Jews. Facing increasing troubles—fighting with his uncle over money, censorship pressures, rising anti-Semitism in Germany, and his inability to find a job, Heine left for France in May 1831, where he would remain for much of the rest of his life and where he would compose "Der Tannhäuser."

France in 1831 was facing major upheavals, with the beginnings of rapid industrialization and the decreasing power of the Catholic hierarchy. 1830 had marked the end of the French Restoration of the Bourbon dynasty after the fall of Napoleon, when the bourgeois used their power to establish a constitutional monarchy with King Louis-Philippe at the helm. In a power share of sorts, the king worked with the parliament until the brief 1848 restoration of the Second Republic. Reforms were put into place during the July Revolution and the Catholic hierarchy began to weaken its hold. The Jewish population, which had been emancipated in the previous century during the French revolution, for the most part eagerly embraced the promise of assimilation. Paris was the center of this rapidly changing world with a regular influx of immigrants, a heady mix of culture, and pockets of rampant poverty worsened by cholera outbreaks.

For Heine, France offered mixed blessings. On the one hand, he enjoyed being at the center of world culture and found Paris to be extremely liberating in mind, spirit, and body, especially in comparison to Germany, which was becoming increasingly repressive. Heine at first found it easy to enter the intellectual and social scene and was soon friends with some of the most important artists and writers of the day, including Honoré Balzac, Victor Hugo, George Sand, Frederic Chopin, and Richard Wagner, who had moved to Paris in 1839. French translations of Heine's books were popular and his dry wit made him well liked among his peers. On the other hand, he remained for the most part a lonely figure, unable to fully become French and longing for his homeland and parents. Exactly as Theodor Herzl would do, he became a foreign correspondent reporting on the cultural scene.

His 1834 hook up with the uneducated and coarse "Mathilde" (so renamed by Heine, although her birth name was Crescence Eugénie) would make it increasingly difficult for him to navigate the Parisian art scene, and over the years he would retreat more and more from social engagements into his own cell-like home. Moreover, within a few years of his arrival in Paris his health began to decline, and he would spend his final years bedridden and in profound physical decay. From the first exciting Parisian years marked by illuminating social interactions and a liberation from German repressiveness, Heine began a sharp decline in his social and physical interactions with the Parisians who esteemed him.

The Prussian government, though free of him physically, still held Heine to be such a dangerous figure that he was kept under surveillance by both French and Prussian agents. In 1835, Prussia took the next logical step and banned his writings, supposedly because of his role in the Young Germans movement. This was a group of German intellectuals with whom Heine briefly associated, becoming its most prominent representative. Heine, who had only been loosely involved with the group, discovered that in 1835 his name was officially added to the edict banning their writings in Prussia. The decree, which Campe managed to circumvent as much as he could, must have been humiliating, frustrating, and economically crippling for Heine. Here he was one of Germany's greatest poets, in physical exile in Paris, and now finding himself in intellectual exile as well. Moreover, the Young Germans he was being tied to could often be anti-Semitic. For Heine and Campe, it likely seemed that it was merely an excuse for the Prussian government to ban the works of a writer who challenged the government from a subversive position. Heine was now permanently banished and orders were generated that he should be arrested if he ever sought to return. Heine was no longer an expatriate but a political exile, and this only increased his homesickness.

To the Prussians he was a radical, although in reality Heine was a typical liberal. Though sympathetic to notions about ending government repression, he never entirely believed in democratic government. In this way he was like many liberals of the time, who did not embrace democratic principles of equality for all since they were fearful of giving full rights to the poor and uneducated. Moreover, as a Jew who had experienced firsthand the dangerous anti-Semitic mobs of the Hep-Hep riots, he was reluctant to extend full rights to groups that could so easily turn violently against the Jews.[31] Finally, Heine was too much his own man and too wary of ideologies of any type to fully embrace a liberal platform.

Not long after his arrival in France, Heine realized to his dismay that the ideals of the French Revolution were not being implemented at all and poverty was as rife as anywhere else in the dirty, congested streets. His turn towards the sensualist, radical philosophies of the St. Simonian cult was in part a response to his understanding that Paris had not fulfilled its revolutionary promises of the social emancipation of all men. St. Simonianism offered him the means to attack Catholicism and social repression while also offering a ready-made social sphere.

"Der Tannhäuser"

In 1836, when Heine composed "Der Tannhäuser," he was going through a midlife crisis of sorts,[32] and the poem is an expression of all that he was then battling with physically, spiritually, and psychologically. Physically, he was recovering from a bout of extreme jaundice that left him weak and more depressed than usual and that would also mark the beginning of his health decline. (The following year, he would have brutal headaches, a weak arm, and his eyesight would go from bad to worse.) Financially, he was having problems. Even though his book income was steady he had no regular full-time job and he saved little. Socially, he was finding that his relationship with the coarse Mathilde was narrowing his ability to move easily through educated French circles. Artistically, he was in a dry spell. The combination of his health, financial, artistic, and relationship concerns left him house bound and morose.

The darkly comic poem, "Der Tannhäuser," which draws a caustic portrait of Germany, was written while undergoing all this turmoil in 1836 and appeared in print in 1837 in the volume *Der Salon* (The Salon). The poem is based on the medieval 1515 ballad as it was rewritten and slightly altered in the immensely popular 1806 German song collection *Des Knaben Wunderhorn* (The Wondrous Horn of the Boy) of Arnim and Brentano, as well as Heinrich Kornmann's 1614 often republished book *Mons Veneris,* about the evolution of Venus motifs in German literature. *Des Knaben Wunderhorn* had brought about a new interest in literary circles with German folk motifs in general, and with *Tannhäuser* in particular. For Heine, as he would assert in his book *Der Romantic Shule* (The Romantic School): "I cannot praise this work enough; it contains the fairest flowers of German spirit and feeling, and he who would know the people from their best side should know these songs."[33] *Des Knaben Wunderhorn* showed Heine that Germany's "best side" was its folklore creations.

Moreover, for Heine undergoing a bitter time in Paris, the song collection offered a remedy for homesickness because it was his literary means to reconnect with the place that had banished him.[34] His own version of Tannhäuser thus shows at the same time a complicated melding of love and rage for Germany. The love is located temporally in a past idyllic epoch of the Tannhäuser myth. The rage appears when the past myth is transported and transformed into present day Germany, which has lost its heroic edge and has sunk into the mire. Heine's reworking of the poem marks out his ambivalent feelings towards home. On the one hand, he admires the cultural ethos of the folklore, while on the other hand, he admonishes what that country has become.

The return to folklore in German circles at the turn of the century often went hand in hand with anti-Semitism. The editors of the *Wunderhorn* volume, for instance, had anti-Jewish tendencies. For Heine to take the folk creation of Tannhäuser and transform it into an attack on current day Germany was, according to Ritchie Robertson, to "adapt folk-poetry and folk-tales so as to bring out their latent revolutionary content, link it to the political programme of emancipation, and thus deprive the German nationalists of one of their best weapons."[35] When average readers picked up a poem entitled "Der Tannhäuser," they likely expected a recognizable version of the original ballad. When instead they encountered Heine's bawdy and satiric rewrite, the dissonance between the serious ballad and the sarcastic version by Heine caused the reader to laugh at a folktale held in great esteem by German nationalists. It also shed a light on the great talent of Heine for evoking humor out of everything and anything, from a popular folktale to a serious account of religious heresy.

The opening words of Heine's "Der Tannhäuser" are saturated with irony:

> Good Christians, do not be ensnared
> By Satan's sly suborning!
> I sing you this Tannhäuser song
> To give your souls a warning.[36]

What any "good Christian" would find in the poem is not a warning about the danger of sin. Rather, from the first words, the tone is ironic and a direct challenge to the morality lessons of the Christian church and the folk ballad as a morality teacher.

What remains of the original work are the characters of Tannhäuser, Venus, and the Pope. However, the motivations of each change as they are transformed into human, rather than archetypal, figures. Venus is now a sexual woman with a history of many partners but who is desperate to have Tannhäuser be her only bedfellow. She is also an abused woman whom Tannhäuser regularly beats. She, nevertheless, prefers his punches to his cruel words:

> Tannhäuser, oh my noble knight,
> That's not the way to treat me;
> I'd much prefer to be beat up
> Just as you've often beat me.
> I'd much prefer to be beat up
> Than hear such insults spoken.

In contrast to Venus, who against all reason still wants to keep the relationship going, Tannhäuser has grown tired of their love. He asserts that his

> soul is sick of kisses too—for bitterness I hanker
> We've laughed and jested long enough, It's tears for which I'm pining
> I'd like a crown of thorns around
> My head, not roses twining.

Sick of the daily routine, Tannhäuser wants anguish and adventures. He is a disaffected youth seeking "a crown of thorns." Heine is thus playing with Catholic iconography and turning Tannhäuser into an anti-Jesus, Gothlike youth who seeks out suffering. As S.S. Prawer notes, "It is not anxiety for his soul which drives Heine's Tannhäuser out of the Venusberg, but a perverse and very modern longing for bitterness after so much sweetness."[37] This representation of the knight is similar to how Tannhäuser was portrayed in 1799 by the popular German Romantic writer Ludwig Tieck in his "Der getreue Eckart und der Tannenhäuser" (Faithful Eckart and Tannhäuser). However, where Tieck drew the knight in a serious light, in Heine's version, Tannhäuser's moodiness is an object of humor.

Heine's Tannhäuser is thus a reversal of the original 1515 ballad. There, the young man is "seduced" by sensual love while here he is overfull of sex and is instead "seduced" by the promise of suffering. Moreover he is a bully and an abuser. The ironic tone and his addressing of himself as "Tannhäuser, a noble knight" shows that he is a character aware that he is housed in a literary work, which makes the poem in many ways is a highly modern literary production.[38] This sets "Der Tannenhäuser" in relationship with and in opposition to its previous incarnations. In the current version, Tannhäuser is a figure representative of an ironic perspective on the world.

When Tannhäuser leaves Venus and goes to Pope Urban instead of seeking absolution for his sins, he begs the Pope to "deliver" him "from the pains of hell / And from the devil's embraces." The Pope says he cannot do this since:

> The devil that has Venus' name
> Is the worst in all creation,
> And from those lovely claws no one
> Can ever get salvation.
> Your soul must pay for lustful flesh
> And the sins you gave performance;
> For you are lost, you are condemned
> To hell's eternal torments.

The tone of the narrative undermines Tannhäuser's intentions for repentance. It is possible, then, that when Tannhäuser addresses the Pope, his tongue, as is the poet's, is firmly planted in his cheek. For the critic Heinz W. Puppe, the dialogue between the Pope and Tannhäuser is a "metaphor for the conflict and interplay of Sensualism and Spiritualism," and with the Pope's "pathetic admission of impotence" to Tannhäuser, he shows that "Spiritualism has no defense against the joys and ecstasies of Sensualism."[39] In Puppe's view, "Der Tannhäuser" thus works through many of the anti-Catholic themes that Heine had delved into while involved with the St. Simonian group.

Once home, the fecund Venus is overjoyed:

> Red blood was running from her nose
> Tears in her eyes were teeming
> Over her lover's countenance
> Her tears and blood were streaming.

She brings him some bread and soup, having clearly forgiven him for the beatings, his cruel words, and his departure. His time away has worked to mend and mature their relationship, and to turn her into a proper housewife.

The poem then switches to a humorous first-person account of Tannhäuser's travels from Rome back to the Venusberg. It is a rather abrupt shift from a love story to a travelogue, but still delivered in an ironic tone.[40] Tannhäuser begins by telling Dame Venus that he had some business to do in Rome

And came home in a hurry
Now, Rome is built on seven hills
Through it the Tiber's fleeting
Oh yes, in Rome I saw the Pope—
He sends you his best greeting.

In one fell swoop, Tannhäuser has undermined the Pope's consignment of him to hell for all eternity. He has comically turned the Pope's harsh indictment into a frivolous greeting, thus completely deflating its power.

Tannhäuser's account of his German travels include stanza-long, humorous descriptions of the cities and towns of St. Gothard, Frankfurt, Dresden, Weimar, Potsdam, Gottingen, and Celle, ending with three stanzas on Heine's favorite geographical "butt of his satire and scorn," Hamburg.[41] It is a whirlwind tour of major German locations, and at each place Heine sends jabs at those who have recently enraged him, or at the very least, have played a prominent role in his negative experiences of Germany. Thus he states that

In Dresden I saw a wretched dog
He was always big and strapping
But now his teeth are falling out
He's just good for pissing and yapping.

Critics have pointed out that the wretched dog is the Romantic nationalist Tieck.[42] Heine may have attacked Tieck not only because he had personal malice against him, but also as a way to downplay the influence of Tieck's 1799 story "Der getreue Eckart und der Tannenhäuser" on Heine's poem.

Heine sends his ire against the outdated and stagnant cult of Goethe that keeps German literature looking backwards to outdated models:

In Weimar, seat of the widowed Muse
Rose wails and laments unforgiving
They wept and moaned that Goethe was dead
And Eckermann still was living.[43]

Heine's satiric attacks do not only land on Germans, but Jews as well, as with his rendition of the leader of the *Wissenschaft* movement, Edward Gans. In Heine's verse, the *Wissenschaft* movement is as outdated as the Goethe cult:

In Potsdam I heard a great uproar
I cried, "What is all that clatter?"
"That's Gans in Berlin, he's lecturing on
Last century's subject matter."

Gans is backward looking and with Hegel now dead, the University of Berlin has no major cultural personalities, and instead focuses all its energies on worn-out models.[44]

There are three mentions of Jewish matters in the poem. When Tannhäuser arrives in Frankfurt the Christian knight asserts that

> I got to Frankfurt on Schabbes and ate
> Schalet and dumplings blended
> They have the best religion there
> And their goose giblets also are splendid.

The stanza points out that not only is Jewish food delicious, but that the Jews "have the best religion there." Three stanzas later, Edward Gans is derided for his loud voice, and in the following stanza Heine writes,

> In Hamburg I asked why the streets stank so
> And from what the stink emanated
> The Jews and Christians both agreed
> From the city canals, they stated.

Jewishness in "Der Tannhäuser" is deeply tied up with Germany and its culture, so much so that the famous Catholic knight eats Jewish food. The Jewish population is not, however, included in the indictment of Christian Germany. Their food and religion is better and they do not stink (in all senses) like their Christian brethren.

Overall, the portrait of Christian Germany depicts a land in serious intellectual and cultural stagnation where "no fruit is found growing." Prussia has kicked out Heine, who as a poet helped keep German literature moving forward. His expulsion is typical of the government's reactionary tendencies as it sought to freeze time and clamp down on revolutionary leanings. Moreover, with each negative rendition of a filthy, stagnant German city or town, Heine is challenging the positive view of the nation then being propagated.

In the 1844 reissue of "Der Tannhäuser," Heine added a final stanza with an open ending:

> In Hamburg I went to Altona too
> It's a very pretty section
> Some other time I'll tell you what
> Befell me at that connection.

This sole mention of something positive about Germany is not explained, leaving the reader nothing tangibly good to know about the country. An open ending resists the expected closure of a legend or of a folktale and transforms the poem into an unfinished narrative that resists an easy interpretation. The tale, in which real travels are not undergone but described after the fact, ends in mid-dialogue. Since no real action happens any longer in Germany, Tannhäuser's exploits do not occur in the present but as events from the past that he tells Venus about. The perpetually endless travelogue is Tannhäuser's verbal offering to the permanently housebound Venus. The couple will forever remain stagnant in the Venusberg while turning for amusement and a false sense of movement to his travel tales. This will fill the hours of their relationship, since for all intents and purposes Tannhäuser will remain as still as the housewife Venus. The future of Germany is embodied in this housebound, stagnant couple endlessly recounting tales of previous journeys.

S. S. Prawer views the final section as showing "a way of escape" for Tannhäuser, since in recounting his travelogue Tannhäuser "has acquired a new freedom, a superiority of mind that enables him to look outwards as well as inwards, to survey the world and then to *choose* the Venusberg."[45] I believe that Prawer is putting far too optimistic a spin on an ending that instead shows a young man who finds no viable options—neither remaining in the stagnant Venusberg, nor in entering the stagnant German society he has just travelled through.

As a whole, the poem turns a beloved character of German folklore into someone no better, and perhaps worse (after all he is a wife beater) than the average man. It is as if Heine is saying that if this knight represents the best of the German folk then they are not worthy of esteem. Heine does not even offer his readers the expectation that the situation in Germany, or in the life of its archetypal young man, Tannhäuser, can improve.

Publication History

Heine wrote "Der Tannhäuser" in 1836, and first published it with an introduction in 1837 in the third volume of his collection *Der Salon* (The Salon) that had been partially published in 1834 in Heine's French volume *De l'Allemagne*. In 1844 he published a second French version of the collection *Neue Gedichte* (New Poems), with the new open-ended version discussed above. With both versions of the poems he added explanatory notes that helped to illuminate his intentions.

In the 1837 publication the poem was placed within an essay entitled "Elementargeister" (Elemental Spirit), which can be seen as illuminating aspects of the poem.[46] In "Elementargeister," Heine challenges Romanticism and Christianity. His dispute with Romanticism is that it focuses endlessly on the idealized past rather than concentrating on what is useful about how we understand the present. The essay also challenges the Christian basis of the Romantic movement. Heine's condemnation of Christianity plays out in the poem when the Pope is presented as a ridiculous figure, totally useless against the pull of the pagan goddess.

Heine also inserted a copy of the original Tannhäuser ballad from Arnim and Brentano's *Des Knaben Wunderhorn* directly before his version of the poem. Heine, however, claimed in the introductory notes that his poem, "Der Tannhäuser" had been written by an anonymous author.

Along with the two Tannhäuser poems, there is an explanation by Heine that he initially read of Tannhäuser in Kornmann's collection of Venus folktales entitled *Mons Veneris*. According to Heine, when he first read the ballad he felt as if he had "suddenly discovered a vein of gold, in a dark, deep tunnel in a mountain." For Heine, the ballad contained the "tones of those nightingales of nonbelievers during the time of the passion right before the middle ages" that had to keep their songs against Catholicism quiet, although they would on occasion arise as in the poem.[47] Heine is thus linking the original version of Tannhäuser with an anti-censorship and anti-Catholic politics, matching his own desire at the time to challenge the Prussian authorities. Thus, while Heine wanted "Elementargeister" as a whole to steer clear of the censors' notice, the Tannhäuser poem overtly challenges them.

In the explanatory notes, Heine also claims that he read a 1515 loose-leaf, decaying version of the ballad given to him by the Young German poet Herr Bechstein.[48] This edition was more "poetic" than the one found in *Des Knaben Wunderhorn*, but Heine was not sharing it with his readers because its language was dated. Rather, he was passing on a more recent version of the poem that he had received and, he claimed, was not written by him. This is the common literary trick, popularized in Cervantes' *Don Quixote*, of inventing a false author for a text.

Why hide behind a nom de plume? First it disassociates Heine from his poem and seemingly averts intense scrutiny by censors. Second, claiming that it is a real, found version makes it a poem generated in Germany. It becomes an authentic insider's vision of Germany rather than the angry scribbling of a rebellious, marginalized Jewish poet. Yet the reality, as Heinz Puppe points out, is "Heine prided himself in writing in such a distinct style that he expected his reading public to identify the true author of his poem without fail."[49] This is a game that his readers would be well aware of. Moreover, by having his poem follow the original ballad, he is establishing a "pedigree" between his version and that of the original.[50]

In the later French edition of "Elementargeister," Heine wrote additional explanatory notes where he confesses that the poem is his own and dissects the differences between his version and the older one to see how two poets from different eras and epochs work around the same framing device.[51] According to Heine, the divergences between the old and contemporary versions display the temperament of the ages, with the modern edition showing skepticism towards the old clerical, didactic religious dogmas of the past and a reluctance to propagate the virtues of absolution.

Taken as a whole, both sets of comments strategically place Heine's "Der Tannhäuser" in a direct relationship with the 1515 original and show that it was created to oppose certain tendencies in German culture. His poem reworks the geography of Germany, and uses it as a literary site on which to express the dark underbelly of German life and how it has undermined Heine's own literary efforts. Later, when stressing how his work differs from the original, he effectively clears a space for himself and his own unique and original voice.

Venus

In the introduction to the second printing of the poem in 1844, Heine claims that the flesh-and-blood inspiration for his Venus was not his permanent companion Mathilde, but an elegant woman whom he spotted on a Parisian street while he was walking with Honoré Balzac.[52] According to Heine, Balzac asserted that she looked like a "kept" woman while Heine insisted that she was a noblewoman. Later, they learned who she was and that each had been in part correct: she was a kept noblewoman.[53] This anecdote is interesting because it points out how Heine viewed himself in those early days in Paris. Heine is the naïve visitor while Balzac is an insider privy to the gossip of the city's underbelly, where women who appear to be upper class are in fact whores. Where Heine sees respectability and nobility, Balzac sees the unvarnished truth. Heine is the tourist, Balzac the true Parisian, able to unpack subtle social codes embedded in a woman's dress and walk. Yet because he was partly right, perhaps Heine is not as naïve as he may seem; in fact, he may know things that the native French are too jaded to see. Moreover, the anecdote places him with Balzac, proof that Heine is moving in the inner circles of Parisian intelligentsia. This of course is in marked contrast with his exile from German cultural life. And finally, this most seductive woman is neither German nor pagan: she is French! Heine's banishment from Germany to France is matched by his making Venus a Parisian.

Another inspiration for his use of Venus may have been a personal vendetta against Ludwig Tieck who had recently attacked Heine in one of his novels.[54] As discussed earlier, Tieck had composed a version of the Tannhäuser story matching his interest in reviving positive German folk heroes of the past. In Tieck's version, Venus is not the pantheistic heroine, but Tatiana. For Heine to make Venus into a debased woman is to challenge Tieck's use of the figure as a positive folklore heroine. For Heine to exclude Tieck from those mentioned in "Elementargeister" as having influenced his writing of "Der Tannhäuser" was certainly an intentional way to downplay the importance of Tieck and his work.[55]

Heine also saw Venus as a tool to challenge Catholicism by showing the continuing powerful lure of paganism. This matches Heine's writing of the time where he asserts a belief in the vitality of the pantheistic gods versus dry, arid Catholicism. Heine saw Catholicism (but not Protestantism, which he viewed as much less repressive) as creating an artificial division between humans and their animalistic sides. These beliefs developed from Heine's dabbling in the cult of St. Simonianism in 1831, the year he came to Paris. It was a group that was prosensual, advocating the liberation of desires and thus contradicting and challenging repressive Catholicism.[56] Heine found much in St. Simonianism silly and never became a devout follower, but he was clearly taken with their dislike of Catholicism and their willingness to challenge society when it was repressive. His "Der Tannhäuser" ends with a description of a sensual, modern relationship that arises from the Pope's (or Catholicism's) rejection of Tannhäuser, reflecting Heine's desire to elevate the sensual and deride the repressive.

Heine's decision to rewrite the famous folktale also may have been inspired by a personal search to understand his relationship with his girlfriend. The story of a man seduced by an erotic woman matched his own love affair with the plebeian Mathilde with whom he had started living the year that he composed the poem (and whom he would marry a few years later). Critics have been unrelenting in painting her as extremely stupid; as someone whom Heine could mold and influence and who was in every possible way wrong for him.[57] Where she was dumb he was brilliant; where she was barely literate he was well read; where she was a devout Catholic he was Jewish; where she had expensive tastes he was perpetually broke; where she was an open page he had an extremely complicated and often mischievous personality. The physical attraction, however, was obvious: she was a dark-haired beauty with a round face, gentle eyes, and an erotic, full mouth. Plump, sensual, and extremely voluptuous, she was Heine's first real love after his failed relationships with his cousins.

Despite their differences, in many ways the relationship actually makes perfect sense. Both were in their own way quite childlike and needy and she provided Heine with unquestioning love and devotion. The year she moved in with him, the intoxication he must have felt toward the young and naïve beauty was expressed in Tannhäuser's inability to leave Venus. In 1836, at the time of his work on "Der Tannhäuser," Heine wrote of his relationship: "My recent stay in Paris was very pleasant, and Mathilde brightens my life with the consistent inconsistency of her moods. I think only rarely of poisoning or asphyxiating both of us; we shall probably take our lives in some other way—by reading a book which will bore us to death."[58]

Heine found Mathilde a dangerous addiction he could not break free of, much as Tannhäuser returns in the end to Venus. As an intellectual, surely it annoyed him that his partner could not be his equal and that, as he commented, she never read his work. It says quite a bit about Heine's personality that he would choose someone so seemingly unworthy: that he was extremely insecure and wanted to be adored by a woman he could consider his lesser and that a physical relationship was less important than a brotherly-sisterly friendship that would produce no offspring. His relationship with Mathilde is not, however, entirely negative since it points to strengths in his character—even at the cost of being socially ostracized he remained true to himself and his relationship.

Post-Tannhäuser Life and Death

After the publication of "Der Tannhäuser," Heine spent the rest of his life in France, although he did manage to revisit Hamburg to see his mother and Campe. In 1846, he returned to the theme of Tannhäuser and Venus in his poem *Die Göttin Diana* (The Goddess Diana). In it he describes an erotic ballet between Tannhäuser and Venus. As will be discussed in the chapter on Richard Wagner, Wagner likely stole the idea to add a sensual ballet to his 1861 French version of the opera from Heine's *Die Göttin Diana*.

The 1840s were marked by Heine's return to questions of Jewish identity, sparked in large measure by the Damascus Affair of 1840 in which there was a "blood libel" directed against the Jewish community of Damascus, Syria. A blood libel was a common, anti-Semitic accusation in which the Jews were blamed for killing Christians, usually children (although in this case it was a monk), in order to use their blood to make Passover matzo. The Damascus Jewish community was terrorized, and there were anti-Jewish riots throughout the Middle East. The most shocking aspect of the affair was not the blood libel itself, which had occurred many times before, but that the French consul supported the accusations of the Muslims. France, the world's most "enlightened" society, should have stopped the terror. They did nothing and instead it was England that intervened for the community.

For Heine, this was a turning point that marked his return to issues of Jewish identity downplayed during his first decade in France. He began work again on his unfinished novel, *The Rabbi of Bacharach*. Soon thereafter, near the end of his life, he also composed his *Hebrew Melodies* which visits Jewish themes such as the Sabbath from a contemporary and edgy perspective. Like his "Der Tannhäuser," the *Hebrew Melodies* transplant iconic images into a contemporary cadence. Thus he writes of "Princess Sabbath":

> She allows all to her lover,
> All except tobacco-smoking:
> "Darling, smoking is forbidden,
> Since today's the Sabbath day.
> But instead you will, at midday,
> Get a dish steamed up to please you.
> A divinely tasty morsel—
> You will feast today on schalet!"
> Schalet, shining gleam from Heaven,
> Daughter of Elysium!—
> Schiller's ode would sound like this if
> He had ever tasted schalet. [59]

The *Melodies* again shows Heine's contradictory view of Jewishness (and his obsession with Jewish food). He mines the culture in a loving way for icons yet he does not imbue them with a reverent status. As with his use of German folklore in "Der Tannhäuser," so too his use of Jewish iconography gives a feeling that Heine is an outsider to the culture.

In the years after the publication of "Der Tannhäuser," Heine remained a major figure on the cultural scene and ironically he became the person to whom numerous pilgrimages were made by German writers. He continued to fight the ban on his works and built a friendship with another expatriate in France, Karl Marx. Heine remained the rebellious figure throughout his life and continued to refuse to embrace any type of totalizing ideology, including Marx's socialism. Yet both were figures enraged at the German authorities and radicals who sought emancipation. For Marx it was economic emancipation, while for Heine it was spiritual and sensual emancipation (as seen in "Der Tannhäuser"). They came

increasingly under the ire of the Prussian authorities and in 1844 an arrest order
was issued for both if they ever attempted to cross the border.

Heine's final years, from 1848-1856, were spent in a "mattress grave" of
horrendous physical decline that had begun in 1836 and had never let up.[60] In
1848, his legs became permanently paralyzed; he was never able to walk again.
The paralysis that destroyed his legs would randomly attack other parts of his
body, including his eyes, which had to be propped open for him to be able to
read. The cause of the horrific attack of his body on his body is generally considered to have been venereal disease that ate at his spinal cord, although it may
have been multiple sclerosis.[61]

Heine became as helpless as a child, relying on others to feed, clothe, and
change him, in agonizing pain, and ingesting steady doses of morphine and other
painkillers. However his brain remained intact and engaged with the world and
he continued to write, even making fun of the horrific state of his body in his
poem "Bequest":

> Now my life is nearly spent—
> Here's my Will and Testament.
> Christianlike, I offer these
> Presents to my enemies.
> . . . I bequeth you diabolic
> Griping pains of belly colic,
> Bladder troubles, and the wiles
> Of the treacherous Prussian piles.
> You shall have my cramps, and pus,
> Bloody spittle, limbs that twitch,
> Spinal rot, and scaly itch—
> Lovely gifts of God to us. [62]

His health worsened precipitously throughout 1855 and on February 17, 1856,
he died. His last words have been recounted as "Write . . . paper . . . pencil" and
"God will pardon me. It is his trade." Over a hundred people, including Parisian
literary figures, attended his simple funeral at Montmartre, the cemetery of note
for famous writers of the day.

Concluding Remarks

Heine's "Der Tannhäuser" expresses the poet's attempt to ridicule the culture that
he had loved and that had banished him and his writings. Using a beloved figure
of German legend, Heine turned Tannhäuser into a debased and debasing cad
who ends up perpetually housebound with Venus, locked together for all time
in endless ruminations over past glories. By taking a popular German ballad
and making fun of every aspect of it, Heine was using literature as a weapon
to challenge and subvert the authority of the German cultural elite. The poem

was Heine's means to show Germany as a spent culture, frozen in time, which was destroying itself by expunging from its terrain its native geniuses. Germany's culture was like a house of cards that lacked any stability to confront the present.

The poem clearly worked as a rebuke, and the perceived danger of Heine, the rebellious Jewish subverter, would remain so strong that a myth would grow that Hitler's first act on invading Paris would be to send his storm troopers to Montmartre.

Notes

1. Hugo Bieber also puts forth this myth of Hitler's destruction of Heine's grave on the opening page of his edited volume, *Heinrich Heine: A Biographical Anthology* (Philadelphia: Jewish Publication Society, 1956), 1.
2. For a detailed discussion of the erection of the obelisk for Heine at the turn of the century, see the chapter "Heine's Grabdenkmal in Paris 1901," in Dietrich Schubert, *"Jetzt wohin?" Heinrich Heine in seinen verhinderten errichteten Denkmälern* (Cologne: Böhlau, 1999), 145-66.
3. For an examination of the evolution of criticism about Heine, see George F. Peters, *The Poet as Provocateur: Heinrich Heine and His Critics* (Rochester NY: Camden House, 2000).
4. Jefferson Chase, *Inciting Laughter: The Development of "Jewish Humor" in Nineteenth-Century German Culture* (New York: Walter de Gruyter, 2000), 3.
5. The best source for biographical information on Heine is Jeffrey L. Sammon, *Heinrich Heine: A Modern Biography* (Princeton: Princeton University Press, 1979). I wish to thank Jeffrey L. Sammons for his incredible generosity in sharing insights with me via email as I prepared this chapter. The rest of the biographies are a mixed bag, many offering contradictory information about Heine. Other biographies I referred to include E. M. Butler, *Heinrich Heine: A Biography* (Westport, CO: Greenwood Press, 1956), Philip Kossoff, *Valiant Heart: A Biography of Heinrich Heine* (New York: Cornwall Books, 1983), Hanna Spencer, *Heinrich Heine* (Boston: Twayne Publishers, 1982), and Max Brod's well known (but not always trustworthy), *Heinrich Heine: The Artist in Revolt*, trans. Joseph Witriol (New York: New York University Press, 1957). For an excellent bibliography in English of Heine's writing and writing on Heine, see George F. Peters, *The Poet as Provocateur: Heinrich Heine and his Critics* (Rochester, New York: Camden House, 2000), 193-216. For German sources see Jan-Christoph Hauschild and Michael Werner, *"Der Zweck des Lebens ist dat Leben selbst": Heinrich Heine: Eine Biographie* (Köln: Kiepenheuer and Witsch, 1997), Gerhard Höhn, *Heine-Handbuch: Zeit, Person, Work* (Stuttgart: Metzler, 1997), and Jochanan Trilse-Finkelstein, *Gelebter Widerspruch: Heinrich Heine Biographie* (Berlin: Aufbau-verlag, 1997).
6. For an analysis of this period and what it meant for the daily life of the Jews of Germany, see Steven M. Lowenstein, "The Beginning of Integration: 1780-1870," in *Jewish Daily Life in Germany, 1680-1945*, ed. Marion A. Kaplan (Oxford: Oxford University Press, 2005), 93-173. This quote is from page 93.
7. Jost Hermand, "Tribune of the People or Aristocrat of the Spirit: Heine's Ambivalence Towards the Masses," in *Heinrich Heine's Contested Identities: Politics, Religion, and Nationalism in Nineteenth-Century Germany*, ed. Jost Hermand and Robert C. Holub (New York: Peter Lang, 1999), 155.

8.   Of Düsseldorf , Heine humorously wrote, "The town of Düsseldorf is very beautiful
      . . . I was born there . . . When I say home, I mean the Bolkerstrasse, and the house
      where I was born. The house will some day be famous, and I have told the old woman
      who now owns it under no circumstances to sell it . . . The paper laurel wreath with
      which they have crowned my brow has not yet spread its fragrance throughout the
      world, and when elegant green-veiled English ladies come to Düsseldorf, they do not
      so much as look at the famous house, but go straight to the market place to inspect
      the colossal, black equestrian statue standing in the middle of it." The quote is from
      Memoiren in Heinrich Heine, *Sämtliche Werke* (Düsseldorf: Artemis and Winkler
      Verlag, 2006), 2:114-15. The English translation can be found in Heinrich Heine,
      The Poetry and Prose of Heinrich Heine, ed. and trans. Frederic Ewen (New York: The
      Citadel Press, 1948), 302.
9.   For a discussion of the popularity of conversion for practical reasons, see Amos Elon,
      The Pity Of It All: A History of Jews in Germany, 1743-1933 (New York: Metropolitan
      Books, 2002), 81-83.
10.   Harry was not the only family member whose name would change (for him it would
      become Christian Johann Heinrich after his conversion)—all his siblings and his
      mother also switched names during their lives: his sister Sarah, born in 1800, was
      called Charlotte, his brother Gottschalk, born in 1803, was called Gustav, and his
      other brother Meyer, born in 1805, was later called Maximillian, while his mother
      Piera was called Betty. And later in life Heine would rename his wife Crescence as
      Mathilde. The changes show his and his family's ease changing their names from
      ones that had implied Jewish resonances, such as Harry, Sarah, and Meyer, to more
      commonplace German Christian ones.
11.   Jeffrey Sammon, *Heinrich Heine: A Modern Biography* (Princeton: Princeton
      University Press, 1979), 17-18.
12.   The quote is from Heine's poem, "An meine Mutter, B. Heine, geborne v. Geldern"
      in *Buch der Lieder* in Heinrich Heine, *Sämtliche Werke* (Düsseldorf: Artemis and
      Winkler Verlag, 2001), 1:53. The English translation, "To My Mother, B. Heine, nee
      v. Geldern" is in *The Complete Poems of Heinrich Heine: A Modern English Version*,
      trans. Hal Draper (Boston: Suhrkamp/Insel, 1982), 46.
13.   The quote is from *Memoiren* in Heinrich Heine, *Sämtliche Werke* (Düsseldorf:
      Artemis and Winkler Verlag, 2006), 2:828. The English translation can be found in
      The Poetry and Prose of Heinrich Heine, ed. and trans. Frederic Ewen (New York: The
      Citadel Press, 1948), 325.
14.   Amos Elon, *The Pity Of It All: A History of Jews in Germany, 1743-1933* (New York:
      Metropolitan Books, 2002), 91.
15.   The quote is from Heinrich Heine, *Ideen. Das Buch Le Grand*, in *Sämtliche Werke*
      (Düsseldorf: Artemis and Winkler Verlag, 2006), 2:128. The English translation
      can be found in Heinrich Heine, *The Poetry and Prose of Heinrich Heine*, ed. and
      trans. Frederic Ewen (New York: The Citadel Press, 1948), 327. Perhaps Heine's
      adult description of his love for Napoleon is so extreme in its adulation in order to
      annoy his German readers, many of whom saw France and Napoleon as the enemy
      of German culture.
16.   For a collection of essays that considers, from a variety of angles, how critics view
      Heine and also challenges a fixed notion of Heine's identity, see Jost Hermand and
      Robert C. Holub, eds., *Heinrich Heine's Contested Identities: Politics, Religion, and
      Nationalism in Nineteenth-Century Germany* (New York: Peter Lang, 1999).

17. See *Memoiren* in Heinrich Heine, *Sämtliche Werke* (Düsseldorf: Artemis and Winkler Verlag, 2006), 2:819-820. These recollections in English translation can be found in Heinrich Heine, *The Poetry and Prose of Heinrich Heine*, ed. and trans. Frederic Ewen (New York: The Citadel Press, 1948), 321-22.

18. For Sammon's discussion of Heine's return to his Jewish roots, see *Heinrich Heine: A Modern Biography* (Princeton: Princeton University Press, 1979), 89-91.

19. See David Blackbourn, *History of Germany 1780-1918: The Long Nineteenth Century*, 2nd ed. (Oxford: Blackwell, 2003), 92-93. While he shows the suppressions of the era, he also argues that the "gloomy picture" of the time needs to be "qualified."

20. The letters can be found sprinkled throughout Hugo Bieber, ed., *Heine: A Biographical Anthology*, trans. Moses Hadas (Philadelphia: Jewish Publication Society, 1956).

21. As quoted in Amos Elon, *The Pity Of It All: A History of Jews in Germany, 1743-1933* (New York: Metropolitan Books, 2002), 124.

22. This quote can be found in *Aufzeichnungen* in Heinrich Heine, *Sämtliche Schriften* (München: Carl Hanser Verlag, 1975), 6:622. The English translation can be found in *The Poetry and Prose of Heinrich Heine*, ed. and trans. Frederic Ewen (New York: The Citadel Press, 1948), 700.

23. For a discussion of Heine's conflicted Jewish identity, see Jeffrey L. Sammon, "Who Did Heine Think He Was?" in *Heinrich Heine's Contested Identities: Politics, Religion, and Nationalism in Nineteenth-Century Germany*, ed. Jost Hermand and Robert C. Holub (New York: Peter Lang, 1999), 1-25. This quote is from page 10.

24. See, for instance, S. S. Prawer, *Heine's Jewish Comedy: A Study of His Portraits of Jews and Judaism* (Oxford: Clarendon Press, 1983).

25. This quote is from "Lyrisches Intermezzo" in *Buch der Lieder* in Heinrich Heine, *Sämtliche Werke* (Düsseldorf: Artemis and Winkler Verlag, 2001), 1:79. The English translation can be found in Hal Draper, ed., *The Complete Poems of Heinrich Heine: A Modern English Version* (Boston Inc: Suhrkamp/Insel, 1982), 69.

26. This quote is from "Die Harzreise" in *Reisebilder* in Heinrich Heine, *Sämtliche Werke* (Düsseldorf: Artemis and Winkler Verlag, 2006), 2:7. The English translation can be found in Hal Draper, ed., *The Complete Poems of Heinrich Heine: A Modern English Version* (Boston Inc: Suhrkamp/Insel, 1982), 123.

27. Heinrich Heine, *The Poetry and Prose of Heinrich Heine*, ed. and trans. Frederic Ewen (New York: The Citadel Press, 1948), 343.

28. As quoted in Amos Elon, *The Pity Of It All: A History of Jews in Germany, 1743-1933* (New York: Metropolitan Books, 2002), 120.

29. Johann Wolfgang van Goethe, *Johann Wolfgang van Goethe: Selected Poems*, ed. Christopher Middleton, trans. Michael Hamburger, David Luke, Christopher Middleton, John Frederick Nims and Vernon Watkins (Boston: Suhrkamp/Insel Publisher, 1983), 30-31.

30. Jeffrey Sammon, *Heinrich Heine: A Modern Biography* (Princeton: Princeton University Press, 1979), 125.

31. See Jost Hermand, "Tribune of the People or Aristocrat of the Spirit: Heine's Ambivalence Towards the Masses," in *Heinrich Heine's Contested Identities: Politics, Religion, and Nationalism in Nineteenth-Century Germany*, ed. Jost Hermand and Robert C. Holub (New York: Peter Lang, 1999), 159.

32. For a discussion of the crisis Heine was going through in 1835-1836, see Michael Werner, "Crossing Borders Between Cultures: On the Preconditions and Function of Heine's Reception in France," in *Heinrich Heine and the Occident: Multiple Identities,*

Multiple Receptions, ed. Peter Uwe Hohendahl and Sander L. Gillman (Lincoln: University of Nebraska Press, 1991), 56.

33. This quote is from *Die Romantische Shule* in Heinrich Heine, *Sämtliche Werke* (Düsseldorf: Artemis and Winkler Verlag, 2006), 3:343. The English translation can be found in *The Romantic School* in Heinrich Heine, *The Works of Heinrich Heine*, trans. Charles Godfrey Leland (London: William Heinemann, 1892), 2:6-7.

34. For a discussion of this, see Jochen Zinke, "Tannhäuser im Exil. Zu Heines Legende Der Tannhäuser," in *Gedichte und Interpretationen*, vol. 4, *Vom Biedermeier zum bürgerlichen Realismus*, ed. Günther Hantzschel (Stuttgart: Reclam, 1983), p. 212.

35. See Ritchie Robertson's *Heine* (New York: Grove Press, 1988), p. 27.

36. The English translation of Heine's "Der Tannhäuser" can be found in Heinrich Heine, *The Complete Poems of Heinrich Heine: A Modern English Version*, ed. and trans. Hal Draper (Boston: Suhrkamp/Insel, 1982), 348-53. I have made a number of amendments to the translation. The original German version can be found in Heinrich Heine, *Heinrich Heine: Sämtliche Schriften* (München: Carl Hanser Verlag, 1971), 3:696-703. The notes that Heine wrote in the *Elementargeister* discussing the original versions from Kornmann and *Des Knaben Wunderhorn* are found on 692-96.

37. S. S. Prawer, *Heine the Tragic Satirist: A Study of the Later Poetry 1827-1856* (Cambridge: Cambridge University Press, 1961), 42.

38. See Mary A. Cicora, *From History to Myth: Wagner's Tannhäuser and its Literary Sources* (Bern: Peter Lang, 1992), 146.

39. Heinz W. Puppe, "Heinrich Heine's Tannhäuser," in *Monatshefte* (1974), 66:350.

40. Critics have been mixed about the final section. S. S. Prawer find's it unconvincingly jarring, see *Heine the Tragic Satirist: A Study of the Later Poetry 1827-1856* (Cambridge: Cambridge University Press, 1961), 46; and Laura Hofrichter finds that his "blending of political and lyrical was not quite successful." See *Heinrich Heine*, trans. Barker Fairley (Oxford: Oxford University Press, 1963), 150. Jochen Zinke, in contrast, finds the final section a natural continuation of the ironic tone of the earlier sections of the poem; see "Tannhäuser im Exil. Zu Heines Legende Der Tannhäuser," in *Gedichte und Interpretationen*, vol. 4, *Vom Biedermeier zum bürgerlichen Realismus*, ed. Günther Hantzschel (Stuttgart: Reclam, 1983), 216. Jeffrey L. Sammons views it as Heine seeking to shift the tone into satire. See *Heinrich Heine: The Elusive Poet* (New Haven: Yale University Press, 1969), 197.

41. Jeffrey Sammon, *Heinrich Heine: A Modern Biography* (Princeton: Princeton University Press, 1979), 48.

42. For a detailed analysis of why and how Heine attacks Tieck in his poem, and the difference between Heine's and Tieck's versions of Tannhäuser, see Günter Oesterle, "Heinrich Heine's Tannhäusergedicht-eine erotische Legende aus Paris" in *Heinrich Heine und das neunzehnte Jahrhundert: Signaturen: neue Beitrae zur Forschung*, ed. Rolf Hosfeld (Berlin: Argument, 1986), 6-11. And, according to Mary Cicora, it is of particular interest that Tieck had written his own version of Tannhäuser. Heine thus viewed him as another Romantic who misused medieval literature. See Mary A. Cicora, *From History to Myth: Wagner's Tannhäuser and its Literary Sources* (Bern: Peter Lang, 1992), 138-39.

43. Johann Peter Eckermann was the main editor and promoter of Goethe's poems.

44. Interestingly, Gans seemingly took little offense at his caricature in the poem, writing a light hearted letter in 1838 about his portrayal in the poem. See S. S. Prawer, *Heine's*

Jewish Comedy: A Study of his Portraits of Jews and Judaism (Oxford: Clarendon Press, 1983), 22.

45. See S. S. Prawer, *Heine the Tragic Satirist: A Study of the Later Poetry 1827-1856* (Cambridge: Cambridge University Press, 1961), 45.

46. See Mary A. Cicora, *From History to Myth: Wagner's Tannhäuser and its Literary Sources* (Bern: Peter Lang, 1992), 139.

47. Heinrich Heine, *Heinrich Heine: Sämtliche Schriften*, (München, Carl Hanser Verlag, 1971), 3:695. Trans. Petra Sertic.

48. The explanatory notes by Heine can be found in Heinrich Heine, *Heinrich Heine: Sämtliche Schriften*, (München, Carl Hanser Verlag, 1971), 3:692-96.

49. Heinz W. Puppe, "Heinrich Heine's Tannhäuser," in *Monatshefte* (1974), 66:346.

50. Ibid.

51. The notes to the French version can be found in Heinrich Heine, *Heinrich Heine: Sämtliche Schriften*, (München, Carl Hanser Verlag, 1971), 3:1023-26.

52. For a discussion of the anecdote about Balzac and how it enables Heine to transfer the Tannhäuser motif to France, see Günter Oesterle, "Heinrich Heine's Tannhäusergedicht-eine erotische Legende aus Paris," in *Heinrich Heine und das neunzehnte Jahrhundert: Signaturen: neue Beitrae zur Forschung*, ed. Rolf Hosfeld (Berlin: Argument, 1986), 14-20.

53. This anecdote can be read in Heinrich Heine, *Heinrich Heine: Sämtliche Schriften* (München, Carl Hanser Verlag, 1971), 3:1025-26.

54. See Günter Oesterle, "Heinrich Heines Tannhäusergedicht- eine erotische Legende aus Paris," in *Heinrich Heine und das neunzehnte Jahrhundert: Signaturen: neue Beitrage zur Forschung*, ed. Rolf Hosfeld (Berlin: Argument, 1986), 6-11.

55. See Deiter Borchmeyer, *Drama and the World of Richard Wagner*, trans. Daphne Ellis (Princeton: Princeton University Press, 2003), 107.

56. See Jeffrey L. Sammon's discussion of St. Simonianism in *Heinrich Heine: A Modern Biography* (Princeton: Princeton University Press, 1979), 159-68. See also Ritchie Robertson, *Heine* (New York: Grove Press, 1988), 37-38.

57. See, for instance, E. M. Butler, *Heinrich Heine: A Biography* (Westport, CO: Greenwood Press, 1956), 103.

58. Heinrich Heine, *The Poetry and Prose of Heinrich Heine*, ed. and trans. Frederic Ewen (New York: The Citadel Press, 1948), 420-21.

59. This quote is from "Prinzessin Sabbat" in *Hebräische Melodien* in Heinrich Heine, *Sämtliche Werke* (Düsseldorf: Artemis and Winkler Verlag, 2001), 1:542-43. Translation in Heinrich Heine, *The Complete Poems of Heinrich Heine: A Modern English Version*, trans. Hal Draper (Boston Inc: Suhrkamp/Insel, 1982), 653.

60. For an examination of Heine's final years, see Ernst Pawel, *The Poet Dying: Heinrich Heine's Last Years in Paris* (New York: Farrar, Straus, Giroux, 1995).

61. From an email from Jeffrey Sammons (June 22, 2007). The major work on Heine's disease is Henner Montanus' *Der kranke Heine* [The Sick Heine] (Stuttgart and Weimar: Metzler, 1995).

62. This quote is from "Vermächtnis" in *Romanzero* in Heinrich Heine, *Sämtliche Werke* (Düsseldorf: Artemis and Winkler Verlag, 2001), 1:538-39. Translation in Heinrich Heine, *The Complete Poems of Heinrich Heine: A Modern English Version*, trans. Hal Draper (Boston Inc: Suhrkamp/Insel, 1982), 19.

Chapter Three

Richard Wagner

The Castle

In April 1842, a decrepit horse and buggy was travelling through the Wartburg valley in Thüringia, Germany. Inside the carriage were Richard Wagner (1813-1883) and his first wife, Minna, returning from two-and-a-half years in Paris. The air was cold and damp and they shivered in their inadequate clothing.

The couple was glad to be finally coming home. Wagner's stay in Paris had been difficult to say the least. While in France, Wagner had been stifled in his attempts to put on his works, faced serious money problems, and constantly fought with his wife. He had, however, met some of the leading members of the Parisian cultural world, even becoming friends with the exiled German Jewish poet Heinrich Heine. Wagner's time in France cemented his belief that Paris represented the worst aspects of the modern world. This was a common view of German nationalists who considered France to be the negative opposite of Germany which, by contrast, had a rich culture of the volk stretching back in time and was filled with heroes and heroines who embodied the highest noble virtues.

So far the journey back to Dresden had been hellish, with terrible weather and roads jammed with people heading to the Leipzig Easter Fair. While travelling through Thüringia, Richard spotted the Wartburg castle atop a steep hill overlooking the valley. On seeing the castle Wagner had an epiphany, and the trip transformed from one filled with difficult drudgery to a redemptive quest of homecoming: "Whereas I had already sensed the deep significance of the fact that I had crossed the legendary German Rhine for the first time on my way home from Paris, it seemed a particularly prophetic indication that I should first sight the Wartburg, so rich in history and myth, at precisely this moment."[1] The castle had an important historical legacy stretching back to medieval times and was a favorite symbol for German nationalists. It was there that Martin Luther had holed up in 1521 after his excommunication and where he had penned his German translation of the *New Testament*. It had also been the home of the thirteenth-century Saint Elisabeth who was an archetype of Christian charity and self-sacrifice. And in 1817, 500 students had gathered there in a nationalist festival to mark the Battle of Leipzig when a massive array of soldiers had fought against the Napoleonic onslaught.[2] This was particularly portentous for Wagner, since the festival had been hosted by the *Burschenschaft* assembly of student fraternities that, like Wagner himself, imbued anti-French and anti-Jewish hatreds into their radical and xenophobic politics.[3]

The castle was Wagner's antidote, as he later wrote, to the "wind and the weather, Jews and Leipzig Fair." Moreover, he added, that while riding through the valley he constructed "the scene for the third act of my *Tannhäuser* in an image so clear that I could always recall it vividly."[4] In Wagner's *Tannhäuser*, the final scene would take place in the valley facing the Wartburg castle. In his opera, the Wartburg would symbolize a positive and rich German space that had, however, lately become inhabited by individuals whose reactionary ethos was in opposition to the creative impulses of the artist Tannhäuser. The Wartburg inhabitants would show how Wagner construed the current Prussian government as a petty, overly bureaucratic, and stifling state. The Venusberg would be the other setting of his opera and would symbolize positive and negative traits: positive because it was a free unbridled space that appealed to Wagner, who was then exploring the ideas of the pro-sensualist, hedonistic, anti-bourgeois Young German group, but negative because the excess on display there reminded him of the vapid, indulgent Paris he was happily escaping.

Seeing the castle crystallized the final act of an opera that Wagner had begun working on while in Paris. For him, his initial interest in *Tannhäuser* grew out of an attraction for all things "inherently German,"[5] and the knight was the antidote for his homesickness: "The picture which my homesick fantasy had painted, not without some warmth of color, in the departing light of a historical sunset, completely faded from my sight so soon as ever the figure of Tannhäuser revealed itself to my inner eye." This was a knight who expressed "the spirit of the whole Ghibelline race for every age."[6]

The opera would offer a positive and compelling portrait of a German knight while at the same time be an indictment of the modern art prevalent in Paris:

> When I reached the sketch and working-out of the *Tannhäuser* music, it was in a state of burning exaltation which held my blood and every nerve in fevered throbbing. My true nature—which in my loathing of the modern world and ardor to discover something nobler and beyond all noblest, had quite returned to me—now seized, as in a passionate embrace, the opposing channels of my being, . . . With this work I penned my death-warrant: before the world of Modern Art, I now could hope no more for life.[7]

Shortly after returning to Dresden following the long journey that brought him past the Wartburg castle, he took a trip to the Bohemian mountains where he "jotted down the complete dramatic sketch of *Tannhäuser*."[8]

And so we have Richard Wagner's masterful spin on how he wrote his latest opera, *Tannhäuser and the Song Contest on the Wartburg* (Tannhäuser und der Sängerkrieg auf der Wartburg).[9] It arose like a beacon from the German soil, and it was based on the mythos of the volk as exemplified by the castle and the medieval accounts of German knights and saints. The opera was home grown, German, and a buffer against modernism.

But of course none of this was really true. Wagner could not let anyone know that a central inspiration for his German volk opera was to be found within the writings of the Jewish poet Heinrich Heine.

Early Life and Work

Wagner's life prior to his 1842 return to Germany had been filled with drama and turmoil.[10] He was born to a large bourgeois, artistic family in Leipzig, where he was raised by his mother, Johanna, and his stepfather, the actor and playwright, Ludwig Geyer. In 1814, they moved to Dresden, where he became captivated by his stepfather's theatrical life and began taking piano lessons. When Wagner was eight, Ludwig died, and in 1827 the family returned to Leipzig. By the age of 20, Wagner had completed his first opera, *The Fairies* (Die Feen), and was working as a chorus master in Würzburg. In 1834, he returned again to Leipzig, and became friends with members of the Young German group, who combined a sensualistic aesthetics with a liberal worldview. Throughout the first part of his life, as Mitchell Cohen has shown, Wagner held a series of "radical" ideas, from supporting the revolutionaries of 1830, to joining with the Young Germans, to his anarchic ties in the late 1840s. This worldview, which saw events as a clash of contrasting sympathies or "colliding worlds," would play out in his pre-1849 operas, including *Tannhäuser*.[11]

In 1836, Wagner began a troubled marriage to the actress Christine Wilhelmine "Minna" Planner which lasted for thirty years. In March of 1839, Wagner's contract as musical director in Riga was not extended, and he and Minna, in serious debt to a variety of creditors, escaped Riga like bandits in the middle of the night. After nearly being ship-wrecked off the coast of England, they arrived in Paris. This was the era of the July Monarchy in Paris, where society was stagnant and stratified into the elite, with money, and all the rest, without. Without money, Wagner found he could not make social contacts with the movers and shakers of French society.

While in Paris he completed his third opera, *Rienzi,* and the time in Paris served to lead him back to his roots in German Romantic music, particularly Beethoven.[12] In 1842, the Wagners decided to return to Dresden, in large part because the Jewish conductor Giacomo Meyerbeer (1791-1864) (whom Wagner would later attack in his antisemitic diatribe *Das Judentum in der Musik*), had influenced the Dresden Court Theatre to put on a production of *Rienzi*.

Wagner was then beginning to make a major mark on opera that would transform the genre from a form of entertainment to the highest type of art. The numerous innovations that he introduced would culminate in the leitmotif technique of his mature masterpiece, *Das Rheingold*. Rather than having the opera unfold in a series of distinct and often unconnected librettos, the leitmotifs were musical themes, all tied together, that expressed different characters, plot elements, or settings. The leitmotifs added a new level of sophistication to opera that made the entire production come together in an integrated, yet often sublime, whole. Furthermore, rather than having the music be the background to the action on stage, as was common at the time, Wagner turned everything around so that in his operas it is the action onstage that sheds light on the music.[13] As he wrote in his essay, "On the Performing of *Tannhäuser*," Wagner wanted his singers to be fully aware of all aspects of the opera rather than just their own parts, since this was the only way that they could do full justice to the work.[14]

Heine and Anti-Semitism

His musical brilliance meant that Wagner was the first German opera composer who was able to extend his influence and popularity beyond Germany. But while Wagner was an extraordinarily gifted composer, he was also one of the most prominent Jew haters of the nineteenth century, the author of one of the most popular and hateful anti-Semitic diatribes, "Das Judentum in der Musik" (generally translated as "Judaism in Music").

During Wagner's time in France between 1839 and 1842 he had been in regular contact with Heine. Paul Lawrence Rose lists the many ways that Heine influenced Wagner during that period:

> The composer had dedicated his musical setting of *Les deux grenadiers* to the poet in January 1840; in March 1841 Heine had passed favorable judgments on Wagner's own efforts at story-writing; and Wagner had come to "an understanding" with Heine about his project for an opera on *Der fliegende Holländer*, a theme inspired by Heine's own account of the legend in Schnabelewopski. There was such a rapport that Heine uncharacteristically even became involved in lending money to Wagner in March 1841.[15]

Years later, in Wagner's autobiography *My Life* (Mein Leben), in a moment of fondness for Heine, he recollected their first meeting in Paris, when Heine joked with the Wagners about their move there.[16] Heinrich and Richard were both German-speaking artists and Heine's works and wit appealed to the staid Wagner. Heine, moreover, taught Wagner to turn to German myths as a well source for motifs that could be used in his opera as a means to showcase his interest in German Romanticism and the perpetuation of volk nationalism.

Wagner's view of Heine evolved and became more negative over time. While in Paris he enjoyed his company, patronage, and insights about German art. Over the years, however, as Heine began to publicly discuss his Jewishness in his works, Wagner sought to distance himself more and more from him. For Wagner, Heine became "the Jewish outsider who speaks about the conditions of our life as an Iroquois would speak about our railroads."[17] Wagner apparently also later turned against Heine because he resented the power that the poet held over him while serving as his benefactor years earlier in Paris.[18]

Wagner's dislike of Heine became overt eleven years after their Paris friendship when he concluded "Das Judentum in der Musik" with an attack on him. The essay was first published anonymously in September 1850 in the journal *Neue Zeitschrift für Musik*. In 1869 it was reproduced with Wagner's name on it along with an explanatory essay entitled "Elucidation of 'Judaism in Music.'" Wagner later claimed that he had published the work anonymously, since he feared that the Jews would suppress his music if they knew he had written it. In 1851, he outlined this fear in a letter that he wrote to the composer Franz Liszt (who was the father of his second wife Cosima). The letter also discussed the intention of "Das Judentum":

> You ask me about "Judaism." You know of course that the article is by me: so why do you ask? It was not out of fear, but to prevent that question from being dragged down by the Jews to a purely personal level that I appeared in print pseudonymously. I harbored a long suppressed resentment against this Jewish business, and this resentment is as necessary to my nature as gall is to the blood. The immediate cause of my intense annoyance was their damned scribblings, so that I finally let fly: I seem to have struck home with terrible force, which suits my purpose admirably, since that is precisely the sort of shock that I wanted to give them. For they will always remain our masters—that much is as certain as the fact that it is not our princes who are now our masters, but bankers and philistines.[19]

Wagner believed that there was a massive Jewish conspiracy against him, and he intended to make it public. His claimed that his essay was a weapon with which to lead a counterattack against the Jews who controlled the economic and cultural life of Germany.

In "Das Judentum in der Musik," Wagner's venom flows in an array of directions.[20] According to him, the Jews represent the corrupted world of capitalism and are a soulless group that lack the depth to create real music. They have "be-Jewed" art and turned it into an expression of their decadence. Everything about the Jew, in fact, makes it impossible for him to create transcendent music: his speech (probably referring to Yiddish) is a grotesque babble and thus his words cannot access the sublime; his tradition of synagogue music is so crass that nothing refined can develop out of it; and he is so money obsessed that he cannot access the "true soul" of music, but only the superficial aspects. There is in fact no solution, since in the essay Wagner disavows both emancipation and baptism as ways to "solve" the Jewish problem. This viewpoint sets the groundwork for biological anti-Semitism.

The second part of "Das Judentum" is a pointed attack on Wagner's two Jewish enemies: the composers Giacomo Meyerbeer and Felix Mendelssohn. Their music manifests all the negative qualities of Jewish artistic production. While Mendelssohn's compositions are technically proficient, they are nevertheless "vague and fantastical outlines," since they lack the depth of real art.[21] Meyerbeer also creates uninspiring shallow works that attempt to mimic true art but fall short.

The essay concludes with the vicious assault on Heine:

> I said earlier that the Jews have never produced a true poet. We must now consider H. Heine. At the time when Goethe and Schiller were writing poetry, we certainly knew of no Jewish poets: but from the time when our poetry became a lie, and when there was nothing that our utterly unpoetical earth could not produce except a true poet, it became the task of this uncommonly gifted Jewish poet to reveal this lie with charming contempt, and to lay bare the Jesuitically jejune hypocrisy of modern verse mongering with all its attempts to achieve poetic expression. He even ridiculed his illustrious fellow tribesmen, pillorying them mercilessly for their claims to be artists; it was impossible to deceive him for long. He was driven restlessly on by the implacable demon of denial, a demon who denies all that merits denial, feeling cold and scornful self-content as he exposed the illusions of modern self-deception. He was the conscience of Judaism, just as Judaism is the conscience of our modern civilization. [22]

The mixture of awe and hatred that Wagner felt towards Heine is evident in this paragraph. On the one hand he acknowledges Heine's gifts as an author who is able to shed light on the lack of depth of his fellow writers. Yet Wagner also derides Heine's desire to bring others down to size. In fact in Wagner's diatribe, Heine's role is so important that he is the "conscience of Judaism," which is negatively construed as the "conscience of modern civilization." The converted, assimilated Heine who struggled throughout his life with his relationship with his own Jewish identity would have likely been appalled, and perhaps a bit amused, to find himself labeled the "conscience of Judaism."

"Das Judentum in der Musik" as a whole is quite shocking to read since it is such a malicious and virulent assault on the Jews. I would suggest that anyone who is prone to make excuses for Wagner's anti-Semitism reread this work. Nevertheless, critics have been divided about how to view Wagner's anti-Semitism. Was Wagner "revolutionary" and "freedom loving" or was he a "reactionary, [a] racist"?[23] Was he the precursor to Hitler, who also formulated a type of anti-Semitism based on German Romantic nationalism? Or, was his anti-Semitism the type that was so common at the time that it merely reflected a troubling, but widespread, trend?[24] Marc Weiner, in a thought-provoking essay entitled "Lingering Discourses: Critics, Jews, and the Case of Gottfried Wagner," argues that there is a deep friction in Wagner studies between foregrounding and downplaying Wagner's anti-Semitism. These attempts at negating Wagner's anti-Semitism have ranged from Dieter Borchmeyer asserting that he had consciously omitted most of Richard Wagner's anti-Semitic essays from a ten-volume edition of his works that he edited to Dieter David Scholz arguing that Richard Wagner could not be an anti-Semite since he was not a Jew. Weiner suggests that to help lessen the polarization between the two sides, we must acknowledge the "traces of racism discernible within [the operas], even as we admire and take enjoyment from them."[25]

Part of the confusion about how to view Wagner is tied to his reluctance when he was younger to express his hatred of the Jews publicly, since he asserted that a conspiracy of powerful Jews would respond by trying to destroy him. In the first part of his life, his anti-Semitism thus mostly showed up in private correspondences and in "Das Judentum in der Musik," which was originally published anonymously. Reading through Wagner's letters, his biography, and the diary notes of his second wife Cosima, however, it is extremely difficult to dismiss Jew hatred as a minor quirk of his personality. Even granting that Cosima's diary entries were not completely trustworthy, since she may have manipulated Wagner's words to express her own, extremely deep anti-Semitism, Wagner's hatred for the Jews constantly crops up and is so vehement and personal that it reads as an obsession that overshadowed many aspects of his life. His comments on the Jews frequently make them into scapegoats for all his troubles. He truly believed that the Jewish people reacted to finding out that he was the author of "Das Judentum in der Musik" by using their power to prosecute and persecute him. As he writes in his autobiography:

> The unheard-of enmity which has pursued me to this day from the newspapers of Europe is comprehensible only to those who took note of that article ["Das Judentum in der Musik"] and the commotion it caused at the time, and remember now that the newspapers of Europe are almost exclusively in the hands of the Jews. Those who seek the reason for this unceasing and vicious persecution solely in some kind of theoretical or practical disapproval of my views or my artistic works can never get at the truth of the matter.[26]

Wagner was not merely falling into the Jew hatred of his contemporaries; he was using it as a basis for defining his life. Moreover, Wagner's influence on German culture was so strong that it is naïve to think that the propagation of anti-Semitism in his essays and comments did not influence Hitler and the Nazi movement; Hitler himself named his one predecessor as Wagner.[27] In contrast to a number of German critics who downplay Wagner's anti-Semitism and argue that we must separate the artist from his art are those such as Paul Lawrence Rose who assert that Wagner's operas embodied the anti-Semitism that would lead to Nazism and that to listen to his works is to spread his hatred. He writes: "There was a Holocaust, and Wagner's self-righteous ravings, sublimated into his music, were one of the most potent elements in creating the mentality that made such an enormity thinkable—and performable."[28] For Lawrence Rose there is an "anti-Jewish agenda which can be elicited from every one of his mature operas."[29] As Marc Weiner argues in his book, *Richard Wagner and the Antisemitic Imagination*, both Wagner and his audience would have been very much aware of the anti-Semitic stereotypes hidden below the surface, particularly in his opera *Parsifal*, and that his work reflected an anti-Jewish world view.[30] And in his article "Nuremberg Trial: Is There Anti-Semitism in *Die Meistersinger*?" Barry Millington asserts that "anti-Semitism is woven into the ideological fabric of *Die Meistersinger*, and that the representation of Beckmesser incorporates unmistakable antisemitic characteristics."[31] Moreover, as Thomas S Grey convincingly argues in his recent essay, "The Jewish Question," Wagner could not readily present overtly negative, caricatured stereotypes of Jews in his operas, since this "would have jeopardized their claim to being serious, timeless works of art." Therefore, "the importance of his own scurrilous pamphlet 'Judaism in Music' (in its independent reincarnation of 1869) in mediating between personal ideology and public art. If Wagner could not plausibly represent 'real' Jews in his operas, he might construct characters who could be perceived as acting, sounding, and behaving 'like Jews,' and this might involve various levels of his synthetic Gesamtkunstwerk: language, singing, gesture, and orchestral music."[32] To attend Wagner's operas, to read his essays, and to view his role in German culture, is thus to engage the völklische mentality that was the basis for his, and later Hitler's, "revolutionary anti-Semitism."

Heine responded to Wagner's attack with an out-of-character silence.[33] For Heine, the assault must have been a painful punch in the face from someone he had previously assisted and even mentored. The essay's attack on Jewish creativity must have been particularly troubling for Heine, who was certainly aware of the central role that his poem "Der Tannhäuser" had played in the creation of Wagner's opera.

Wagner's Debt to Heine

Dieter Borchmeyer asserts that there is no doubt that Wagner actually first encountered the Tannhäuser ballad in its entirety in Heine's "Elementargeister" essay book, which republished the version from *Des Knaben Wunderhorn* of Arnim and Brentano (along with Heine's poem).[34] Heine's essay in "Elementargeister," which accompanies his reproduction of the ballad along with his own poem, "Der Tannhäuser," discusses the contrast between paganism and Christianity. This contrast would become embodied in Wagner's opera in the figures of Venus and Elisabeth, with Venus a pagan seductress, and Elisabeth a representation of the saint.

The greatest difference between Wagner's opera and Heine's poem, "Der Tannhäuser" was in the tone and intent: Wagner's opera reconstituted his poem from a satiric attack on German culture to a representation of its greatest aspects. Wagner also inserted an extremely strong Christian parable, in contrast to Heine, who turned the encounter with the Pope into a comic moment. Like Heine, Wagner was drawn towards the Tannhäuser myth while in Paris, although Wagner's opera would be a love letter to Germany, while in Heine's hands, "Der Tannhäuser" would become a bitter indictment of the homeland.

In a further twist on Wagner's debt to Heine, Heine's "Venusberg ballet," entitled *The Goddess Diana* (Die Göttin Diana), was probably another inspiration for his opera.[35] Heine composed the ballet in Paris in 1846. When Wagner created his 1861 "Paris version" of *Tannhäuser* he introduced "striking similarities"[36] between his ballet sequence, set in the Venusberg, and the one found in *The Goddess Diana*. In Heine's piece, there is a frenzy of bacchic dancing in the Venusberg that reaches a climax when, to quote from the Heine ballet, there is the entrance of "Frau Venus with Tannhäuser, her *eavaliere servente*. Scantily clad, with garlands of roses on their heads, these two dance an intensely sensual pas de deux reminiscent of the most illicit dances of the modern period."[37] The ballet sequence that Wagner inserted into the opening scene of his opera exactly mimics this: it is also set in the Venusberg with frenzied bacchic dancing that introduces Venus and Tannhäuser. This is how Wagner describes it: "what I have in mind is an epitome of everything the highest choreographic and pantomimic art can offer: a wild, and yet seductive chaos of movements and groupings, of soft delight, of yearning and burning, carried to the most delirious pitch of frenzied riot."[38] Both, moreover, are set in castles where there is a major confrontation of cultures. In Heine's *The Goddess Diana* it is between what Heine describes "as the 'decorous' world of a medieval court and the world of the gods."[39] In Wagner's *Tannhäuser* there is a similar clash, but in this case between the court singers and Tannhäuser.

Borchmeyer is perhaps too generous to Wagner when he suggests that the ties between the two works may be coincidence.[40] Wagner's 1861 Parisian version of *Tannhäuser* has so many parallels to Heine's *The Goddess Diana*, many of which Borchmeyer charts, that there is little doubt that Wagner lifted numerous aspects of it from three Heine sources, the "Elementargeister" essay, the poem, "Der Tannhäuser," and *The Goddess Diana*.

It is to Wagner's discredit that he never mentioned any of this and later further dug in the knife by writing that Heine was a bad poet, a bad man, and a bad German. Wagner chose to deny the large influence of Heine on his opera for four reasons: his anti-Semitism made him uncomfortable connecting his work with the writings of a Jew, he was loathe to confess that anything he had created had been cribbed from outside sources, his admission of Heine's influence would go against his desire to present the opera as homegrown, and he did not want his grand and serious opera connected with Heine's unpleasant, satiric version of the medieval legend. When, in an 1873 diary entry, Cosima discusses her anger that a fellow German poet writes about Tannhäuser without "giving the least acknowledgement to R[ichard]" it is a typical moment of hypocrisy, since this is exactly what Richard did to Heine, but on a much larger scale.[41]

Rather than having his work directly tied to Heine's, Wagner asserted that the character of Tannhäuser "sprang from my inmost heart."[42] Wagner would, however, reluctantly admit his debt to versions by fellow prominent German cultural figures. For instance, he acknowledged the influence of Ludwig Tieck's "The Faithful Eckart and Tannenhäuser" (Der getreue Eckart und der Tannenhäuser) and E. T. A. Hoffmann's piece about a Wartburg singing contest entitled *The Singers' Contest* (Der Kampf der Sänger). But he also downplayed their roles: as for Tieck's version, Wagner asserted that the "Catholic frivolity had not appealed in any definite way to my sympathy," while Hoffman's tale "left me without the slightest incitation to dramatic treatment."[43]

The other main influence that Wagner did acknowledge was a mysterious "volksbuch" or chapbook that he claimed "fell into his hands."[44] Critics are divided about whether this chapbook really existed and if it did, what it contained. Most now think the book was not a chapbook but instead a collection of legends put out by Ludwig Bechstein (the same poet that Heine mentions as having introduced him to the medieval ballad) in the 1830s entitled *Der Sagenschatz und die Sagenkriese des Thüringerlandes*. This book not only contains a reprint of the original sixteenth-century ballad the *Lied von dem Danheüser*, but also throws in discussions of the real life thirteenth-century knight Tannhäuser and Saint Elisabeth. This book is supposed to be *the* volksbuch because Wagner's opera added a new twist to *Tannhäuser* by combining two different legends: that of the knight and that of the song contest. This is evident in the opera's full title: *Tannhäuser and the Song Contest on the Wartburg* (Tannhäuser und der Sängerkrieg auf der Wartburg), which mimics the manner in which Bechstein's book mistakenly conflates the knight Tannhäuser, who was a real historical minstrel singer, with the protagonist of the legend. The former took part in a song contest, the latter, as found in the medieval sources of the legend, did not. Wagner's intention in bringing together both legends was perhaps to ground the story of the knight Tannhäuser in a symbolically positive German setting, the Wartburg castle.

In fact, paradoxically, Wagner was creating a myth about how his version of *Tannhäuser* came into existence, in much the same manner as Heine, by claiming to have found a chapbook with the Tannhäuser tale in it that inspired him to create his own adaptation. Heine's fabricated story of a found version was a trick. He did it in order to declare an authentic volk lineage for his poem, which the poem's content then undermined by portraying a stagnating German culture. For Wagner, in contrast, the intent was to show how very German his opera was: its main source was a text of the folk, or, volksbuch. Where Heine's "Der Tannhäuser" was a means to destroy the culture, Wagner's version intended to build it up. By stressing the linkage to the mysterious chapbook—this "wonderful creation of the folk"[45] as Wagner labels it—in one fell swoop he both disassociates his opera from the work of a Jew and ties it to a myth of the German people.

Tannhäuser und der Sängerkrieg auf der Wartburg

The first act of *Tannhäuser* was completed in January 1844, and the second act that October. The complete draft of the opera appeared in 1845, followed shortly thereafter by its first performance in Dresden. In 1861, Wagner created a new "Paris" version of the opera.[46] The plot described below is based on the Paris version. Because in Wagner's operas the actions on stage are inextricably bound with the music, it does his work a huge disservice to describe it in terms of the plot alone. For this reason a brief discussion of the music will allow the reader to gain a sense of the larger dramatic picture. The opera is divided into three acts.

Before the curtains open the hall is filled with the rising sounds of the opera's overture. The opera's many admirers have ranged from Queen Victoria to Charles Baudelaire; Oscar Wilde even had his iconic character Dorian Gray attend the opera where he found himself relating to the knight. The overture in particular deeply moved the admirers.[47] Upon hearing the overture, recapitulated at the end of the opera, it is clear why Theodor Herzl became so infatuated with the opera that he would return to hear it, night after night, while he was a correspondent in Paris.

The curtains part to display the Venusberg, located, according to the production notes, in Germany in "Horselberg near Eisenach." Onstage, a ballet is taking place with gyrating nymphs and sirens. The music expresses the "hyperactive excesses" being acted out on stage.[48] Onstage is a grotto with a brook flowing through it. Everything is bathed in a rich and erotic fecundity. The pagan goddess Venus is draped over a couch with Tannhäuser lying over her knees and with his harp next to them. Tannhäuser jolts up as if awakened from a dream or a spell, and sings of his desire to leave. In particular, he yearns to escape the grotto, which although overgrown with greenery, is in fact completely cut off from the natural world. It is a cloistered, a temporal space in contrast to the earth above that he longs for. He sings:

> The time that I have been here
> no longer can be measured
> daytime, night-time, mean no more to me
> how long since I have felt the sunlight
> or glimpsed the stars that glimmer in the darkness
> the grass no more I see, so fresh with promise
> of summer's healing warmth
> the nightingale no more I hear that sings of spring's awakening.[49]

From the outset Tannhäuser is a hero with romantic aspects.[50] Yearning to again hear the nightingale's song he longs for escape and the freedom to plot his own destiny. Like the protagonist in Heine's version, he desires to leave a place where all his sensual desires are met so that he can experience the real world of longing and suffering:

> I am a man, I yearn for change
> In joy alone lies no tomorrow
> I long to suffer in human sorrow.

He wants to escape Venus' clutches and return to a world of meadows "fresh with dew," a "songbird's carefree singing," and "the sound of church bells ringing."[51] Specifically, it is the German landscape that he yearns for with its valleys and forests. The pull between Germany and the Venusberg represents Wagner's desire to show the German landscape as intrinsically positive and virtuous in contrast to the debased space of the Venusberg. It is supposed that by simply returning to Germany, he will be transformed by the landscape from a sinner to a man who is capable of being redeemed.

Unlike Heine's knight, who lacks the self-reflection to critique the "sin" of his life with Venus, Wagner's German knight feels that his life in the Venusberg "shames" him. Tannhäuser's pleas to leave are matched in intensity by Venus's entreaties that he stay. Finally he calls out

> All you can offer is love
> You have not the power to give what I seek
> my hope lies in Maria!"[52]

Tannhäuser's call to Maria is not to some sweetheart, of course, but Mary, the mother of Jesus. Thus Maria becomes at this moment a third figure battling for his affection, and she is as real to him as the Saintly Elisabeth, who he eventually chooses. Enraged, the huffy goddess disappears.

Tannhäuser finds himself in a beautiful valley with a shepherd singing about the spring. A band of Christians appear on a pilgrimage to Rome. Tannhäuser decides to join them, but before he does so he is spotted by a group of minstrel singers. He begs to leave them and they implore him to stay. In contrast to when he intoned the name "Maria," which broke Venus's spell, when one of the minstrel singers, his friend Wolfram, says "Elisabeth," he is unable to tear himself free. Wolfram reminds Tannhäuser how he had been the master singer of the group, able to "bewitch" Elisabeth with his singing. He tells Tannhäuser that if he will only join them, then Elisabeth will agree to attend the song contest. Clearly Wolfram hopes that if Elisabeth comes to hear the contest his own songs will entice her to dismiss her longing for Tannhäuser and to choose him instead. Tannhäuser takes up the offer, crying out, "To her, to her/ Oh, take me to her now!"[53] He joins the group and the curtains close on the first act.

Act one establishes a triangular set of competing pulls at Tannhäuser. In one corner is the pagan Venus with her profusion of erotic love. However her space, the Venusberg, is so cut off from the real world that it is too cloying and claustrophobic for the knight. In the second corner is the Christian realm of Maria and the pilgrims who are devoted to Jesus Christ. However, although calling out the name Maria gives him the strength to break free of the Venusberg, the Christian pull is not strong enough to entice him to join the pilgrims. The third corner, which is ultimately victorious at the end of act one, is the pull of the German landscape as symbolized by the Wartburg home of Elisabeth and the minstrels. The question that now hangs in the air is which will ultimately be victorious: pagan sinning, Christian redemption, or noble German love for Elisabeth.

The second act takes place in the hall of minstrels in the Wartburg castle. Onstage Elisabeth is excitedly singing of the return of her beloved Tannhäuser, soon followed by Wolfram leading him in. Elisabeth asserts that Tannhäuser was the master singer of the hall where he ruled "as king." She chants how his songs bewitched her and awoke in her "a strange new world of feeling."[54] Tannhäuser's songs were the catalyst for her erotic awakening, much as Venus had awoken Tannhäuser's sexuality. Tannhäuser responds that his songs were all about love: "Love has inspired my song to you; / Love spoke to you through all I sang here."[55] The piece reaches its height when they both take turns praising the power of love, which has "broken the spell" of Venus. It ends with Wolfram in the background singing that his own "love remains unspoken."

Another triangle is being formed this time between Elisabeth, Tannhäuser, and Wolfram. Elisabeth's uncle, the Landgrave, enters to lead the song contest. He intones that

> the magic that the power of music unleashes and inspires
> today we shall discover, and with fulfillment crown it
> The world of art will be transformed to deed.[56]

In other words, music is the ultimate bewitcher of the souls of men and women. Tannhäuser channeled it to intoxicate Elisabeth and Venus to seduce Tannhäuser. With this claim Wagner is asserting the power of his own art to reveal the world's truths and to inspire the passions of men. This is an appealing notion for the nineteenth-century opera audience: they need to merely give themselves over to music to become intoxicated by the fervor it unleashes. Moreover, in theory, they, like Elisabeth, will experience their solitary and dull selves swept away as they ride to the heights of the music's glory.

When the Landgrave officially opens the song contest, he reminds the group of the role that music has played in building the nation as well as the part it has played "in battle." Again Wagner is stressing the role of his music in inspiring both the individual man and the German nation. The contest officially begins with Wolfram's noble song of undefiled love directed at "virtuous ladies." It is a lovely piece but it also strikes a somewhat insipid note. Will the new and improved Tannhäuser also share a similar song of noble love? If so, will it bewitch Elisabeth again? As Tannhäuser's song gets underway, it becomes evident that he is finding his true voice as an artist. He thus sings an honest ode to the love he knew with Venus; a love that slaked his "body's longing" from which he did "drink both deep and long."[57]

As James M. McGlathery notes, Tannhäuser is put in an impossible position during the song contest.[58] If he is to sing powerfully enough to intoxicate Elisabeth, his song will have to be a true expression of his passions, passions that were recently devoted to Venus. If instead he sings a tepid song about virtuous love that is untrue to his experience, it will not be inspiring enough to bewitch Elisabeth. It is a no-win situation, because in either case he risks losing Elisabeth, either by singing a bland song or by singing an exciting yet offensive one.

For the other singers, "true love" can only be directed at a noble, virginal maiden (like Elisabeth). Any other love is offensive and sordid. This is the classic Madonna/whore split. It also suggests the "traditional juxtaposition of Venus and the Virgin Mary as the twin divinities of profane and sacred love," with Elisabeth representing an earthly form of the Virgin.[59] For Tannhäuser, in contrast, there are two types of pure love, which he synthesizes in his attraction to Elisabeth: the erotic, pagan and the emotional, Christian. As Wagner wrote of Elisabeth, she is the "woman who, star-like, showed to Tannhäuser the way that led from the hot passion of the Venusberg to heaven."[60] Elisabeth, in return, finds Tannhäuser a man who fuses both her physical and emotional attractions. In the medieval setting of the opera there is, however, no cultural acceptance of a love that is both sexual and Christian.

For Wagner as well, the only response to the dual physical and spiritual pulls is to repress the physical side. As he wrote in a letter discussing his earlier operas, including *Tannhäuser*, "if there is any single poetic feature underlying these works, it is the high tragedy of renunciation, the well-motivated, ultimately inevitable and uniquely redeeming denial of the will."[61] If Tannhäuser and Elisabeth are to succeed, they must both sublimate their sexuality. Only in the realm of death can they share both aspects of love, the physical and the intellectual. On earth no such thing is possible: here the only choice is the repression of desire.

The knights respond angrily to Tannhäuser's honest song: they are the knights of "love pure and holy" and Tannhäuser has debased all of them. When Tannhäuser responds by reasserting his passion for Venus and admonishing these "poor mortals, who true love have never tasted" to "make haste, haste to the Venusberg,"[62] Elisabeth has to jump in to stop them from killing him. Unexpectedly, Tannhäuser's song of love and lust for Venus has succeeded in pulling Elisabeth even closer to him by making her come to his rescue. The song has thus made her more intoxicated by him than ever.

When listening to the opera, the spell cast by Tannhäuser's song on Elisabeth is understandable, since in contrast to Wolfram's chaste ode, Tannhäuser's song is much more passionate and compelling. Moreover, Elisabeth probably recognizes her own sexual feelings for Tannhäuser in his words about the joys of physical love.

In Elisabeth's intercession, she tells the others that they "are not fit to judge him," particularly when he has been "possessed by devils, his mind bewildered by a spell." She also reminds them that "it was for him, too, that our Saviour died."[63] Like the saint that she is, she saves Tannhäuser's life by asserting traditional Christian beliefs. Her words not only jolt awake the knights from their murderous frenzy, but they also redirect Tannhäuser to the true Christian path of redemption. Like Tannhäuser and Venus, Elisabeth has shown herself to be a master of song who can influence and "bewitch" her listeners. In this case, she has brought the entire room back to the true and noble Christian path.

Tannhäuser responds to her intercession by asserting that he now realizes that his sin was not that he lived with Venus, but that he lusted after Elisabeth:

> To save a sinner from damnation
> an angel came to guard my days,
> but I, I saw her, and desired her,
> soiled her with sly and lustful gaze.
> O Thou, high above this vale of sorrow,
> who sent this angel that I might repent,
> have mercy, Lord, on one who, steeped in evil,
> dared to profane the messenger you sent.
> Have mercy, Lord, I cry to Thee.[64]

Wagner asserted that "in this verse and in the music to which it is sung lies the entire meaning of Tannhäuser's catastrophe, nay, it is the unique expression of Tannhäuser's entire being, which made him such a moving figure for me."[65] What the passage shows is that Tannhäuser has improperly dirtied chaste love with sinful lust. His actions have thus brought the lusty realm of the Venusberg into the space of the noble German Wartburg. By so doing, he has recklessly superimposed pagan love upon a Christian saint who was only there to save him. In fact his erotic longing was so all-consuming that his vision was clouded and he was unable to see that Elisabeth was a messenger sent by the Christian god. With this realization, Tannhäuser has finally internalized the chaste values of the Wartburg while at the same time repressed the sensual world of the Venusberg.

The knights agree to release Tannhäuser to a group of pilgrims heading to Rome to seek redemption. The second act draws to a close with the young pilgrims' chorus:

> And so to Rome my steps I trace
> to pray that God grant me His grace
> For he who puts his father in Heaven
> if he repent, may be forgiven.

This is followed by Tannhäuser passionately singing out "To Rome," followed by Elisabeth, Landgrave, the Minstrels, and the Knights responding "To Rome."[66] Where the first act concluded with three pulls, the pagan Venus, the Christian

Maria, and the German Wartburg, the second act concludes with all the characters drawn toward the site of Christian redemption, Rome.

Unexpectedly, the third and final act does not open in Rome, where the
audience imagines that everything will be resolved. Instead, the curtain rises in
the same locale as the end of the first act: the valley in front of the Wartburg.
Tannhäuser is nowhere to be seen. Elisabeth is on the right-hand side, praying
before a statue of the Virgin Mary. As in the first scene, when Tannhäuser cried
out for help from Maria, Elisabeth is also seeking the Virgin. Wolfram enters
from the woods on the left looking for her. He sings that she has been constantly
praying for Tannhäuser's redemption while awaiting the return of the pilgrims.
Immediately the chorus of the returning pilgrims is heard, a "pious hymn /
sung by those who have been granted absolution." When Elisabeth realizes that
Tannhäuser is not among the redeemed group, she implores the Virgin: "Let me
in death once purified / rise as an angel to Your side."[67] She further sings,

> But if my sins are not forgiven
> just as I am, please take me still
> that I might kneel to You in heaven
> to hear one favor if You will
> for him I loved once, hear me pray
> let all his sins be washed away."[68]

She wants to make the ultimate sacrifice: her death so that Tannhäuser will be
redeemed.

Hearing this, Wolfram asks Elisabeth if he can walk with her. She gently
refuses and makes her way up the path towards the Wartburg. When night falls, a
haggard and broken Tannhäuser enters the valley. He is wearing an old pilgrim's
dress and carrying his pilgrim's staff. Wolfram admonishes him for returning
without a pardon from the Pope. Tannhäuser responds that he is merely cutting through the valley on the way back to the Venusberg. A stunned Wolfram
asks Tannhäuser to recount exactly what has happened and why he has not been
absolved.

Reluctantly, Tannhäuser shares his tale and here Wagner mimics Heine's
poem in which Tannhäuser describes, rather than shows, what happened in
Rome.[69] The audience does not experience firsthand the encounter with the Pope
but rather must trust Tannhäuser's account of it. This structure stresses that what
is most important is how Tannhäuser has understood and interpreted the event.

Tannhäuser asserts that he was the most contrite penitent "that has ever
been" and that his repentance was true, honest, and complete. Moreover, on the
trip to Rome he did numerous acts of contrition, far more than any of the other
pilgrims. While they slept in shelters on the way, he lay outside in the "snow and
ice." When they were thirsty they drank from fountains, while he instead "drank
the scorching heat of sun alone."[70] For the other pilgrims their songs of atone-
ment were enough. Tannhäuser offered remorse with his body as well as his soul.

His experience of penitence, like his experience of love, required the full force of both his physical and spiritual sides. Yet, when it was his turn to have an audience with the Pope, again the truth got the better of him and he

> confessed with growing desperation
> to evil lust and uncontrolled desires
> to longings that no penance ever stilled,
> and for a respite from these raging fires.[71]

This was a critical mistake, since he did not tell the Pope that he was seeking absolution from previous sins. Instead, he asked the Pope to intervene and quiet his raging lusts. In other words, he wanted the Pope to perform some type of magic that would stop him from feeling his desires. The Pope responded:

> You who in evil lust have dealt,
> you who have knocked at Satan's door,
> if in the Venusberg you dwelt,
> then you are damned for evermore.
> Just as this staff here in my hand
> never will blossom into flower,
> so from the torments of the damned
> to save you lies beyond my power.[72]

In Wagner's opera, the powers of the pagan goddess are stronger than those of the Catholic Pope. No wonder that Tannhäuser also gives in and decides to return to Venus: if even the Pope is weaker than she is, there is no hope for him.

Again someone comes and intervenes for Tannhäuser. In the first act, it was the Virgin Mary. In the second act, it was Elisabeth who stopped the knights from killing him. In the third act, first it was Elisabeth who offered her life to save his, and now it is Wolfram who intercedes by stopping Tannhäuser from returning to the Venusberg. As has occurred earlier in the opera, Wolfram invokes a name: "Elisabeth" which jolts Tannhäuser out of his spell. In response, Venus disappears and a chorus of minstrels is heard singing in mourning for Elisabeth.

As the pilgrims and minstrels enter carrying Elisabeth's body on an open bier, Tannhäuser realizes that she has died. Typical of Wagner's works, the opera does not show what killed her. It is unclear if she committed suicide by jumping off the Wartburg hill, or if she had so much control over her body that she decided to die naturally so that she could enter heaven. By leaving her death offstage, Wagner imbues it with a powerful mysterious force that enables it to be an act of divine intervention. Tannhäuser's final words in the opera, as he sinks dying over Elisabeth's body, are "Blessed Saint Elisabeth, pray for my soul." At that moment she has transformed from a woman to a saint.

Although at first glance Tannhäuser and Elisabeth seem like opposites, they are in many ways a perfect match. Both are master singers able to sway their listeners. Both have strong sensual passions, although initially Elisabeth's are directed at Tannhäuser and Tannhäuser's at Venus. And while Elisabeth sublimates her desires somewhat, nevertheless she is "intoxicated" by Tannhäuser's song, much as Tannhäuser is by the song of Venus. Their passions lead them to love the wrong people. The more correct match for Elisabeth is perhaps the chaste, noble Wolfram, who loves her unconditionally. Her attraction to Tannhäuser is so strong, however, that she follows her heart rather than her head. For Tannhäuser the correct match is Elisabeth, but he only fully accepts this upon her death. They are both torn figures who in the end find each other and unify the severed spheres of physical versus spiritual longing.

In response to Tannhäuser's death, the chorus of the young pilgrims declares that the staff which the Pope claimed would never blossom, since Tannhäuser's sins were eternal, has now "put forth leaves of freshest green."[73] The power of Saint Elisabeth is stronger than that of the Pope; she has won his absolution. Tannhäuser's redemption should be chanted everywhere since, according to the pilgrim's chorus, it shows that "High over all the Lord doth reign / man shall not call on Him in vain." The Pope was mistaken in suggesting that the Christian God was weaker than the pagan one. Tannhäuser's death has shown this. The final words, sung by the unified community of voices on the stage, are: "The grace of God to the sinner is given / his soul shall live with the angels in heaven!" [74] In heaven, then, the couple is united.

The Music

In *Tannhäuser*, the music matches the theme of the pagan and Christian worlds both pulling for the soul of the knight. Wagner at the time held revolutionary tendencies and believed in the liberation of the artistic soul. He also disliked the pettiness of the bureaucratic world, particularly during the 1830s, when Germany was in a reactionary mode of clampdown. This ethos was exemplified in the music. Thus the music of the Wartburg, the central location of the German conservative bureaucracy, is much more dull than the music that Wagner uses for the Venusberg. The Venusberg, in contrast, reflects his interest in the Young German group's hedonistic call for liberation and breaking free of old shackles. However, his opera cannot be reduced into this simple binary, since the Venusberg also represents the vacuous, showy French culture that Wagner was repulsed by during his Paris years, while the Wartburg is an inspiring nationalist icon.

The contrast between the "holy" and "sinful" music is what gives the opera its power because, when listening to it, the audience is enveloped in a full blanket of competing sounds drawing them, like Tannhäuser, in the two directions of the Wartburg and the Venusberg. As Hans Mayer writes:

> In the libretto the French and pagan world of the Venus is to be overcome by the German landscape, by the ideal of German art, by purity and holiness. But the musical expression of this Germanness, of German courtly

love and the knightly tradition, is abundantly conservative, not to say routine . . . In contrast, Wagner provided the world of Venus with music of the
utmost originality which, in its rhythmic complexity, imaginative harmony,
and novelty of orchestration, marks a step beyond anything that had been
created by him before.[75]

The discord between the pagan and the Christian, the sensual and the intellectual, the body and the soul, come together in it as well as in its repetition at the
opera's conclusion. As Wagner himself noted, the replaying of the overture at
the end shows that the two aspects of love have been unified: "both dissevered
elements, both soul and senses, God and Nature, unite in the atoning kiss of hallowed Love."[76]

The Characters

Of the four main characters, Tannhäuser, Elisabeth, Wolfram, and Venus,
Tannhäuser and Elisabeth have divided souls. While Elisabeth is seemingly the
counterpart to the sensual Venus, her soul is as troubled as Tannhäuser's. If she
really was truly chaste then she would love the chaste Wolfram. In contrast, Wolfram and Venus have far less complex personalities: Venus is all about lust and
Wolfram is all about virtue. Because Tannhäuser and Elisabeth are torn personalities, they need to be reconciled. On earth the only proper form of love is that
of Wolfram: chaste and virtuous and, frankly, tepid and dull.

The knight Tannhäuser, while representing aspects of the Young German
movement's espousal of sensualism, is also a challenge to their beliefs because in
the pagan realm he is deeply unhappy. In fact, everywhere he is unhappy, especially in the "asexual" Wartburg. Wherever he is, he seeks the opposite. When
he is with Venus he longs for Maria and Elisabeth, when he is with Elisabeth he
sings of Venus, when he is in the Venusberg he wants to be back in the Wartburg,
and once he is in the Wartburg he is pulled towards Rome. He is a rebellious
figure who, rather than enjoying this aspect of himself (as does Heinrich Heine's
character Tannhäuser) is tormented by it. He is thus less a figure embodying the
sensualistic views of the Young Germans and more a mirror of Faust, seeking ful-
fillment but never finding it since the "obstacle to be overcome is as much within
himself as outside."[77] He is a force that knocks down all the conventions imposed
to keep order along a hierarchical structure with the chaste Christian world of
the Wartburg as the pinnacle and the sinful pagan world of the Venusberg as the
nadir. This is made apparent by the Wartburg's location at the top of a mountain
and the Venusberg's location below the earth.

Wagner wrote that Tannhäuser the man is a "German from head to toe."[78]
His herculean struggles to redeem himself show that the German everyman should
seek out his true path even in a chaotic world where there are numerous competing pulls (although in Tannhäuser's case his redemption occurs in death). He is he-

roic for confronting his problems and seeking to solve them in an appropriate way. However, he is also extremely masculine. Where Tannhäuser is the representation of the German male, Elisabeth represents the German female archetype.

Wagner claimed that an inspiration for Elisabeth was a portrait of the Madonna that he saw in a local church: "In the parish church at Aussig I asked to be shown the Madonna of Carlo Dolci: it is a quite extraordinarily affecting picture, and if Tannhäuser had seen it, I could readily understand how it was that he turned away from Venus to Mary without necessarily having been inspired by any great sense of piety. At all events, I am now firmly set on Saint Elisabeth."[79] Elisabeth is pure and beautiful and for Wagner clearly she combines erotic and virginal aspects. She is thus conflated with both the Madonna and Saint Elisabeth. She represents the ideal German woman. When casting the parts for the original production of the opera, Wagner would first offer the role to his niece Johanna who had, as he wrote, an "unmistakably German cast of her features."[80]

Just as Tannhäuser misunderstands his relationship with Elisabeth, Elisabeth's tragedy is that she represses her real feelings about Tannhäuser. She cannot fully accept her deep love for him as a man, since to do so would be to confess that she has base desires. Moreover, her home is the conservative Wartburg, not the pagan Venusberg. Like Tannhäuser, she is out of place with her surroundings. However, she does not have the possibility, as does Tannhäuser, of sinking into the Venusberg to feed her erotic hungers; she must remain on earth, denying her real feelings. No wonder that she chooses to sacrifice herself and leave behind a life of utter repression. Since she is not comfortable living life as "the whore," she dies to become the Madonna. According to the pilgrim's chorus, her death, and the staff's blooming that follows it, signify that she has saved all humankind. She has died to save the world, as did Jesus. In Elisabeth, Wagner gives his audience a beautiful symbol of the virtues of self-sacrifice for the greater good, suggesting perhaps that the volk as a group also should sacrifice themselves for the greater benefit of Germany. This idea would become the strongest and most influential motif in the opera for both Theodor Herzl and I. L. Peretz.

Venus is perhaps the least developed character and the one most infrequently discussed by critics. Originally the opera was actually named after the Latinized form of Venusberg: *Mons Veneris*. However, Wagner changed the title when he learned that medical students used the term "Mount of Venus" as an obscene "sexual metaphor."[81] Venus and her abode presented deep problems to Wagner.[82] He thought that the character was originally written in a "clumsy way"[83] and wanted to make her have more weight to serve as an oppositional figure to the very well-defined Elisabeth. When casting her in the Paris version she was appropriately played by, as he wrote, a "grotesque Jewess."[84] In the opera, she comes off as a one-sided character, far less defined than Wolfram, Elisabeth, or Tannhäuser.

Wagner struggled to write a version of the opera that he was happy with and it was the sole uncompleted opera that plagued him throughout his life.[85] The bizarre dream he shared with Cosima about *Tannhäuser* sheds a light on how deeply the opera concerned him: "Richard had an exciting night, he dreamed of a performance of *Tannhäuser* in Vienna in which Lulu and Boni were to have appeared, but it fell through; suddenly, after Elisabeth's exit, he heard a cabaletta being sung which he had found inserted in the theater score and had cut; speechless with rage, he leaped onto the stage and there encountered his sister-in-law, Elise Wagner, who said to him, 'But it all sounds very lovely' while he, searching desperately for words, at last said loudly and clearly, 'You swine!' and woke up."[86] The dream shows the toll on him of continually reworking, cutting, and pasting the opera, which remained his obsession right up to his death. Days before he passed away he told Cosima that he "still owes the world *Tannhäuser*."[87] The opera represented a "Janus faced cornucopia of [Wagner's] obsessions"[88] that he could never fully reckon with.

Wagner bristled at the notion that his opera was merely a Christian morality tale. He wrote, "How absurd, then, must those critics seem to me, who, drawing all their wit from modern wantonness, insist on reading into my *Tannhäuser* a specifically Christian and impotently pietistic drift!"[89] He was correct to deny this type of interpretation, since the opera's use of Christian motifs and iconography shows a real ambivalence towards the topic. While the Virgin Mary becomes a prominent force for redeeming Tannhäuser, the Pope is very weak: after all, it is Elisabeth rather than the Pope who saves him. Moreover, the Pope mistakenly predicts Tannhäuser's future of eternal damnation. The chaste Elisabeth, based on the Christian saint, also is a complex character who hints at having a "sinful" nature. The story is therefore less a Christian morality tale than one that shows the complex struggles of the human soul. All the characters, music, and settings reflect such an array of Wagner's interests and beliefs, often in a contradictory form, that the complex characters and profound music work against any type of singular interpretation. For all these reasons it appealed deeply to men as varied as I. L. Peretz and Theodor Herzl, who found in the opera the room to create their own interpretations of the plot and to understand its universal, rather than specifically Christian, insights.

The opera not only represented a lifelong struggle for Wagner, it also had a large role in Cosima's life. She began a relationship with her first husband, Hans von Bülow, after von Bülow conducted a disastrous performance of the overture. And of all Wagner's works she claimed that *Tannhäuser* affected her the "most deeply."[90] When Richard was sweet talking Cosima he would even liken her to Elisabeth (but not to Venus, which may suggest something about the state of their sex life).[91]

The Paris Version

There were two primary renderings of the opera; the "Dresden version" that was completed in 1845 during Wagner's stay there three years after sighting the Wartburg castle, and the 1861 Paris version.[92] The Dresden version was neither a critical nor a popular success, primarily because it had an obscure, open ending. Rather than showing the reappearance of Venus, the death of Elisabeth, and the sprouting of the leaves on the staff signifying Tannhäuser's redemption, Wagner laid hints. Thus, he had a bell toll onstage to suggest that Elisabeth had died. The Dresden version, however, was closest to Heine's poem, which also did not have the staff bloom at the end. In 1847, Wagner wrote the final draft of the Dresden version with a new ending that included having Elisabeth's coffin appear onstage, next to which the knight collapses in death.

The Paris version was the one that Theodor Herzl would see reproduced while a Paris correspondent for the *Neue Frei Press*. According to Wagner, the Paris version was "linked with an unbroken series of experiences of the most wretched kind."[93] In 1859, Wagner returned to Paris to oversee a production of the opera. This had been arranged by the wife of the Austrian ambassador, Princess Pauline Metternich, who had long been a big fan of his work. The Princess, however, was despised in France, especially considering the anti-Austrian sentiment prevalent at the time. The much hated Princess had pressured Emperor Napoleon III to put on *Tannhäuser* in France and part of the hatred of the audience for the opera was really directed against the Wagner and Metternich friendship.[94]

Wagner's xenophobia made him believe that there could not be a "French *Tannhäuser*."[95] Moreover, the translation presented him with additional problems. As he wrote in a September 1859 letter, "if an attempt is to be made to perform *Tannhäuser* in Paris, no one who is a Frenchman through and through can possibly understand the poem and translate it properly."[96] Working one-on-one with a series of translators, Wagner was eventually able to write to a friend that "the thing I had least believed in—a good translation—has now in fact come off, at least as far as such a thing is possible."[97]

According to Wagner, however, he needed to stick with the production no matter what, since his German opera would inspire and teach the French: "Anyone who can calmly observe the life of such a talented but incredibly decadent nation as the French and who can summon up an interest in everything that may be seen as useful in developing and ennobling this race can scarcely be blamed for regarding the acceptance of a French *Tannhäuser* as a matter of the most vital concern for the educability of these people."[98] Even before the opera was on stage, the battle lines were clearly drawn by Wagner. The tale of the knight represented the virtues of the Germans as against the "decadent" French. If the Parisian public did not appreciate the opera, they were clearly manifesting their debauched nature.

By March of 1860, rehearsals had begun, and over the months the opera was reworked numerous times. Major changes included the addition of a ballet sequence (based on Heine's ballet, *The Goddess Diana*) and an expansion of the first act in the Venusberg. The ballet was probably a concession to the male opera goers who liked the chance to glimpse a bit of flesh and who saw opera more as entertainment than as art. The expansion of the Venusberg scene made more artistic sense, particularly if Venus and her abode were meant to be a counter-weight to the Christian Wartburg space.

There was considerable friction between Wagner, the director, and the man cast in the role of Tannhäuser, Albert Niemann. The conflicts with the director were primarily over the latter's desire for a ballet sequence, although in the end, Wagner agreed to put one in. The battles between Wagner and Neimann were between two prima donnas: Niemann insisted that Wagner cut some of Tannhäuser's verses because he was worried that they would ruin his voice, and Wagner rejected any demands made upon his great opera. There were at least 164 rehearsals, which led to an impending sense that the project was spiraling out of control.

The first performance was on March 13, 1861. During the show the Jockey Club, a loose affiliation of young aristocrats, interrupted the performance with loud clapping and blowing on dog whistles. They probably did this because they had arrived late to the opera after first going out for dinner and had missed the "ballet sequence," where they would have been able to glimpse the ballerinas, many of whom were their lovers. They were also upset at the power of the Austrian ambassador's wife, Princess Metternich, and her ability to sway the emperor to put on the opera of a German upstart like Wagner. Disrupting the opera while she was in attendance was a way to get even. At the second performance the Jockey Club again interrupted the show, but Wagner hoped that the third performance would succeed, since the Jockey Club members usually did not attend on a Sunday. Having stayed home rather than risk attending, he was dismayed to learn that this performance had also been destroyed by the Jockey Club, who unexpectedly showed up. According to Wagner, he then decided to pull the opera for the sake of his singers.[99]

Wagner did a remarkable spin on the Paris disaster in his autobiography, letters, and particularly in his essay, "A Report on the Production of Tannhäuser in Paris."[100] He claimed that the audience had in fact absolutely loved the work and that the disturbances had only been the result of a small clique opposed by the majority. He even labeled the run a "huge success" and asserted that it received as much applause as it did boos. Moreover, the real cause for the fiasco was not just the Jockey Club but a Jewish conspiracy, led by none other than his arch enemy, the composer Giacomo Meyerbeer, who apparently had the press "in his hands."[101] The French public, according to Wagner, in fact supported him entirely, were aware of his genius, and were proud of his attempt to challenge the power of a group of decadents who were devoted to excess. If the opera was not fully appreciated it was because a "French audience" could not fully understand this story of a German knight: Wagner and his opera symbolized German supremacy against this debased culture. In typical fashion, Wagner the self-publicist and self-deluded and solipsistic conspiracy theorist, was more interested in reinventing history than with being honest.

Concluding Remarks

Wagner's version of *Tannhäuser* restored the knight to a place of dignity, since in the end Tannhäuser succeeds in suppressing his individualistic desires and accepts the Christian values of Elisabeth. Having experienced the excesses of the July Monarchy in Paris, Wagner used the knight to transport himself and his audience to an idealized medieval German world of heroic actions and noble self-sacrifice. Where Heine's knight made fun of the land of Germany and showed how debased it had become, Wagner used him to restore the grandeur of the German territory. In Wagner's spin on how he came to the tale, rather than admitting the great influence of Heine, he constructed a myth of Parisian decadence followed by a return to German chasteness and nobility as exemplified in his sighting of the Wartburg castle upon his return to Germany in 1842. It is from this soil that *Tannhäuser* springs forth.

In order to fully express the story of the knight, Wagner created some of the most inspiring and unforgettable music of his oeuvre. It is no wonder that the work had such an influence on Theodor Herzl and I. L. Peretz. However, ironically, where Wagner would propagate the Germanness of the opera, the universality of the tale is what appealed most to Herzl and Peretz. For them, Tannhäuser, Venus, and Elisabeth were not specifically German figures but archetypes expressing notions of love and self-sacrifice. Thus, where Wagner aimed to inspire Germans to raise their volk consciousness, Herzl and Peretz would use it to encourage Wagner's enemies, the Jews, to raise their own Jewish consciousness. As the poets have always said, "irony is the revenge of slaves." Wagner, not known for his ironic sense of humor, would definitely have missed the joke.

Notes

1. Richard Wagner, *My Life*, trans. Andrew Gray (Cambridge: Cambridge University Press, 1983), 219. The German original can be found in Richard Wagner, *Mein Leben*, ed. Eike Middell (Leipzig: Carl Schünemann Verlag, 1986), 1:254.
2. See David Blackbourn, *The Long Nineteenth Century: A History of Germany, 1780-1918* (Oxford: Oxford University Press, 1998), 121.
3. See Mitchell Cohen's "To the Dresden Barricades: The Genesis of Wagner's Political Ideas," in *The Cambridge Companion to Wagner*, ed. Thomas S. Grey (Cambridge: Cambridge University Press, 2008), 55.
4. Richard Wagner, *My Life*, trans. Andrew Gray (Cambridge: Cambridge University Press, 1983), 219. The German original can be found in Richard Wagner, *Mein Leben*, ed. Eike Middell (Leipzig: Carl Schünemann Verlag, 1986), 1:253-54.
5. Ibid., English, 212, German, 247.
6. See Richard Wagner, "A Communication to My Friends" [Eine Mitteilung an meine freunde], in *Richard Wagner's Prose Works*, trans. William Ashton Ellis (New York: Broude Brothers, 1966), 1:315.
7. Ibid., 362.
8. Ibid., 316.

9. Dieter Borchmeyer discusses Wagner's "rewriting of the genesis of Tannhäuser" in his chapter entitled "Venus in Exile: *Tannhäuser* Between Romanticism and Young Germany," in *Drama and the World of Richard Wagner*, trans. Daphne Ellis (Princeton: Princeton University Press, 2003), 101-46. Paul Lawrence Rose, "Heine and Wagner Revisited: Art, Myth and Revolution," in *Heine-Jahrbuch*, 1991, 93-122 also has excellent analysis of Wagner's desire to downplay the influence of Heine.

10. For biographical information on Wagner, see Joachim Köhler, *Richard Wagner: The Last of the Titans*, trans. Stewart Spencer (New Haven: Yale University Press, 2004); *The Life of Richard Wagner*, 4 vols. (New York: Cambridge University Press, 1976); Curt Von Westernhagen, *Wagner: A Biography*, trans. Mary Whittall (London: Cambridge University Press, 1980); Barry Millington, *Wagner* (Princeton: Princeton University Press, 1984); Barry Millington, *The Master Musicians: Wagner* (London: J. M. Dent, 1984). For a discussion of the difficulties of using Wagner's writings to dissect his life, see John Deathridge, "Wagner Lives: Issues in Autobiography," in *The Cambridge Companion to Wagner*, ed. Thomas S. Grey (Cambridge: Cambridge University Press, 2008), 3-17. For Wagner's autobiography see Richard Wagner, *My Life*, trans. Andrew Gray, ed. Mary Whittall (Cambridge: Cambridge University Press, 1983). The German original, which includes a biography, is Richard Wagner, *Mein Leben*, 2 vol., ed. Eike Middell (Leipzig: Carl Schünemann Verlag, 1986). There is also some biographical information sprinkled throughout Ulrich Müller and Peter Wapnewski, eds., *Wagner Handbook*, trans. John Deathridge (Cambridge: Harvard University Press, 1992).

11. See Mitchell Cohen, "To the Dresden Barricades: The Genesis of Wagner's Political Ideas," in *The Cambridge Companion to Wagner*, ed. Thomas S. Grey (Cambridge: Cambridge University Press, 2008), 47-48.

12. See Thomas S. Grey, "Meister Richard's Apprenticeship: The Early Operas (1833-1840)" in *The Cambridge Companion to Wagner*, ed. Thomas S. Grey (Cambridge: Cambridge University Press, 2008), 23.

13. See Carl Dahlhaus, "Wagner's Place in the History of Music," trans. Alfred Clayton, in Ulrich Müller and Peter Wapnewski, eds., *Wagner Handbook*, trans. John Deathridge (Cambridge: Harvard University Press, 1992), 103.

14. See Richard Wagner, "On the Performing of *Tannhäuser*," in *Richard Wagner's Prose Works*, trans. William Ashton Ellis (New York: Broude Brothers, 1966), 3:172-73. The German original, "Über die Ausführung des *Tannhäuser*" can be found in Richard Wagner, *Sämtliche Schriften und Dichtungen*, (Leipzig, 1911-1916), 5:123-59. This passage can be found on pp. 126-27.

15. Paul Lawrence Rose, "Heine and Wagner Revisited: Art, Myth and Revolution," in the *Heine-Jahrbuch*, 1991, 94. For additional analysis of the relationship between Heine and Wagner, see Dieter Borchmeyer, "Heinrich Heine—Richard Wagner: Analyze einer Affinität," in Dieter Borchmeyer, Ami Maayani, and Susanne Vill, eds., *Richard Wagner und die Juden* (Stuttgart, Weimar: J. B. Metzler, 2000), 20-33.

16. Richard Wagner, *My Life*, trans. Andrew Gray (Cambridge: Cambridge University Press, 1983), 180. The German original can be found in Richard Wagner, *Mein Leben*, ed. Eike Middell (Leipzig: Carl Schünemann Verlag, 1986), 1:211.

17. As quoted in Martin Gregor-Dellin and Dietrich Mack, eds., *Cosima Wagner's Diaries: 1869 – 1877*, trans. Geoffrey Skelton (New York: Harcourt Brace Jovanovich, 1976), 1:234.

18. See Paul Lawrence Rose, "Heine and Wagner Revisited: Art, Myth and Revolution," in the *Heine-Jahrbuch*, 1991, 111-12.

19. See Richard Wagner's letter to Franz Liszt written on April 18, 1851 from Zurich. The translation into English can be found in Richard Wagner, *Selected Letters of Richard Wagner*, trans. and ed. Barry Millington and Stewart Spencer (New York: Norton, 1987), 221-22. The German original can be found in Richard Wagner, *Briefe*, ed. Wilhelm Ultmann (Leipzig: Bibliographisches Institut, 1925), 1:254-256.

20. The best English translation of "Judaism in Music" can be found in the journal *Wagner* [Journal of the London Wagner Society], trans. Stewart Spencer, 9, no. 1 (1988): 20-33. The German original is found in Richard Wagner, *Sämtliche Schriften und Dichtungen* (Leipzig, 1911-1916), 5:65-85.

21. Ibid., English, 30; German, 81.

22. Ibid., English, 32-33; German, 84-85.

23. See Paul Lawrence Rose, *Wagner: Race and Revolution* (New Haven: Yale University Press, 1992), 1.

24. This insight was suggested to me in an email from Dieter Borchmeyer on March 24, 2008.

25. See Marc Weiner, "Lingering Discourses: Critics, Jews, and the Case of Gottfried Wagner," in *Richard Wagner for the New Millennium*, ed. Matthew Bribitzer-Stull, Alex Lubet, and Gottfried Wagner (New York: Palgrave Macmillan, 2007), 151.

26. Richard Wagner, *My Life by Richard Wagner*, trans. Andrew Gray, ed. Mary Whittal (Cambridge: Cambridge University Press, 1983), 467. The German original can be found in Richard Wagner, *Mein Leben*, ed. Eike Middell (Leipzig: Carl Schünemann Verlag, 1986), 2:23-24.

27. For an entire book devoted to Wagner's influence on Hitler, see Christopher Nicholson, *Richard and Adolf: Did Richard Wagner Incite Adolf Hitler to Commit the Holocaust?* (New York and Jerusalem: Gefen Books, 2007).

28. Paul Lawrence Rose, *Wagner: Race and Revolution* (New Haven: Yale University Press, 1992), 192.

29. Ibid, 191.

30. See Marc Weiner, *Richard Wagner and the Antisemitic Imagination* (Lincoln: University of Nebraska Press, 1995).

31. See Barry Millington, "Nuremberg Trial: Is There Anti-Semitism in *Die Meistersinger?*" *Cambridge Opera Journal* 3, no. 3 (1991), 247.

32. See Thomas S. Grey, "The Jewish Question," in *The Cambridge Companion to Wagner* (Cambridge: Cambridge University Press, 2008), 212.

33. For a discussion of Heine's response to the essay, see Paul Lawrence Rose, "Heine and Wagner Revisited: Art, Myth and Revolution," in the *Heine-Jahrbuch* (1991), 116-18.

34. See Dieter Borchmeyer, *Drama and the World of Richard Wagner*, trans. Daphne Ellis (Princeton: Princeton University Press, 2003), 105.

35. *Die Göttin Diana* can be found in Heinrich Heine, *Heinrich Heine: Sämtliche Werke* (Düsseldorf: Artemis & Winkler Verlag, 2001), 2:731-39. I could find no translation of the work into English.

36. See Dieter Borchmeyer, *Drama and the World of Richard Wagner*, trans. Daphne Ellis (Princeton: Princeton University Press, 2003), 134.

37. As quoted in Dieter Borchmeyer, *Drama and the World of Richard Wagner*, trans. Daphne Ellis (Princeton: Princeton University Press, 2003), 136.

38. See Richard Wagner, "On the Performing of *Tannhäuser*," in *Richard Wagner's Prose Works*, trans. William Ashton Ellis (New York: Broude Brothers, 1966), 3:194. The German original can be found in Richard Wagner, "Über die Ausführung des *Tannhäuser*," in *Sämtliche Schriften und Dichtungen*, (Leipzig, 1911-1916), 5:150.

39. See Dieter Borchmeyer, *Drama and the World of Richard Wagner*, trans. Daphne Ellis (Princeton: Princeton University Press, 2003), 135-36.
40. Ibid.
41. See Martin Gregor-Dellin and Dietrich Mack, eds., *Cosima Wagner's Diaries: 1869 – 1877*, trans. Geoffrey Skelton (New York: Harcourt Brace Jovanovich, 1976), 651.
42. See Richard Wagner, "A Communication to My Friends" [Eine Mitteilung an meine freunde], in *Richard Wagner's Prose Works*, trans. William Ashton Ellis (New York: Broude Brothers, 1966), 1:315.
43. Ibid., 311-12.
44. Ibid., 311.
45. Ibid.
46. For a full overview of the opera as well as documents relating to it, see Attila Csampai and Dietmar Holland, eds., *Richard Wagner: Tannhäuser, Texte, Materialien, Kommentare* (Hamburg: GmbH, 1980). For another study of the opera and its sources, see Mary A. Cicora, *From History to Myth: Wagner's Tannhäuser and its Literary Sources* (New York: Peter Lang, 1992).
47. For Queen Victoria's diary response to the "overpowering" overture, see Curt von Westernhagen, *Wagner: A Biography*, trans. Mary Whittall (Cambridge: Cambridge University Press, 1978), 1:207. Charles Baudelaire wrote an entire essay on attending *Tannhäuser* in Paris entitled, "Richard Wagner and *Tannhäuser* in Paris," in his *Selected Writings On Art and Artists*, trans. P. E. Charvet (Cambridge: Cambridge University Press, 1972), 325-57.
48. The full text of the opera in both German and in English that I am quoting from is found in Nicholas John, ed., *Tannhäuser*, English National Opera Series Guide 39, trans. Rodney Blumer (New York: Riverrun Press, 1988), 61-93. The page numbers I give refer to both the German original and the English translation of the text.
49. See "Tannhäuser and the Song Contest on the Wartburg," in *Tannhäuser*, English National Opera Series Guide 39, ed. Nicholas John, trans. Rodney Blumer (New York: Riverrun Press, 1988), 62.
50. In Johann Nestroy's 1857 parody of Wagner's opera, he transforms Tannhäuser from a Romantic hero to a pathetic drunk. For the full text of his parody, see Johann Nestroy, *Stücke 36: Tannhäuser*, ed. Peter Branscombe (Vienna: Franz Deuticke, 2000), 5-38.
51. See "Tannhäuser and the Song Contest on the Wartburg," *Tannhäuser*, English National Opera Series Guide 39, ed. Nicholas John, trans. Rodney Blumer (New York: Riverrun Press, 1988), 64.
52. Ibid., 67.
53. Ibid., 72.
54. Ibid., 74.
55. Ibid.
56. Ibid., 75.
57. Ibid., 78.
58. See James M. McGlathery, *Wagner's Operas and Desire* (New York: Peter Lang, 1998), 39.
59. See Timothy McFarland, "Wagner's Most Medieval Opera," in *Tannhäuser*, English National Opera Series Guide 39, ed. Nicholas John, trans. Rodney Blumer (New York: Riverrun Press, 1988), 25-32. The discussion of the Virgin versus Venus is on p. 25.

60. See Richard Wagner, "A Communication to My Friends" [Eine Mitteilung an meine freunde], in *Richard Wagner's Prose Works*, trans. William Ashton Ellis (New York: Broude Brothers, 1966), 1:340.

61. See Richard Wagner's letter to August Röckel, Waldheim of August 23, 1856. The translation into English can be found in Barry Millington and Stewart Spencer, eds. and trans., *Selected Letters of Richard Wagner*, (New York: Norton, 1987), 357. The German original can be found in Richard Wagner, *Briefe*, ed. Wilhelm Ultmann (Leipzig: Bibliographisches Institut, 1925), 1:384-85.

62. See "Tannhäuser and the Song Contest on the Wartburg" in *Tannhäuser*, English National Opera Series Guide 39, ed. Nicholas John, trans. Rodney Blumer (New York: Riverrun Press, 1988), 80.

63. Ibid., 81-82.

64. Ibid.

65. See Richard Wagner's letter to Franz Liszt of May 29, 1852. The translation into English can be found in Barry Millington and Stewart Spencer, eds. and trans., *Selected Letters of Richard Wagner*, (New York: Norton, 1987), 258.

66. See "Tannhäuser and the Song Contest on the Wartburg" in *Tannhäuser*, English National Opera Series Guide 39, ed. Nicholas John, trans. Rodney Blumer (New York: Riverrun Press, 1988), 84.

67. Ibid., 86.

68. Ibid.

69. Isaac Leyb Peretz's later Yiddish version of the opera will also present the Rome scene retrospectively rather than in real time.

70. See "Tannhäuser and the Song Contest on the Wartburg" in *Tannhäuser*, English National Opera Series Guide 39, ed. Nicholas John, trans. Rodney Blumer (New York: Riverrun Press, 1988), 89.

71. Ibid.

72. Ibid.

73. Ibid., 93.

74. Ibid., 83.

75. See Hans Mayer, *Portrait of Wagner: An Illustrated Biography*, trans. Robert Nowell (New York: Herder and Herder, 1971), 43.

76. See Richard Wagner, "Overture to "Tannhäuser." in *Richard Wagner's Prose Works: The Theatre*, trans. William Ashton Ellis (New York: Broude Brothers, 1966), 3:231.

77. See James M. McGlathery, *Wagner's Operas and Desire* (New York: Peter Lang, 1998), 33.

78. See Richard Wagner's June 5, 1845 letter to Karl Gaillard. Translated into English in Barry Millington and Stewart Spencer, eds. and trans., *Selected Letters of Richard Wagner*, (New York: Norton, 1987), 122. The German original can be found in Richard Wagner, *Briefe*, ed. Wilhelm Ultmann (Leipzig: Bibliographisches Institut, 1925), 1:142-46.

79. See Richard Wagner's September 6, 1842 letter to Ernst Benedikt Kietz. Translated into English in Barry Millington and Stewart Spencer, eds. and trans., *Selected Letters of Richard Wagner*, (New York: Norton, 1987), 94-95. The German original can be found in Richard Wagner, *Sämtliche Briefe*, ed. Gertrud Strobel and others (Leipzig: Deutscher Verlag für Musik, 1967-2007), 2:153.

80. Richard Wagner, *My Life*, trans. Andrew Gray (Cambridge: Cambridge University Press, 1983), 308. The German original can be found in Richard Wagner, *Mein Leben*, ed. Eike Middell (Leipzig: Carl Schünemann Verlag, 1986), 1:354.

81. See Dieter Borchmeyer, *Drama and the World of Richard Wagner*, trans. Daphne Ellis (Princeton: Princeton University Press, 2003), 121.

82. See, for instance, Richard Wagner's early August 1860 letter to Mathilde Wesendonck. Translated into English in Barry Millington and Stewart Spencer, eds. and trans., *Selected Letters of Richard Wagner*, (New York: Norton, 1987), 498 and Martin Gregor-Dellin and Dietrich Mack, eds., *Cosima Wagner's Diaries: 1869 – 1877*, trans. Geoffrey Skelton (New York: Harcourt Brace Jovanovich, 1976), 1:311. The German original can be found in Richard Wagner, *Briefe*, ed. Wilhelm Ultmann (Leipzig: Bibliographisches Institut, 1925), 2:139-40.

83. Richard Wagner, *My Life*, trans. Andrew Gray (Cambridge: Cambridge University Press, 1983), 310. The German original can be found in Richard Wagner, *Mein Leben*, ed. Eike Middell (Leipzig: Carl Schünemann Verlag, 1986), 1:357.

84. Richard Wagner, *My Life*, trans. Andrew Gray (Cambridge: Cambridge University Press, 1983), 625. The German original can be found in Richard Wagner, *Mein Leben*, ed. Eike Middell (Leipzig: Carl Schünemann Verlag, 1986), 2:204.

85. See Carolyn Abbate, "Orpheus and the Underworld: The Music of Wagner's *Tannhäuser*" in *Tannhäuser*, English National Opera Series Guide 39, ed. Nicholas John, trans. Rodney Blumer (New York: Riverrun Press, 1988), 33-50.

86. Martin Gregor-Dellin and Dietrich Mack, eds., *Cosima Wagner's Diaries: 1869 – 1877*, trans. Geoffrey Skelton (New York: Harcourt Brace Jovanovich, 1976), 1:505.

87. Martin Gregor-Dellin and Dietrich Mack, eds., *Cosima Wagner's Diaries: 1869 – 1877*, trans. Geoffrey Skelton (New York: Harcourt Brace Jovanovich, 1976), 2:996.

88. See Mike Ashman, "*Tannhäuser*—An Obsession," in *Tannhäuser*, English National Opera Series Guide 39, ed. Nicholas John, trans. Rodney Blumer (New York: Riverrun Press, 1988), 7.

89. See Richard Wagner, "A Communication to My Friends" [Eine Mitteilung an meine freunde], in *Richard Wagner's Prose Works*, trans. William Ashton Ellis (New York: Broude Brothers, 1966), 1:323.

90. Martin Gregor-Dellin and Dietrich Mack, eds., *Cosima Wagner's Diaries: 1869 – 1877*, trans. Geoffrey Skelton (New York: Harcourt Brace Jovanovich, 1976), 1:773.

91. Ibid., 290.

92. For a discussion of the production and reception history of the Dresden and Paris versions, see Curt Von Westernhagen, *Wagner: A Biography*, trans. Mary Whittall (London: Cambridge University Press, 1980), 69-79, 277-93. For his essay on the French production, see Richard Wagner, "A Report on the Production of Tannhäuser in Paris," in *Richard Wagner's Prose Works*, trans. William Ashton Ellis (New York: Broude Brothers, 1966), 3:347-60. Wagner also discusses the Paris productions in detail Richard Wagner, *My Life*, trans. Andrew Gray (Cambridge: Cambridge University Press, 1983), 611-21. For a detailed analysis of the changes that Wagner implemented in the Paris version of the opera, see Carolyn Abbate, "The Parisian 'Venus' and the 'Paris' Tannhäuser," *The Journal of the American Musicological Society* 36 (1983): 73-123.

93. Martin Gregor-Dellin and Dietrich Mack, eds., *Cosima Wagner's Diaries: 1869 – 1877*, trans. Geoffrey Skelton (New York: Harcourt Brace Jovanovich, 1976), 1:887.

94. See Barry Millington, *The Master Musicians: Wagner* (London: J. M. Dent, 1984), 69.

95. As quoted in Richard Wagner's March 3, 1860 letter to Mathilde Wesendonck. Translated into English in Barry Millington and Stewart Spencer, eds. and trans., *Selected Letters of Richard Wagner*, (New York: Norton, 1987), 486. The German

original can be found in Richard Wagner, *Briefe*, ed. Wilhelm Ultmann (Leipzig: Bibliographisches Institut, 1925), 2:121-24.

96. Richard Wagner's September 19, 1859 letter to Cosima Von Bülow. Translated into English in Barry Millington and Stewart Spencer, eds. and trans., *Selected Letters of Richard Wagner*, (New York: Norton, 1987), 467.

97. Richard Wagner's June 8, 1860 letter to Julie Ritter. Translated into English in Barry Millington and Stewart Spencer, eds. and trans., *Selected Letters of Richard Wagner*, (New York: Norton, 1987), 492.

98. Richard Wagner's April 10, 1860 letter to Mathilde Wesendonck. Translated into English in Barry Millington and Stewart Spencer, eds. and trans., *Selected Letters of Richard Wagner*, (New York: Norton, 1987), 487. The German original can be found in Richard Wagner, *Briefe*, ed. Wilhelm Ultmann (Leipzig: Bibliographisches Institut, 1925), 2:125-26.

99. See Richard Wagner, "A Report on the Production of Tannhäuser in Paris," in *Richard Wagner's Prose Works*, trans. William Ashton Ellis (New York: Broude Brothers, 1966), 3:357.

100. Ibid., 347-60.

101. Richard Wagner, *My Life*, trans. Andrew Gray (Cambridge: Cambridge University Press, 1983), 628. The German original can be found in Richard Wagner, *Mein Leben*, ed. Eike Middell (Leipzig: Carl Schünemann Verlag, 1986), 2:208.

Chapter Four

Theodor Herzl

A Night at the Opera

On the evening of May 11, 1895, the crowd was seated and nervously waiting for the curtain at the Académie de Musique, better known as the Paris Opera; it was an invited audience of political luminaries, journalists, and artists at the dress rehearsal for Richard Wagner's opera, *Tannhäuser*.

The audience was anxious, because when *Tannhäuser* had first been performed in the City of Light in March 1861 it had been an infamous disaster discussed in the previous chapter. When Wagner heard of the failure of the third production he realized that the best thing to do was to pull the opera. He ended the run and vowed never to show *Tannhäuser* in Paris again. Wagner died in 1883, having kept his promise. However in 1895, some brave souls decided that the Parisian public should be provided with another chance to attend one of the late maestro's famous works.

Among the seated audience waiting for the curtain that night in 1895 was a tall bearded man in a black frock coat with a top hat laid across his knees. This was Theodor Herzl. As correspondent for the most prestigious newspaper in Central Europe, the *Neue Freie Presse*, he was attending *Tannhäuser's* dress rehearsal to report on an important event in Parisian society. Herzl was a sophisticated music lover, and a part of him wanted Wagner's music to succeed, yet Herzl was also Jewish and very much aware of Wagner's well-known and deep-rooted anti-Semitism. In fact, Herzl's first personal confrontation with anti-Semitism had been in 1883 when he was a Viennese college student attending memorial ceremonies for Wagner's death.

Herzl attended the performance to report how an audience reacted more than thirty years after the original disaster. Much water had flowed under the

Rhine bridges between France and Germany since 1861; in 1861 there was no Germany, and France was an empire. Now, Wilhelm was emperor of the Germans and the Parisians lived in the Third Republic. Germany was transforming into a self-confident, proud Reich, and France was becoming a moribund democracy that had only recently been defeated and occupied by German armies. Would a group of patriotic, wealthy Parisian aristocrats again undermine Wagner or had he become so well established that the crowd would approach his work with solemn respect?

On May 14, 1895, three days after the performance, the *Neue Freie Presse* published Herzl's feuilleton on *Tannhäuser*, where he announced his verdict. The opera goers had in fact generally responded very warmly because they had listened with the expectation that the music would be good since it was created by a composer who was now popular: "A different time has arrived and it listens differently with a different set of ears. Now they sit in anonymous reverence in the dress rehearsal and happily roll their eyes. How loved this music is! Who managed to achieve this? Who? The mysterious, the great matchmaker: success."[1]

Herzl's reaction to the opera is enthusiastic but restrained, and reading the feuilleton one would never guess that the father of Zionism was so inspired by Wagner's opera that he made sure to attend nightly performances while formulating his 1897 political tract *Der Judenstaat* (The Jewish State). This key pamphlet of Herzl's life was written in the months after attending the opera and it was published in Vienna the following year. "Der Judenstaat" became a central Zionist manifesto and the ideas put forth in it helped to start the process that culminated in the creation of the State of Israel in 1948. In Herzl's feuilleton about *Tannhäuser*, there is in fact only one mention that the music is good. Reading it, one gets a sense that Herzl's favorite part was explaining to the readership how humiliated Wagner had been at the original performance thirty years earlier. He writes that "the famous musicians were of course all against Wagner . . . A comment made by Auber between acts is also preserved. He said, 'It is as if one was reading a book without breathing and in which there is no punctuation.'"

Typical of the feuilleton, Herzl's comments and impressions are ironic, detached, and unemotional. It is interesting to compare the article from the *Neue Freie Presse* with what he later wrote in his diary:

> During the last two months of my stay in Paris I wrote the book *Der Judenstaat*. I cannot remember ever having written anything in such a mood of exaltation. Heine tells us that he heard the flapping of eagles' wings above his head when he wrote certain stanzas. I too seemed to hear the flutter of wings above my head while I wrote *Der Judenstaat*. I worked at it daily until I was completely exhausted. My one recreation was on the evenings when I could go to hear Wagner's music, and particularly *Tannhäuser*, an opera which I go to see as often as it is produced. And only on those evenings where there was no opera did I have any doubts as to the truth of my ideas.[2]

Herzl went to Wagner's opera in his role as Paris correspondent for the *Neue Freie Presse*, but continued to attend, night after night, to clear the thoughts in his head. As he states, only when he was not at the opera did he "have any doubts as to the truth" of his ideas.

For years Herzl had been trying to solve the dilemma of Jewish life in Europe. He was raised in a family that believed wholeheartedly in the promise of emancipation, and as a young man he thought that if the Jews assimilated then anti-Semitism would stop. Yet when anti-Semitism kept spreading, and the liberals who were supposed to assist the Jews acted as cruelly as the most staunch conservatives, the assimilationist model looked as though it would crack. After giving up on assimilation, Herzl thought up several bizarre solutions, such as having the Jews perform a dignified mass conversion to Catholicism in front of the Pope in Rome and trying to instigate duels with leading anti-Semites.

In 1895, when Herzl attended the opera, things were reaching a new level of crisis for European Jews. In April, Vienna, which had been quaffing from the cup of intolerance since the stock market crash of 1892, decided to drink the whole poisoned chalice by electing as mayor the anti-Semitic Karl Lueger. The Lueger victory forced the Jewish population, usually advocates for democracy, to back Emperor Franz Josef's executive order to overturn the election. The Jews were in a bad situation in Vienna, one that looked as if it would only worsen rather than improve.[3] Paris, on the contrary, had less overt and entrenched anti-Semitism, which was easier to dismiss as a temporary problem that might just go away. However, recent events, such as espionage charges leveled against the extremely patriotic, assimilated French Jewish Captain Alfred Dreyfus, had made the situation there troubling.

Herzl was also inspired by the medium in which the opera was delivered:

> In the evening *Tannhäuser* at the opera. We too will have such splendid auditoriums-the gentlemen in full dress, the ladies dressed as lavishly as possible. Yes, I want to make use of the Jewish love of luxury, in addition to all other resources. This again made me think of the phenomenon of the crowd. There they sat for hours, tightly packed, motionless, in physical discomfort—and for what? For something imponderable, the kind that Hirsch does not understand: for sounds! for music and pictures! I shall also cultivate majestic processional marches for great festive occasions.[4]

Tannhäuser suggested to him that to motivate the masses he should turn to spectacle and large events where the Jews would be swept up by the pressure of the crowd.

Herzl's experiences in France had cast a new light on how to solve the Jewish problem. Moving in the corridors of power in Paris, he received firsthand knowledge of how politics worked, yet as a Jew, Herzl had little chance of becoming a politician, even though his personality and bearing would have made this a natural choice. Zionism, as described in *Der Judenstaat*, gave him the chance to become a Jewish statesman, not for Vienna or Paris, but for the Jews at large. Wagner's opera, and the self-sacrificing love of Elisabeth for Tannhäuser, was a potential inspiration, showing how redemption could be brought through the abnegation of the self. Where a Christian Viennese or Parisian was also required to sacrifice herself or himself in numerous daily ways for the state, for the Jews the story was different. Herzl's aim was nothing less than the salvation of the entire European Jewish population, and the means to do this was mass self-sacrifice: the Jews would undertake the seemingly impossible task of relocating out of Europe and building a new Jewish state somewhere else.

Early Life and Work

Theodor Herzl was born in 1860 in the town of Pest.[5] Situated on the Eastern shore of the Danube River, Pest fused with the conjoining towns of Buda and Obuda in 1873 to become the Hungarian capital Budapest. Throughout his life, Herzl found himself drawn towards three different identities, while not associating completely with any of them: the Hungarian world of his childhood, the German culture he was attracted to, and his Jewish roots. His parents, Jacob and Jeannette, were wealthy, middle-class Jews who believed in the doctrine that promised emancipation for the Jewish population in exchange for assimilation. As with Heine's and Peretz's mother, Jeannette both doted on and dominated her son, while his father was a more gentle presence who was often away on business. Herzl's parents thought that he was born for great things and throughout his life he remained extremely close to them, even living with them for a time while he was married. They were his rock, supporting him financially, psychologically, and spiritually throughout his entire life.

Like Heine, Judaism played only a small role in his upbringing. Instead of a Bar Mitzvah, he had an assimilated version, a confirmation, and he only occasionally attended the nearby synagogue. He saw himself and the Jews as sharing a history and culture, rather than a religion. As with Heine, as anti-Semitism rose, Herzl increasingly identified himself as a Jew. Like many middle-class Hungarian Jews, the Herzl family's emotional and cultural attachment was to Germany; they all spoke fluent German and Hungarian and at a young age Herzl began reading German literature, particularly Heinrich Heine. Along with his sister, Pauline, the nuclear family was a tight-knit group, well off and optimistic about the future which was for them German.[6] Throughout his young adulthood Theodor's question was whether he identified himself more strongly as Hungarian or German; to privilege his Jewishness was not a possibility.

As a young man, Herzl briefly attended a Jewish day school and then switched to a technical school devoted to math and science. Soon he discovered that he preferred the humanities, and in 1876 he transferred to the Evangelical Gymnasium. His new school had a large number of middle-class Jews. While there, Herzl developed such a deep affinity for German culture that he even founded a club devoted to its literature. Herzl thus began to identify less with Hungary and more with its neighbor to the north and west.

Everything changed for the Herzls in 1878, when Theodor's sister Pauline died from typhoid. Herzl was then eighteen. Her death shattered the peace and sent Theodor's parents into a tailspin of grief that ultimately led them to pack up the house, so full of memories of Pauline, and relocate to Vienna. It would be in Vienna that Herzl would find a community that shared the same attachment to Germany. Vienna, like Pest, was a bustling commercial city that was situated on the Danube River, the main waterway of central Europe. Unlike Pest, Vienna was also a thriving arts center, where the middle-class Herzls came into direct contact with European culture. Vienna's energetic art scene focused primarily on the theater; pageants, operas, and theatrical productions were a regular aspect of urban life. The pinnacle of the city's cultural progress was the 1897 appointment of Gustav Mahler as head of the Vienna Opera House.

The Herzl family lived in a large apartment in the primarily middle-class Jewish neighborhood of the Leopoldstadt. Although culturally affiliating themselves with the broader society, like most Viennese Jews they maintained social, economic, and marriage networks with other middle-class Jews. Thus, they were both insiders and outsiders, an empowered marginal group that, like Heine's community before them, could at times navigate the broader culture, but remained separate enough from it to have a critical, outsider's perspective. Edward Timms calls this an "Austrio-Jewish symbiosis" that led to a type of "empowered marginality," where as outsiders Jews could think outside the box and create groundbreaking solutions, while at the same time use their insider status to tap into institutions to support them in their endeavors.[7] This symbiosis led to a phenomenal number of Viennese Jews becoming major cultural figures, such as Gustav Mahler, Karl Kraus, Arnold Schoenberg, Arthur Schnitzler, Ludwig Wittgenstein, Sigmund Freud and, of course, Theodor Herzl.

Although many middle-class Viennese Jews converted to Christianity to gain what they hoped would be full access to the broader society, many more did not and most lived their life with fellow Jews as their closest friends as well as their economic and marriage partners. Thus, it makes sense that someone like Herzl, who believed as a young man in the assimilationist mandate, would nevertheless have no interest in converting and would marry a Jewish woman.[8] The Jews of Vienna were for the most part thus "acculturated" rather than "assimilated."[9] In Vienna, Judaism was on the Reform model, which mimicked in numerous ways the decorum and practices of Protestantism. Reform Judaism also made drastic cuts in the traditional 613 commandments of Halakhah. This enabled Jewish distinctiveness to decrease so that the Jews seemed, externally at least, as Viennese as their Christian brethren. While there had been a large influx of Eastern European, poor, highly traditional Jews to Vienna in 1840, the middle-class residents of Herzl's neighborhood lived their lives associating with other middle-class, acculturated, Jews who also saw their cultural models as Vienna and Germany. At first, like other immigrants, Herzl did not see his identity "as fixed" and he fluctuated between seeing himself as Hungarian and as Viennese.[10] Soon enough, however, he set his identity as Viennese, and associated with the culture so strongly (as did many other Jews of his class), that in 1881, when he was a college student, he joined the nationalistic (and later anti-Semitic) Albia fraternity.

Herzl began law studies in 1878 at the University of Vienna, but soon discovered that he really wanted to be a writer. At the university, Herzl's aloof bearing kept him at a distance from other students and though he continually longed for romantic attachments, he only managed to have trysts with prostitutes and occasional lovers.[11] Much like Heine, he found relationships with women extremely difficult and perhaps the main love of his life was his mother. He also maintained throughout a strange fascination with young girls, in the same vein as Lewis Carroll, more the trait of a man unable to relate to adult women than a pedophile. At the time, universities were "hotbeds of nationalist strife," and like other students, Jew and Christian alike, Herzl was attracted to the cause of German nationalism. He therefore joined the nationalist fraternity, Albia, aware that one of their mandates was that their Jewish members would "shed their Jewish traits and embrace the German."[12] However, this was a futile desire, because as Herzl would soon discover, the non-Jewish world had little interest in accepting him. As a means to appear more European and less "Jewish," Herzl even claimed a Sephardic heritage, since those with Spanish ancestry were deemed to be the intellectual and cultural elite in contrast to the backwards, premodern Eastern European Jews of Russia and Poland.[13]

As strange as it may seem that the leader of Jewish nationalism began as a German nationalist, it actually makes sense. As Jacques Kornberg documents in *Theodor Herzl: From Assimilation to Zionism*, the assimilationist drive, fostered by being a middle-class central European Jew, took as its premise that the Jewish people were crippled beings, overly obsessed with money and backwards in culture. They needed to be reformed. Herzl's unique version of Zionism would do this by creating a means to conflate assimilation and nationalism (two seemingly opposite ideas) in a Jewish state built on a European liberal model. This would thus foster a "new Jew" who was European through and through.

Throughout his life Herzl had embraced German culture. Yet when the nationalists became increasingly anti-Semitic and began to reject liberal values, Herzl started to pull away. The difference between Herzl's version of German nationalism, typical of his generation, that placed Germanness on a pedestal while disavowing Jewishness, and this new anti-Semitism, was twofold. First, anti-Semitism was becoming racial and was thus eliminating assimilation as a means for Jewish emancipation. It asserted that the Jews were biologically inferior and that it made no difference how they acted in the world since they could not really improve. Second, it was becoming extremely conservative and Herzl was a liberal. However, in both forms of German nationalism, the Jews, particularly the poor traditional Eastern European ones, were unacceptable in their current condition. Either, as Herzl at first asserted, they should become Westernized and modernized or, as he later believed, they needed to leave Europe altogether. Unlike racial anti-Semites such as Wagner, however, who sought to erase Jewishness from European life, Herzl's Zionism sought to push the Jews to leave Europe as means to liberate them by giving them a new locale in which to become European.

Herzl went public with his disgust about the rising anti-Semitism within German nationalism when he quit the Albia fraternity in March 1883 in response to their handling of a ceremony marking the death of Richard Wagner. At the memorial service, which was a massive, nationalistic event in honor of the Reich, a member of the Albia fraternity made an openly hostile speech against the Jews. The next day Herzl wrote a public letter denouncing the speech and asserting that the fraternity had approved of all the anti-Semitism on public display. Herzl, who had remained in the fraternity for two years after it stopped accepting Jewish members, was dropping out now because they were propagating a new form of racial anti-Semitism. For Herzl, it was high time to admit that nationalism and liberal politics were no longer in sync and that an increasing intolerance was taking hold. The Albia incident irked him personally, but for a while longer he did not see the event as indicative of a larger problem that he needed to solve.

☆   From 1885 until 1891, Herzl gave up on the law and worked as a neophyte playwright and journalist. He desperately tried to get his bourgeois comedies produced in Europe with the ultimate goal of premiering an original play at the most famous Viennese playhouse, the Burgtheater. Suprisingly, eventually the Burgtheater did accept two of his bourgeois comedies into their repertory: *Der Flüchtling* (The Refugee) and *Tabarin*. He also was able to have his controversial play, *The New Ghetto* staged in Berlin, Vienna, and Prague in 1897 and 1898. *The New Ghetto* is the most interesting of the three. It is about a member of the assimilated Viennese-Jewish middle class confronting rejection by Christians as well as his own self-hatred. The story typifies Herzl's attempt to work through the contradictions of his earlier approaches to anti-Semitism and shows his arrival at a new understanding of Jewishness. Even with these successes, however, Herzl's talents were not deep enough to become anything more than a minor playwright, and for him fame would finally come through his journalism. Yet for Herzl, stagecraft would later be a central aspect of his Zionism.

➷   At the age of twenty-nine, Herzl fell for the beautiful, neurotic, young daughter of a Viennese millionaire, Julie Naschauer. She was a small, pretty blonde woman with curly hair and dark eyebrows. From his writings about Julie, Herzl seems more infatuated with the idea of love than with the real woman he was betrothed to, and soon after their lavish wedding their relationship became deeply troubled. Their sixteen-year marriage was marked by Herzl's constant threats to walk out and the couple spent months and sometimes much longer living apart. It is no surprise that the marriage had so many problems because Herzl was unable to have mature relationships and Julie's mercurial personality, which suggests mental illness, no doubt made things worse.

Although Herzl was a bad husband, he was still a great son to his parents and he attempted to be a good father to his three children by loving them unconditionally and trying to be involved with all aspects of their lives. The fate of the children, Hans, Pauline, and Trude, is one of the saddest legacies in modern Jewish history. The man who was in large part responsible for creating the drive to seek a Jewish state would have no forbears to perpetuate his own legacy, as all three died tragically. The first two, Hans and Pauline, both committed suicide, while his third child, Trude, was taken out of a mental institution and killed by the Nazis. In 1946, two years before the foundation of the State of Israel, his only grandchild, Peter Theodor, also committed suicide.

Early Zionism

In the 1890s, while working as a freelance journalist and playwright, Herzl began a series of proactive attempts to solve the Jewish problem. He wanted to find a means to reassert the dignity of the Jewish people so that they could be considered equal with cultured Viennese and Germans.[14] In a response much more typical of his Eastern European Jewish brethren, Herzl at first played with the idea of having the Jews join with Viennese socialists to overthrow the current government and enact a revolutionary regime. By so doing, they would help to create a utopian society where instead of sticking out, they would submerge into the universal tide of humanity.

Herzl also came up with two other plans: public duels and mass conversion. Dueling was a popular and often deadly pursuit among the indolent wealthy classes as a way to ameliorate social shaming. Herzl's plan was to instigate duels with leading Viennese Jew haters. As he saw it, whether he won or lost he could use the duel as a public, respectable public platform for challenging anti-Semitism. If Herzl succeeded by killing his opponent, he would give a rousing public speech on the evils of anti-Semitism at his trial, and if he lost, the public would feel profound regret that anti-Semitism had led to such a pointless death. Fortunately Herzl never followed through with this plan.

At the same time, he also considered another strange solution: a mass conversion of the Jews in St. Peter's Square, Rome. Although by converting they would cease to be Jews, in Herzl's mind conversion was a means to regain Jewish dignity, since they would convert in a proactive manner that showed the world their regal bearing.[15] In both solutions, public duels and mass conversions, Herzl was utilizing his training and interest in theatrical public spectacles to come up with a response to the problem of anti-Semitism.

Neue Freie Presse

In 1891, Herzl wrote a series of feuilletons for the *Neue Freie Presse* about his recent travels to the Pyrenees. (The trip, financed by his parents, was really a means for him to escape his troubled marriage to Julie.) A feuilleton has no real equivalent today, but is a bit like a pamphlet or an opinion piece in a political magazine. Herzl was a natural at the form since it is a genre in which the author filters the events of the world through his or her personal viewpoint. First made popular with Heine, the feuilleton was decried as a negative product of the "Jewish press," as it was seen to undermine "objective" journalism. [16] It is no wonder that Heine and Herzl were masters of the genre, since in their social position as insecure outsiders seeking to become insiders they were acutely tuned to social mores and could comment adeptly on them. Moreover, to really be capable at the form one had to possess a large personality with set opinions which would permeate the text, since a good practitioner would often try to make the text more exciting by infusing into it personal views. The highly opinionated and confident Herzl had such a personality. The Pyrenees travel pictures were so well written, funny, and engaging that the *Neue Freie Presse* offered him the position of cultural correspondent for Paris. Becoming Paris correspondent for the most important newspaper in central Europe was a huge coup for Herzl, even if what he really wanted was to be a kind of Austro-Hungarian Molière.

The *Neue Freie Presse* was run by two middle class, liberal Viennese Jews, Moritz Benedikt and Eduard Bacher, and the paper's ideology was progressive assimilationist liberalism. In fact, years later when Herzl would ask Benedikt and Bacher to have the paper editorialize for his Zionist endeavors, they would distance themselves from what they saw as a radical and impossible pursuit that was contrary to their assimilationist outlook. Yet, "paradoxically, it was the income he earned from this anti-Zionist newspaper which helped him to develop his Zionist campaign," as Herzl would work for the *Neue Freie Presse* for most of his life. [17]

Herzl was well aware of the status that his job bestowed and used it to gain personal audiences with some of the most important political and financial leaders of the day. He would sign his letters with the reminder, "Perhaps my name is not unknown to you. In any case, you are acquainted with the newspaper which I represent here. Respectfully yours, Dr. Herzl, Correspondent of the *Neue Freie Presse*." [18] One of the most important tools that Herzl had for pushing his later Zionist agenda was his job as a journalist, which enabled him to meet with political and financial leaders. [19]

Paris

When Herzl moved to France in 1891 at the age of thirty-one, Paris, like Vienna, was a cultural center; however, it quickly became evident that Vienna was the poor relation of the grande dame that was Paris. The 1890s was the time of the belle époque, or "beautiful era" when Paris was the world center of bohemianism. These were golden years in France when the arts, music, theater, and salon life were at their most exciting and innovative. The Eiffel Tower had recently been completed, impressionism filled the galleries, and theaters were packed. The great iron tower symbolized that the Parisians were literally reaching towards the sky. Yet the "gay nineties" were also a time of corruption and scandals when the peace was occasionally shattered by anarchist violence, which the public and their newspapers reacted to with both revulsion and fascination. It was an era when anything seemed possible and where nothing was certain. It was certainly a good moment to be a journalist seeking to understand one's own, and the broader, political system.

Herzl was happy to work as a correspondent. It was his first full-time and steady job and it ideally suited his temperament, which was active, curious, and engaged in the world at large.[20] Transforming himself from a playwright to a journalist meant seemingly a switch to a more realistic form of writing, yet by continuing to publish in the feuilleton form, his own creative approach could still be used to the maximum. During his initial stay in Paris, his wife Julie remained with the children in Vienna, and this was probably positive for Herzl, who found the relationship burdensome, even though he missed his children. When homesick he longed not for Julie but for his parents and he begged them to join him. He got more than he bargained for in 1892, when Julie, the children, and Herzl's parents all came to live with him.

In Paris, Herzl attended the main society events. His writings were very popular with the readers and through them he transmitted his pleasure for Parisian culture while also reporting on the French's obsessive interest with anarchic violence. As a correspondent, he also was invited to political events such as parliamentary meetings. According to Haya Harel, "the French parliament . . . was a kind of experimental laboratory for democratic politics and at the same time, it was also Herzl's school of statesmanship."[21] As a correspondent he often wrote pieces satirizing French politics and he, like Heine, came briefly under the watch of the French Secret Service.

The Dreyfus Affair

Herzl started to question whether the assimilationist model would ever work when he saw that even in Paris anti-Semitism had begun to rise, since the Panama scandal of 1892 was blamed on the Jews. At first he was able to tell himself that this increased hostility was a temporary glitch. However, the steady escalation of hatred in France troubled him more and more. In both Vienna and Paris, where the arts dominated and where one would have expected a progressive doctrine to take root, anti-Semitism was becoming respectable. For a liberal like Herzl, who believed wholeheartedly in a progressive social vision, this so-called period of bohemia and culture must have seemed confusingly backwards. Moreover, the rising Jew hatred must have stung him personally. After all, he was doing everything he was supposed to do: he had assimilated into Western culture to such an extent that he even shared many Christians' views about the crippled state of Jewry. He dressed and acted like a Christian gentleman and he was still to be rejected because he was born a Jew. This realization challenged his outlook and he began to distrust the idea of giving the Christian masses full political rights, since they would be bound to turn their wrath at some point against the Jews.

Herzl's growing disillusionment with the Parisian government culminated with the Dreyfus trial, on which he first reported in December 1894. The case revolved around a charge of espionage leveled against the French Jewish Army Captain Alfred Dreyfus, and was a litmus test in French society for liberal, progressive values versus conservative ones. If one, like Émile Zola, was for Dreyfus, then one supported the oppressed and the forces of tolerance. If one was against Dreyfus, as were many conservatives, Catholics, and Royalists, one backed the establishment and the French government. Herzl, who initially was a cheerleader for the old order, at first believed in Dreyfus's guilt, but soon came to realize that the whole thing was a set up. Dreyfus was innocent but he was being made into a scapegoat because he was Jewish. Herzl attended the trial, heard the guilty verdict firsthand, and wrote about Dreyfus's public humiliation. Dreyfus, like Herzl, was an assimilated middle-class Jew who believed totally in the Enlightenment ideals of brotherhood and emancipation. His arrest and indictment were the cruelest betrayals for a man who had devoted his life to France. If someone like Dreyfus could be falsely accused and convicted, then no Jew was safe.

According to Herzl himself and to many critics, the Dreyfus Affair of December 1894 was a turning point in his life. Some commentators see the affair as leading directly to Herzl's "conversion" to Zionism. Others view it as the straw that broke the assimilationist's back; the final in a series of steps in the development of Herzl's ideology. The most historically accurate way to view Herzl's response to Dreyfus, according to Jacques Kornberg, is as a step in a multilayered evolution.[22] Herzl's Zionism did not occur in a day but evolved over time: "Herzl's conversion to Zionism was not a cheaply won certitude, the outcome of an abrupt illumination, as the Dreyfus legend suggests. Such a view trivializes his courageous and highly original struggle with issues of assimilationism, Jewish self-contempt, the pariah status of Jews, and their self-liberation. His conversion was a step-by-step, hazardous passage on trackless terrain."[23] With each step the assimilationist Herzl, ashamed of his Jewishness, found a new model of Jewish salvation that rejected the carrot and stick of European emancipation ideologies.[24] Whether or not the coverage of the trial was a conversion moment, it served to cement Herzl's growing realization that assimilation into European culture would not solve the Jewish problem.

In Paris, Herzl's Zionism thus added two new aspects: a belief in a radical and total solution and a model for implementing it based on French statesmanship. As Herzl would write in his diaries: "In Paris I was in the midst of politics-at least as an observer. I saw how the world is run. I also stood amazed at the phenomenon of the crowd—for a long time without comprehending it. Here too I reached a higher, more disinterested view of anti-Semitism, from which at least I did not have to suffer directly."[25] The Dreyfus affair forced Herzl to accept that anti-Semitism was permanent and not changed by assimilation, culture, or liberal politics. Out of this knowledge arose Herzl's desire to have the Jews leave Europe en masse to establish a new Jewish state.

1894 and 1895 were watershed years in the development of Herzl's Zionism. During that time he witnessed the Dreyfus Affair in December 1894 and the election of the anti-Semite Karl Lueger as mayor of Vienna during a trip there in April 1895. It was also when he attended multiple performances of Wagner's opera *Tannhäuser* in Paris.

Tannhäuser: Public Versus Private Responses

In his cool, detached review of the revival of Wagner's opera in Paris for the *Neue Freie Presse*, Herzl discusses how cultural pressures play a role in individual responses to the arts: "The only difference [between the two audiences] is that back then they were whistling, and today they clap their hands. But the gentlemen still put on their tailcoats every night, jam a glass into the eye, let themselves 'be noticed among those present' just as they did back then."[26] According to Herzl, the audience's warm reaction has less to do with the timeless quality of Wagner's music and rather more to do with changing fashions: Wagner had become in with the in crowd. This was an audience that was more concerned with being seen than with what they were viewing. However, shortly after writing the feuilleton, Herzl noted in his diaries that he doubted his ideas when not attending *Tannhäuser*:

> During the last two months of my stay in Paris I wrote the book *Der Juden-staat*. I cannot remember ever having written anything in such a mood of exaltation. Heine tells us that he heard the flapping of eagles' wings above his head when he wrote certain stanzas. I too seemed to hear the flutter of wings above my head while I wrote *Der Judenstaat*. I worked at it daily until I was completely exhausted. My one recreation was on the evenings when I could go to hear Wagner's music, and particularly *Tannhäuser*, an opera which I go to see as often as it is produced. And only on those evenings where there was no opera did I have any doubts as to the truth of my ideas.[27]

The opera kept him confident about the new ideology he was formulating.

Why this discrepancy, where the feuilleton is a sounding board for ideas about mass culture, while the diary entry shows the important role that *Tannhäuser* plays in his intellectual life? The feuilleton was written for an audience of sophisticated, cultured readers (much like himself) who expected to be amused. It would have been out of place for Herzl to delve into how *Tannhäuser* was affecting him emotionally, because that was not his job as a reporter for the *Neue Freie Presse*. Ever the astute political animal, Herzl would have known that a discussion of Zionism was not appropriate for the editors and readers of the assimilationist paper. These impressions he instead saved for his diaries which were the place where he composed his ideas without any "internal censorship."[28]

Importance of *Tannhäuser*

Critics have been divided about how to view the role of the opera in Herzl's life.[29] For Steven Beller, it marks a turning point, since it offered Herzl an image of redemptive liberation that spoke to his Zionist cause.[30] Others, such as Jacques Kornberg, believe that since we can never really know how important the opera was for him we must be cautious about overplaying its influence.[31]

Although critics are divided about how much weight to ascribe to *Tannhäuser*, most make sure to mention that it was quite central in his intellectual development. Herzl publicly cites or makes use of the opera four times in his life:

1. In his *Neue Freie Presse* feuilleton comparing the 1895 performance with Wagner's first failed attempt in 1861.
2. In the diary note discussing his repeat attendance while in a frenzy composing *Der Judenstaat*.
3. In his diary entry about how the opera inspires the crowd to react in unison.
4. In his decision to open the Second Zionist Congress to the music of *Tannhäuser*.

There are perhaps numerous reasons that *Tannhäuser* appealed to Herzl. First, throughout his life Herzl had evinced an interest in Wagner's music and in Heine's poems. Second, the *Tannhäuser* story seemingly reiterated and worked through topics that for a long time had played a large role in Herzl's intellectual development: the tale's use of a knight to express the highest virtues; the central role of the Pope as a representative of issues of conversion and excommunication; the theme of self-sacrifice and redemption; the figure of Venus to represent ideas about obsessive love; the locale of the grotto, which reminded some critics of the Jewish ghetto. Third, the spectacle of the opera offered a tool to inspire the Jewish masses to follow Herzl's Zionist agenda.

Herzl's attendance at the opera exemplified his complicated relationship with the work of Wagner and his decidedly less complicated feelings towards Heinrich Heine. Herzl's ties to Wagner were both negative and positive. On the downside, Herzl encountered anti-Semitism for the first time at Wagner's memorial service, and in his feuilliton about attending *Tannhäuser* in Paris there is an unmistakable tone of glee about sharing Wagner's disastrous initial performance. But on the plus side, Wagner's operas represented for him the music of refined society that the Jews should aspire to. In fact, in his Zionist novel, *Altneuland* (Old-New Land), Herzl has Miriam, an idealized member of the new Jewish state, sing "Wagner, Veri, Gounod, the music of all the nations . . . The melodies flowed in a ceaseless stream."[32]

As for Heinrich Heine, the relationship was entirely positive: Heinrich Heine had been one of Herzl's major literary inspirations and in 1897 he wrote a sentimental feuilliton about Heine's love affairs.[33] Also, he made at least one pilgrimage to Heine's grave at the Montmartre cemetery—the same site where I would search for the obelisk over a hundred years later. He would doubtless have been familiar with Heine's poem, "Der Tannhäuser."

The story of Tannhäuser likely resonated quite deeply with Herzl. For instance, he had a lifelong affinity with knights as embodiments of the highest form of inner grace. As a young man, Herzl extensively read German chivalric tales and he related strongly to their representation of the nobility's idealization of valor, honor, and self-sacrifice.[34] The topic of Venus also held a longstanding appeal for him: Herzl had titled his first collection of feuilletons about love *News from Venus*.

⭐ Private and Public Self-Sacrifice and Redemption

The opera's theme of self-sacrifice and redemption likely spoke to him. For Herzl, a journalist who always wanted to be a great writer and who found himself in an ugly marriage from which he believed he could not escape, the journey of Tannhäuser potentially offered a mirror to his own life. It showed him how a man burdened by an unhealthy love could cut loose and find inner salvation. While Herzl would not leave his wife Julie as Tannhäuser had left Venus, he could break free from the spiritual morass of a life uncommitted to a large, noble cause.

The notion of redemption probably also spoke to Herzl philosophically and politically. Herzl, who at the time was seeking a solution to the Jewish problem, could glean from *Tannhäuser* that the Jews needed to embrace self-sacrifice for the greater cause, much as Elisabeth had done for her man. And like Tannhäuser, they had to find a way to leave the seductive ghetto/grotto of a crippled, premodern existence. For both Tannhäuser and the Jews, the ghetto/grotto was a "scourge" that needed to be transcended through an act of will. In order to help the Jews to do this, Herzl himself first had to learn to relate to, and even appreciate, the ghetto which symbolized the poor Jewish masses he felt distanced from. Only then could he help them to liberate themselves.[35]

The New Jewish Knights

Perhaps Herzl believed that if the Jews could learn to be brave fighters for the cause of freedom, they, like Tannhäuser, could serve as an example to the world and gain its respect. And their prowess would culminate in the creation of an

honorable Jewish state much as Tannhäuser had been transformed himself into
an honorable Christian knight. Through their self-transformation, the Jews
would stop being crass, crippled, and backwards and become bourgeois. This
would lead them to be accepted into the Western world.[36] In *Tannhäuser*, the
redemption is individual, in Herzl's Zionism, it is national.

Spectacle as a Propaganda Tool

The opera also was inspiring for Herzl because, as he wrote in his diaries and
in his feuilleton, it showed him the importance of spectacle as a means of mass
persuasion. In other words, Wagner's opera was a lesson in propaganda: how to
manipulate the people through art. When Herzl watched the enraptured crowd
at the opera he found himself appropriating the lesson for his Zionism. The former playwright turned journalist was comfortable mining his background in
theater to further his cause. As in Wagner's *Tannhäuser*, which utilized a model
of Germanic chivalry to motivate the public, Herzl sought his own symbols to
inspire the Jewish masses.

The opera was not only a lesson in spectacle, but in how to perpetuate
specifically bourgeois culture. When he saw the awed audience at the *Tannhäuser*
performance, Herzl likely realized that the Jews could also be brought to appreciate fine culture. For instance, he would soon decide that he had to pressure
his followers to dress in tuxedos for major cultural events and he would even
institute a dress code for the Zionist Congresses. By so doing he thought the Jews
would elevate themselves in their own and the world's eyes, from backward and
premodern poor people, to cultured members of modern society.

The Pope

In 1875, Herzl composed a poem about an excommunication. Entitled "We Shall
Not Go to Canossa," the poem describes the famous occasion when the Holy
Roman Emperor Henry IV went to Pope Gregory VII to beg absolution from
the man who had previously excommunicated him. The poem documents this
moment in 1077 when the church gained the upper hand over the German Em-
perors.

It is interesting to contrast Herzl's interest in papal excommunication, as
documented in his poem, with Wagner's version in *Tannhäuser*. In Herzl's poem
the Pope wins the battle outright, the emperor is shunned, his pathetic attempt to
regain his power fails and, according to Herzl in the poem, only years later with
the ascendency of Luther's Protestantism do the Germans again redeem themselves from papal domination.[37] In Wagner's *Tannhäuser*, the knight redeems
himself though his love for Elisabeth and this act renders futile the Pope's excommunication. Wagner's solution probably appealed to Herzl, who as a young
man believed that the Jews should convert en masse and thereby give themselves

over to papal domination. In Wagner's opera, the absolution is done by an individual outside the confines of organized religion. Perhaps the Jewish masses, like the knight, could also break free of Christianity and absolve themselves on their own terms. This concept may have resonated with ideas Herzl was then mulling over in his head, validating his belief that there were many avenues for Jewish self-redemption.

✮ Ironically, on January 26, 1904, the year he died, Herzl actually gained a meeting with Pope Pius X to ask him to support a Jewish state in Palestine. Usually so astute about how to manipulate things, in their meeting Herzl's identity as a Jew overrode his identity as a politician, and he refused to kiss the Pope's hand: "I was conducted through numerous small reception rooms to the Pope. He received me standing and held out his hand, which I did not kiss. Lippay had told me I had to do it, but I didn't. I believe that I incurred his displeasure by this, for everyone who visits him kneels down and at least kisses his hand." According to Herzl's understanding of the meeting, this was a huge blunder that may have cost him the Pope's support: "I briefly placed my request before him. He, however, possibly annoyed by my refusal to kiss his hand, answered sternly and resolutely 'We cannot give approval to this movement. We cannot prevent the Jews from going to Jerusalem—but we could never sanction it . . . The Jews have not recognized our Lord, therefore we cannot recognize the Jewish pope.'"[38] Like Tannhäuser's pilgrimage to Rome to gain the Pope's blessing, so too Herzl made his way to the Holy City to seek the Pope's support. Both were shunned. And like the knight, Herzl realized he would have to rely on other avenues for redemption.

The Wagner-Herzl Connection

✮ As critics have noted, there is also a dark side to "Herzl's addiction to *Tannhäuser*" because it can seem to suggest that Herzl was mimicking Wagner's anti-Semitism.[39] The tie between Herzl and Wagner has been for some critics both shocking and disturbing, as was made evident most recently when the British theorist, Jacqueline Rose, published her book, *The Question of Zion*, in which she wrote the following anecdote that added Adolf Hitler to the audience of *Tannhäuser* in Paris: "According to one story it was the same Paris performance of Wagner, when—without knowledge or foreknowledge of each other—they were both present on the same evening, that inspired Herzl to write *Der Judenstaat*, and Hitler *Mein Kampf*."[40] Rose is suggesting an ideological link between Zionism and Nazism.[41] Although she was called to task for this mistake and recanted the claim (which was impossible since Hitler would have been six at the performance and was not in Paris at the time), it shows the uncomfortable link between Herzl and Wagner. How to account for the influence of the performance on Herzl without falling into the trap of suggesting that both Nazism and Zionism evolved from the same Wagnerian model? While both movements were rooted in nineteenth-century European Romanticism, they evolved out of two different branches: nationalism, from which Zionism was an outgrowth, and Social Darwinism and racial anti-Semitism, from which Nazism was an outgrowth.[42]

❧ Herzl, especially after the troubling rise in anti-Semitism he experienced at Wagner's memorial service, would not have been able to discard Wagner's anti-Semitism. He must have been keenly aware of it, yet he still felt it was appropriate to use the man's work to inspire him. For Herzl, the goal was to make the Jews strong and assured and he believed that any tool could be used towards this end. Wagner wanted the Jews to "disappear," since only then could an authentic Germanic volk culture be fully revived. Wagner was an anti-Semite seeking an anti-Semitic solution to the Jewish problem. Herzl, in contrast, understood that anti-Semitism was a permanent problem that could not be responded to by anything other than the radical solution of abandoning the ship of Europe to create a new homeland. Herzl's aim was to revive Jewish life, and nothing could have been more antithetical to Wagner's intention.

Der Judenstaat

Following the election of Karl Lueger, the Dreyfus trial, and his attendance at the opera, Herzl wrote his famous text *Der Judenstaat* (The Jewish State) in nine months. As Steven Beller delineates, there were actually four "extant versions of the idea which forms the basis of *Der Judenstaat*":

> There is the original set of notes that Herzl wrote for his initial meeting with Hirsch, which is surprisingly full, and 22 pages long. There are the copious notes in his diary for "The Jewish cause," whose date of commencement is given by Herzl as Whitsun 1895, a remarkable date for beginning the diary of the Zionist movement. These jottings were written on anything available during Herzl's near manic episode after the meeting with Hirsch, when Herzl was completely obsessed with his "mighty dream." This collection of inchoate ideas was then put together by Herzl in a fleshed-out version of his Hirsch notes to produce the third extant, and the first elaborated version, which is his 68-page "Speech to the Rothschilds," written within two weeks of the Hirsch meeting. This, with some variations and additions, became *Der Judenstaat*, of 86 printed pages, published on 14 February 1896.[43]

The collection of notes, the manic second version, was written in Paris, while attending *Tannhäuser* night after night.

Der Judenstaat, unlike other utopian models popular at the time, offered, so Herzl thought, a realizable model for planning, carrying out, and establishing the Jewish state. *Der Judenstaat* outlines how to do this, what is needed, and what the state will look like once it is established. The pamphlet-long book is divided into two sections; in the first section Herzl discusses anti-Semitism and how the Jews have come to be viewed so negatively; in the second part he outlines a practical model for establishing a homeland.

For Herzl, "the Jewish Question is neither a social nor a religious one, even though it may assume these and other guises. It is a national question, and to solve it we must first of all establish it as an international political problem which will have to be settled by the civilized nations of the world in council."[44] Thus, by bringing the problem to the international forum the nations will work together for a political solution.[45] Herzl's role would be to show how to enact this "state forming movement,"[46] and to help organize the subsequent massive Jewish emigration from Europe.

In the second part of the book, Herzl outlines "The Plan." As he writes, "the entire plan is in its essence perfectly simple, as it must be if it is to be comprehensible to all. Let sovereignty be granted us over a portion of the earth's surface that is sufficient for our rightful national requirements; we shall take care of everything else ourselves."[47] By taking care of everything themselves, the Jews would generate internal and external respect for their ability to carry out a massive undertaking for their own good. To help them to do this, two "great agencies" would be created, the Society of the Jews and the Jewish Company. Together these bodies would oversee all aspects of the Jewish departure from Europe.

The Society of the Jews would be in charge of leading the negotiations for a neutral territory for the Jewish state. In *Der Judenstaat* Herzl writes that this can either be in Palestine or Argentina. Clearly, Herzl's primary concern is to get a tract of land and then populate it with Jews, rather than finding a place that already is important in the cultural memory. He is first and foremost focused on the practicalities. For him, Argentina is an excellent possibility because it is a "country with some of the greatest natural resources in the world," while Palestine also appeals to him because it is the "unforgettable historic homeland."[48] It was only at the Sixth Zionist Congress in 1903 that Herzl decided the Jewish state would have to be in Palestine. If it was not, he would risk losing the support of the Jewish masses who were seeking not just a state of the Jews, but a Jewish state. Ironically, when he eventually traveled to Palestine to try and push his Zionist agenda, he was disgusted by the filth, chaos, and the "un-European" Jews that he found there.[49]

The other masthead of the plan, The Jewish Company, would be responsible for setting up the movement of money and property for the Jews leaving Europe. The overall aim of this body would be to minimize any chaos with the exodus. By making everything flow smoothly, non-Jews would be more likely to support the plan. The company would not only do the economic work necessary for leaving Europe, but whatever was needed in the new homeland in terms of purchasing land, building dwellings, and creating an infrastructure for the immigrants.

The final section of the book declares that the new state will have a "modern constitution" and be run along the lines of an "aristocratic republic."[50] Thus, while the country is modern and liberal, it is nevertheless no "socialist utopia." Instead, reflecting Herzl's growing distrust of handing power over to the masses even if they are Jewish, he seeks to remove the real power from them and give it to an enlightened leader.

The book concludes with a final rallying call asserting that this is a realistic venture that is good for the entire world:

> Let me repeat my opening words once more: The Jews who want a State of
> their own will have one. We are to live at last as free men on our own soil
> and die peacefully in our own homeland. The world will be freed by our
> freedom, enriched by our riches, and made greater by our greatness. And
> whatever we attempt there only for our own welfare will spread and redound
> mightily and blessedly to the good of all mankind.[51]

The new homeland will therefore not only free the Jewish people, but it will also free all of humankind. Moreover, it will also improve the Jews by transforming them from being at the mercy of those in power, to those who hold the power.

The ideal Jew of the new state was in essence "liberated" from his or her crippled traits.[52] In other words, Herzl's model for a free, empowered new Jew was based on liberal European values popular at the time. These asserted the virtues of strength, hard work, and a downplaying of one's religion. For Herzl and the Jewish masses, Zionism was the tool to end their "self-contempt" by turning them into strong, modern individuals. This would mean that there would no longer be any aspect of the Jewish civilization to loathe.

Certainly it is troubling to consider how much Herzl's Zionism grew out of the anti-Jewish dogmas prevalent in the broader society at that time. Yet it is important to remember that Herzl took those negative images as an impetus to create a new model of self-sufficiency that entrusted the Jews with the power to decide their own fate. He could have lived a comfortable life as a successful journalist and continued to fill his time with visits to French cultural events, but instead he chose to take a huge risk and be labeled as a utopian dreamer and a laughing stock.

Political Action and Zionist Congresses

To establish a Jewish state, Herzl became a politician meeting with important leaders to further his cause. His personality and looks aided him immeasurably. He was handsome with dark hair and a long and lush black beard. Herzl's upright bearing and charisma made him appear taller than he was and gave him the regal dignity of a born leader who some compared to King David and others to a new Jewish messiah.[53] He was a man of action who not only formulated his Zionist plan but also devoted his short life to implementing it. Extremely politically astute, he was aware of how even seemingly small things such as the color of one's tie could make an impression and had to be manipulated to put forth the correct message. One can see his extraordinary level of self-conscious, intelligent determination in a description of his decision to wear a "broken pair of gloves" to a meeting with the Jewish financial leader, Baron Hirsch: "On Whitsunday morning I dressed myself with discreet care. The day before I had purposely broken in a new pair of gloves so that they might still look new but not fresh from the shop. One must not show rich people too much deference."[54]

From 1895 until 1902, using his ticket as the *Neue Freie Presse* correspondent, Herzl gained an entrance to many courts of power. He had an audience with the Sultan of Turkey, among others. The high point of his diplomatic life was a meeting with Kaiser Wilhelm II in 1898. Unlike Heine, who later in life evolved a negative attitude towards Germany, Herzl always remained a Germanophile. To have a personal visit with the German Emperor must have felt to Herzl as if he was truly fulfilling his destiny as a great statesman. In the end, however, the meetings were practical failures because they did not lead to the granting of a territory or large funds. They were psychological successes, however, because they showed the Jewish masses that Herzl was on the road to empowering them by becoming a statesman for their cause, able to gain audiences with European leaders.

The reaction to *Der Judenstaat* was mixed. It is suggestive of how uncomfortable the pamphlet made many assimilated Jews feel that even his own newspaper made no mention of it.[55] The Viennese public received the book with little enthusiasm. In contrast, news of the book spread quickly through Eastern Europe where the Jewish public was excited that a modern Westerner, the prominent journalist Theodor Herzl, had taken up their cause.[56] In his diaries, Herzl saw his work as a mission sent from God and many Eastern Europeans shared this vision.

Real momentum was gained for Herzl's plan when he organized and headed the first Zionist Congress in Basel, Switzerland in 1897. Working with his greatest supporter and friend, the prominent social critic Max Nordau, they brought together Eastern and Western European Zionists with the aim to create a movement uniting these disparate members. The Eastern Jews, led by Ahad Ha'am, Herzl's main rival, pushed for cultural nationalism. They sought a slow infiltration of Palestine and wanted the movement to have a strong Jewish platform. Herzl believed in a public, political solution to the Jewish problem, and was less concerned with making the movement Jewish than with making it European. In the Congress, Herzl demonstrated his political talents by serving as a bridge between a variety of passionate, disagreeing activists and also by using his incredible managerial skills. Without the careful guidance of this astute politician, it is likely the Congress would have broken into a myriad of competing and resentful groups. Instead, the Congress was a success which resulted in Zionism taking a role on the world stage.

The first Congress was followed by five more presided over by Herzl. The one major rupture in the implementation of Herzl's Zionism occurred at the Sixth Congress in 1903, when the Eastern European delegates walked out over Herzl's proposal of the Uganda plan. The Uganda Plan was based upon an offer made by the British government that the Jewish people could have a tract of land in current-day Kenya on which to build the Jewish state. Herzl eventually managed to fix the rift by backing away from the plan. Thenceforth he was careful to publicly assert that Palestine would be the only place for the Jewish state. Throughout the rest of his short life Herzl continued to write, not only for the *Neue Freie Presse*, but also letters, memoirs, and even a Zionist novel, *Altneuland*, completed in 1902.

Herzl died in 1904 at the age of forty-four, likely of a heart ailment. His death left his family destitute, and his children and grandchildren all died young and tragically, most from suicide. In the wake of Herzl's death a practical form of Zionism took root based on the Eastern European model of slow, quiet, and steady infiltration of Palestine.

Concluding Remarks

Herzl opened the Second Zionist Congress in 1898 to the sounds of *Tannhäuser*. Amos Elon notes that "Herzl's secretary, Heinrich Rosenberger, could not help wondering whether an audience of anti-Semites would have been 'equally generous' in its applause for the Jewish composers Halevy and Meyerbeer, whose works were also played."[57] In other words, Herzl's entourage was aware that while the Jews could appreciate the work of Wagner, the esteem would not be reciprocated. Herzl likely used the music because it was a means to motivate and inspire the delegates towards the cause of Zionist self-sacrifice. Yet one also wonders if it was an insider's joke on Herzl's part: using the work of a German nationalist to inspire Jewish nationalism. It was almost as if he was reaching back to the Wagner memorial and his troubles with the Albia fraternity, showing to himself and the world how much had changed. Here he was, in charge of this grand movement and using Wagner for his own reasons, rather than to perpetuate anti-Semitism. In this case, he was in a sense "Judaizing" the anti-Semite Wagner's work.

Notes

1. From Theodor Herzl, "Feuilleton: *Tannhäuser*," *Neue Freie Presse*, Morning edition (May 14, 1895), 1-4
2. Theodor Herzl, *Zionist Writings: Essays and Addresses*, trans. Harry Zohn (New York: Herzl Presse, 1973), 1:18. The original German version is found in Theodor Herzl, *Zionistische Shriften* (Berlin: Judischer Verlag, 1920), 9.
3. In fact, in 1897, Emperor Josef finally allowed Lueger to become mayor of Vienna and he held the office until 1910.
4. From Theodor Herzl, *The Complete Diaries of Theodor Herzl*, ed. Raphael Patai, trans. Harry Zohn (New York: Herzl Presse and Thomas Yoseloff, 1960), 1:33. The original German is found in Theodor Herzl, *Briefe und Tagebucher*, ed. A. Bein, H. Greive, M. Schärf and J. H. Schoeps (Berlin: Propyläen, 1983), 2:127.

5. For the biographical information, I have refered to the following sources: Jacques Kornberg, *Theodor Herzl: From Assimilation to Zionism* (Bloomington: Indiana University Press, 1993); Amos Elon, *Herzl* (New York: Holt, Rinehart and Winston, 1975), Steven Beller, *Herzl*, Jewish Thinkers Series, ed. Arthur Herzberg (New York: Grove Weidenfeld, 1991); Alex Bein, *Theodor Herzl: A Biography*, trans. Maurice Samuel (Philadelphia: Jewish Publication Society, 1956); Andrew Handler, *Dori: The Life and Times of Theodor Herzl in Budapest (1860-1878)* (Alabama: The University of Alabama Press, 1983); Desmond Stewart, *Theodor Herzl* (New York: Doubleday, 1974).

6. Jacques Kornberg points out that even when living in Vienna, the culture that spoke to Herzl was not Austrian but German. See his *Theodor Herzl: From Assimilation to Zionism* (Bloomington: Indiana University Press, 1993), 16.

7. For an astute discussion of how the Jews of Vienna were both insiders and outsiders and how Herzl used his press badge to gain access to the corriders of power, see Edward Timms, "Ambassador Herzl and the Blueprint for a modern State," in *Theodor Herzl and the Origins of Zionism*, eds. Ritchie Robertson and Edward Timms, Austrian Studies vIII series (Edinburgh: Edinburgh University Press, 1997), 13.

8. Jacques Kornberg, *Theodor Herzl: From Assimilation to Zionism* (Bloomington: Indiana University Press, 1993), 11.

9. My discussion of Viennese Jewry's models of acculturation is based on Marsha L. Rozenblit's essay, "Jewish Assimilation in Habsburg Vienna," in *Assimilation and Community: The Jews in Nineteenth-Century Europe*, ed. Jonathan Frankel and Steven J. Zipperstein (Cambridge: Cambridge University Press, 1992), 225-45. In the essay she argues that Viennese Jews modernized in such a way that they continued to assert Jewish "normative values" and Jewish distinctiveness.

10. Steven Beller discusses his changing identity in his book, *Herzl*, Jewish Thinkers Series, ed. Arthur Herzberg (New York: Grove Weidenfeld, 1991), 4.

11. This was not unusual behavior for a male college student at the time.

12. For a cogent analysis of the Albia fraternity and Herzl's role in it, see William J. McGrath, "Student Radicalism in Vienna," *The Journal of Contemporary History* 2, no. 3 (1967): 183-201. On Herzl's membership, see Jacques Kornberg, *Theodor Herzl: From Assimilation to Zionism* (Bloomington: Indiana University Press, 1993), 6, 48.

13. See Jacques Kornberg, *Theodor Herzl: From Assimilation to Zionism* (Bloomington: Indiana University Press, 1993), 76-77.

14. Jacques Kornberg discusses Herzl's early schemes for dealing with anti-Semitism in his chapter, "The Reabsorption of the Jews," in *Theodor Herzl: From Assimilation to Zionism* (Bloomington: Indiana University Press, 1993), 115-29.

15. Herzl discusses the conversion plan and how the Christian church has been responsible for the Jewish situation in *The Complete Diaries of Theodor Herzl*, ed. Raphael Patai, trans. Harry Zohn (New York: Herzl Press and Thomas Yoseloff, 1960), 1:7-9.

16. See Steven Beller, *Herzl*, Jewish Thinkers Series, ed. Arthur Herzberg (New York: Grove Weidenfeld, 1991), 9.

17. Edward Timms, "Ambassador Herzl and the Blueprint for a Modern State," in *Theodor Herzl and the Origins of Zionism*, eds. Ritchie Robertson and Edward Timms, Austrian Studies vIII Series (Edinburgh: Edinburgh University Press, 1997), 16

18. As quoted in *The Complete Diaries of Theodor Herzl*, ed. Raphael Patai, trans. Harry Zohn (New York: Herzl Press and Thomas Yoseloff, 1960), 1:14.

19. See Edward Timms, "Ambassador Herzl and the Blueprint for a Modern State," in *Theodor Herzl and the Origins of Zionism*, ed. Ritchie Robertson and Edward Timms, Austrian Studies vIII Series (Edinburgh: Edinburgh University Press, 1997), 12-26.

20. According to Carl E. Schorske, Herzl's emotional life in Paris was troubled and this may have led him to embrace a larger social cause: "Disappointed in marriage, bereft of his dearest friends, Herzl's emotional life in the Paris years was thus more than usually impoverished. It may help to explain his readiness to abandon his aloofness from the social world, to identify himself heart and soul with a wider cause." In *Fin-de-Siecle Vienna: Politics and Culture* (New York: Alfred A. Knoph, 1980), 159. I am not sure that the Paris years were actually more difficult than in Vienna: he had a wonderful job, his marriage had always been disturbed, and soon his parents and family joined him, and with Max Nordeau he developed an extremely deep friendship.

21. Haya Harel, "From the Palais Bourbon to Der Judenstaat," in *Theodor Herzl: Visionary of the Jewish State*, eds. Gideon Shimoni and Robert S. Wistrich (Jerusalem: Hebrew University Magnes Press Jerusalem, 1999), 144.

22. This perspective is the central thesis of his book, Jacques Kornberg, *Theodor Herzl: From Assimilation to Zionism* (Bloomington: Indiana University Press, 1993).

23. Ibid., 9.

24. Steven Beller also thinks the influence of the Dreyfus affair has been overstated. See Steven Beller, *Herzl* Jewish Thinkers Series, ed. Arthur Herzberg (New York: Grove Weidenfeld, 1991), 31.

25. From Theodor Herzl, *The Complete Diaries of Theodor Herzl*, ed. Raphael Patai, trans. Harry Zohn (New York: Herzl Press and Thomas Yoseloff, 1960), 1:5.

26. From Theodor Herzl, "Feuilleton: *Tannhäuser*," *Neue Freie Presse*, Morning edition (May 14, 1895), 1-4.

27. Theodor Herzl, *Zionist Writings: Essays and Addresses*, trans. Harry Zohn (New York: Herzl Presse, 1973), 1:18. The original German version is found in Theodor Herzl, *Zionistische Shriften* (Berlin: Judischer Verlag, 1920), 9.

28. See Steven Beller, *Herzl*, Jewish Thinkers Series, ed. Arthur Herzberg (New York: Grove Weidenfeld, 1991), 43.

29. The main work on the *Tannhäuser*-Herzl connection has been done by Steven Beller. See his essays, "Herzl, Wagner, and the Ironies of 'True Emancipation,'" in *Tainted Greatness: Anti-Semitism and Cultural Heroes*, ed. Nancy A. Horowitz (Philadelphia: Temple University Press, 1994), 127-55; and "Herzl's *Tannhäuser*: The Redemption of the Artist as Politician," in *Austrians and Jews in the Twentieth Century: From Franz Joseph to Waldheim*, ed. Robert S. Wistrich (London: St. Martin's, 1992), 38-57. Carl Schorske discusses how *Tannhäuser* may have spoken to Herzl as a "parallel to his own return to the (Jewish) ghetto." See Carl E. Schorske, "Politics in a New Key: An Austrian Triptych," *The Journal of Modern History* 39, no. 4 (1967): 378. For Schorske's further discussion of this, and how Wagner's opera showed Herzl a way toward the "Volk against the mass, the revolt of the young and vital against the old and ossified," see *Fin-de-Siecle Vienna: Politics and Culture* (New York: Alfred A. Knoph, 1980), 163. For an assertion that "it is to Herzl's experience" of Wagner's *Tannhäuser* that we directly owe his advocacy of the Jewish state," see Allan Janik and Stephen Toulmin, *Wittgenstein's Vienna* (New York: Simon and Schuster, 1973), 60.

For additional discussions of Herzl and the influence of *Tannhäuser*, see Desmond Stewart, *Theodor Herzl* (New York: Doubleday, 1974), 182; Daniel Boyarin, "*Goyim Naches*: The Manliness of the Mentsh," in *Modernity, Culture and "the Jew,"* ed. Bryan Cheyette and Laura Marcus (Stanford: Stanford University Press, 1998), 78-82; Carl E. Schorske, "Politics in a New Key: An Austrian Triptych," *The Journal of Modern History* 39, no. 4 (1967): 377-78. Steven Beller points out that Alex Bein's original 1934 German version of his groundbreaking autobiography, *Theodor Herzl: A Biography*, "Romanticized the Wagner connection, making more of it than Herzl had initially," while in the "much-abridged English edition during the Second World War, this detail about *Tannhäuser* had disappeared, along with much else." See Steven Beller, "Herzl, Wagner, and the Ironies of 'True Emancipation,'" in *Tainted Greatness: Anti-Semitism and Cultural Heroes*, ed. Nancy A. Horowitz (Philadelphia: Temple University Press, 1994), 129. Jacques Kornberg begins his chapter, "Herzl as German Nationalist," in his book *Theodor Herzl: From Assimilation to Zionism* (Bloomington: Indiana University Press, 1993), 35 with the quote about Herzl doubting his plans when not attending *Tannhäuser*. Kornberg ties the importance of the opera for Herzl, to his interest in German nationalism during his student days. See p. 52.

30. See Steven Beller, "Herzl's *Tannhäuser*: The Redemption of the Artist as Politician," in *Austrians and Jews in the Twentieth Century: From Franz Joseph to Waldheim*, ed. Robert S. Wistrich (London: St. Martin', 1992), 52-53.

31. Jacques Kornberg was extremely gracious to me in preparing this chapter. Over the course of some months, I emailed him questions I had about my interpretation of the Herzl-Tannhäuser connection. For Kornberg, he stressed in his emails to me that it is important to remember that we "can only speculate about" the significance of the connection and he warned me throughout to be cautious about "overplaying" the tie. From private emails between Kornberg and me dating between September 2006 and January 2007. I am very grateful to him for his insights.

32. Theodor Herzl, *Altneuland* (Leipzig: Seemann, 1902), 302. The English translation can be found in Theodor Herzl, *Old-New Land*, trans. Lotta Levensohn (New York: Bloch Publishing Co, 1941), 263.

33. Theodor Herzl "Heine und die Liebe," in *Feuilletons*, 2nd ed. (Berlin: Benjamin Harz, n.d.), 1:243-53.

34. See Steven Beller, *Herzl*, Jewish Thinkers Series, ed. Arthur Herzberg (New York: Grove Weidenfeld, 1991), 5.

35. For an assertion of the ghetto as grotto concept see Carl E. Schorske, "Politics in a New Key: An Austrian Triptych," *The Journal of Modern History* 39, no. 4 (1967): 378. Desmond Stewart argues that Schorske's interpretation of the grotto as ghetto is "farfetched as well as inaccurate, since Tannhäuser does not return to the grotto once he leaves it (though in Act III he tries to)." See his book, *Theodor Herzl* (New York: Doubleday Presse, 1974), 182.

36. Steven Beller, "Herzl, Wagner, and the Ironies of 'True Emancipation,'" in *Tainted Greatness: Anti-Semitism and Cultural Heroes*, ed. Nancy A. Horowitz (Philadelphia: Temple University Press, 1994), 150.

37. The poem can be found in Leon Kellner, *Theodor Herzls Lehrjahre, 1860-1895* (Vienna: R. Löwit, 1920), 17-18. Jacques Kornberg discusses the poem in *Theodor Herzl: From Assimilation to Zionism* (Bloomington: Indiana University Press, 1993), 15.

38. The English translation can be found in Theodor Herzl, *The Complete Diaries of Theodor Herzl*, trans. Harry Zohn (New York: The Herzl Press, 1960), 4:1602-03.

39. See Steven Beller, "Herzl, Wagner, and the Ironies of "True Emancipation," in *Tainted Greatness: Anti-Semitism and Cultural Heroes*, ed. Nancy A. Horowitz (Philadelphia: Temple University Press, 1994), 127-55.

40. See Jacqueline Rose, *The Question of Zion* (Princeton: Princeton University Press, 2005), 64. Rose emailed me that critics were mistaken in seeing her as equating Zionism with Nazism, a tie she had no intention of making. From a private email dated September 21, 2006.

41. For a brief discussion of the Herzl-Hitler anecdote and a political conclusion that could be drawn from it, see David J. Goldberg, *The Divided Self: Israel and the Jewish Psyche Today* (London: I. B. Tauris, 2006), 210-12.

42. Richard Libowitz offered this insight to me.

43. Steven Beller, *Herzl*, Jewish Thinkers Series, ed. Arthur Herzberg (New York: Grove Weidenfeld, 1991), 37.

44. Theodor Herzl, *The Jewish State (Der Judenstaat): A New Translation*, trans. Harry Zohn (New York: Herzl Presse, 1970), 33.

45. Remarkably, this occurred fifty-three years later when the United Nations recognized the Jewish State of Israel in 1948.

46. Theodor Herzl, *The Jewish State (Der Judenstaat): A New Translation*, trans. Harry Zohn (New York: Herzl Presse, 1970), 37.

47. Ibid., 49.

48. Ibid., 52.

49. See Jacques Kornberg, *Theodor Herzl: From Assimilation to Zionism* (Bloomington: Indiana University Press, 1993), 178.

50. Theodor Herzl, *The Jewish State (Der Judenstaat): A New Translation*, trans. Harry Zohn (New York: Herzl Presse, 1970), 98.

51. Ibid., 110.

52. Jacques Kornberg, *Theodor Herzl: From Assimilation to Zionism* (Bloomington: Indiana University Press, 1993), 177.

53. See Carl E. Schorske, "Politics in a New Key: An Austrian Triptych," *The Journal of Modern History* 39, no. 4 (1967), 383-84.

54. From Theodor Herzl, *The Complete Diaries of Theodor Herzl*, ed. Raphael Patai, trans. Harry Zohn (New York: Herzl Presse and Thomas Yoseloff, 1960), 17-18.

55. David Vital, *The Origins of Zionism* (Oxford: The Clarendon Presse, 1975), 267.

56. Ibid., 273-77.

57. Amos Elon, *Herzl* (New York: Holt, Rinehart and Winston, 1975), 259.

Chapter Five

I. L. Peretz

The Prisoner

In October 1899, the first snow of winter was falling in the courtyard of the Citadel prison in Warsaw. The jail housed the usual motley crew of a Tsarist prison: thieves, murderers, army deserters, anarchists, socialists, revolutionaries, and poets. The political prisoners, who received comforts denied the others, were allowed fifteen-minute nightly turns around the frigid prison yard.[1] Two of the men walked together and talked with chattering teeth as they were pummeled by the snow: the Yiddish storyteller Isaac Leyb Peretz (1852-1915) and his friend and fellow writer Mordechai Spektor (1858-1925).[2] Though Peretz was a nervous type who normally strolled quickly around the prison courtyard, he kept a slow pace for his friend. That night, like most nights, Peretz was excitedly discussing his latest writing plans. This time it was about a new series of stories that he hoped would alter the history of Jewish writing. Spektor liked the idea and encouraged him. As a political prisoner, Peretz was allowed a quota of paper and ink, and after his rejuvenating walk in the October snow with his friend, he returned to his cell to began work on a new story, "Oyb nisht nokh hekher: A khasidishe dertseylung" (If Not Higher: A Hasidic Narrative). This tale marked a massive turn in his writing that would culminate in Peretz's extraordinary rewrite of Richard Wagner's opera *Tannhäuser* as a Yiddish novella entitled *Mesires-nefesh* (Self-Sacrifice).[3]

Peretz, along with countless other Warsaw radicals, had been arrested in a massive police sweep. These activists, inspired by the promise of a new world heralded by the fin de siècle, were writing songs, stories, and poems devoted to a revolution that would wipe out the stale, autocratic, anti-Semitic Tsarist government and bring in a new enlightened regime. Peretz entered prison committed to the socialist cause, but was hardly a full blown radical. According to Mordechai Spektor, he and Peretz were arrested at a workers' rally that they had attended only with the assurance that it was being held with police permission.[4] However, instead of leaving the Citadel a more devoted socialist, as was the case with countless other young radicals, he left a Jewish cultural nationalist. Being locked up with truly committed activists caused Peretz to reconsider his ideological beliefs.

Before his awakening in prison, Peretz's stories often focused on conflicted traditional young Jews seeking the promise of modern life. He also composed tales about life in the shtetl where Jews often displayed hypocritical and troubling ethics. After his incarceration, his art became more reflective and increasingly devoted to reclaiming the ultra-religious heritage of poor Eastern European Jews. His post-prison tales were populated by devout men and women who displayed the highest ethics and deepest belief in Judaism, while at the same time being committed to progressive, Western ideals. The new narratives fused his modernist ethos with a rekindled respect for Jewish values.

As part of the post-prison series, Peretz wrote a new version of Wagner's opera in which he transformed the German knight Tannhäuser into a young Jewish man in premodern Israel. Peretz Judaized the opera to such a degree that it actually became a morality tale about how to live an ethical Jewish life. Peretz used the opera in a way similar to Herzl: as a tool to empower the masses to reclaim and be proud of their Jewish identity. It also taught them that the best way to fight anti-Semitism was to return to an authentic Jewish culture based on religious textual study.

Early Life and Work

Isaac Leyb Peretz, "arguably the most important figure in the development of modern Jewish culture,"[5] was born and raised in the Eastern Polish town of Zamość.[6] This community was originally founded in the sixteenth century by the progressive chancellor and head of the Polish-Lithuanian commonwealth army, Jan Zamoyski (1541-1605). Zamoyski commissioned an Italian architect to design the town in the renaissance style, with a beautiful courtyard in the center. Because Zamoyski was devoted to ideals of tolerance, he allowed the town to be a safe haven for people from a broad array of ethnicities and religions, including a large number of Jews. When Peretz was a boy, the Jewish population was around 8,000, or about 55% of the town's residents. While Zamość had a generally charitable history toward the Jewish population, things began to change when Russia took over following the Congress of Vienna in 1815, 37 years before Peretz's birth. Anti-Semitic occurrences, on both a small and large scale, occasionally began to break out.

When Peretz was born in 1852, the Jews of Zamość were beginning to be influenced by two contradictory cultural pulls. On one side were the Maskilim:

Jews who followed enlightenment ideals. They advocated notions of universal brotherhood, religious toleration, secular (along with religious) education, and a push for the Jews to be more Westernized. The Maskilim, though small in number, had enough influence to open a school in 1886 where Jewish boys not only learned Talmud and Jewish texts, but also studied science, Russian, math, and other secular subjects. Peretz's father shared some of their liberal tendencies, while the father of Peretz's first wife was one of the most important Maskils in the town. Many of the beliefs of the Maskilim play a role in Peretz's early writings.

On the other side of the divide was the small but growing influence of Hasidism, which had gained a late foothold in Zamość. While Peretz only knew one Hasidic rebbe personally, the movement played a disproportionately large role in his post-prison writings. Hasidism was a religious movement founded by Israel Baal Shem, popularly known as the Besht (c.1700-1760), a charismatic miracle worker whose stories were collected in the book *Sippurey Mayses* (Tales) (1815). By the time Hasidism arrived in Zamość in the mid-1800s, it was a mass movement among poor Jews throughout Eastern Europe. Anti-elitist and anti-intellectual, it spoke to an individual, ecstatic relationship between the devotee and God. Hasidism also introduced the rebbe, a figure very different from the traditional Jewish rabbi. Where a rabbi was an intellectual, trained in Jewish texts, who often served as a community leader, the rebbe was a charismatic preacher who devotedly propagated the beliefs of the Hasidic movement.

Different regions of Eastern Europe were grouped around different rebbes, with followers showing regional variations in dress and ritual observances. In Peretz's post-prison works, the Hasidic rebbe was often a figure of profound spiritual depth who devoted his life to the highest ideals of Jewish learning and faith. This picture was a radical departure in representation from the manner in which rebbes had been rendered in Jewish Maskilic enlightenment literature, where they were often portrayed as buffoons, drunkards, and charlatans.

Jewish life in Zamość, though influenced by the Maskilic and Hasidic movements, was in large part run along traditional Jewish lines. Life revolved around the holiday calendar, with each week focused on Friday's preparations for the Saturday day of rest. Jewish folk culture was realized in a myriad of rituals such as spitting thrice after prayer to ward off any evil and sleeping with one's feet towards the door to keep death at bay. Day-to-day life for the young Peretz consisted of long hours at school broken by kosher meals: buttered bagels and coffee for breakfast, kasha, soup and herring, hot lima beans, or sliced onions and salty radishes with sour cream for lunch and dinner, and deserts of egg cookies or the occasional slice of cheesecake. It was a typical, safe, and sheltered Jewish childhood in pre-Holocaust Poland.

The physical set up of Zamość was a great playground for Peretz. It was surrounded by a forest and there was a deserted castle on its perimeter. There were also long abandoned military ramparts where the local children often found empty bullet casings and other things to play with. Except for occasional

anti-Semitic flare ups, the Christian population played only a small part in Peretz's childhood.

Peretz's mother, Rivele (Levin) was very religious and encouraged the same
fervor in her two sons and daughter. His father, Yudele, who traveled quite a
bit for his job as a lumber and alcohol merchant, was much more liberal and
came from a wealthier and more westernized background. Throughout much of
his childhood, Peretz's father was out of town while his mother ran a store. The
family was not poor but middle class, living in a two-story home near the town's
beautiful square.

Although his father was interested in Western trends, his strong willed,
traditional mother decided that rather than going to the Maskilic school, Peretz must attend one of the Jewish day schools or cheders. The lengthy school
days were spent studying and arguing over the great Jewish legal code book, the
Talmud. Jewish memoirs about cheder education tend to focus on two aspects:
stuffy and suffocating classrooms where the children yearn to escape outdoors
and the desire to enact revenge on cheder teachers who were often unintellectual
oafs more interested in beating their students than in teaching them.[7] Peretz was
lucky, however, because his liberal-minded father told the teachers not to hit
him, and to allow him daily time outdoors.

Much of the information on Peretz's childhood comes from his extremely
subjective autobiography, *Mayne zikhroynes* (My Memoirs).[8] Moreover, he only
reluctantly began to write his memoirs in serial form in 1913 near the end of his
life and more than 50 years after the events he was describing. Like Henry Roth's
second blooming, the events he writes of are therefore influenced by how he has
chosen to shape and recall the memories of half a century before.

Peretz excelled at learning but also enjoyed playing tricks and being
a scamp: putting ink in his teacher's tea and sneaking off to ice-skate. From a
young age he showed the intense dual pulls that would mark his literature: a
desire to rebel against the traditional Jewish society, while at the same time, a
need to be the good Jewish son for his mother. His writings would show this with
stories that both challenged and synthesized aspects of traditional Jewish life. A
profound (and perhaps unhealthy) devotion to his mother would also become a
central theme in Peretz's version of Tannhäuser.

As a youth he became interested in literature and began to compose poems at night by candlelight, even writing his first bad Heine poem.[9] According
to Peretz's autobiography, the event that had the greatest impact on his literary
development was receiving keys to the town's library when he was a teenager.
In the library, asserts Peretz, the "books [were] shelved at random, with novels,
scientific works, and serial romances all mixed up and scattered."[10] Peretz worked
his way through them, getting a broad reading in fiction, natural science, history,
and secular languages. For Peretz, the library key was a passport to a forbidden
realm. The Polish, French, and German books thus became "seductions," pulling
him away from traditional Jewish life. After reading a book on natural science,

Peretz's religious outlook was radically shaken: "Something in me froze, something died. I could no longer believe in the mysteries of the Divine Creation of heaven and earth or the mystical speculations on the Divine Chariot. There was no heaven. The blue that we see was the limit of human vision. And there could be no divine reward or punishment if there was no free will."[11] He had become a rationalist. For him, there was seemingly no going back to his earlier, more naïve perspective. The library also educated him in the wonders of Western literature. As an adult writer, he would frequently meld Western and Jewish themes. Peretz would eventually denounce the influence of non-Jewish writing, although his Tannhäuser story masterfully uses a Western trope in a Judaized setting.

Soon after he began his library visits, Peretz's transformation into a radical was stopped in its tracks by his inability to refuse an arranged marriage. While a rebel at heart, outwardly he was a good Jewish boy who bowed to his mother's wishes, and although he desired to leave town and attend college, he married a girl he met for the first time just before the wedding. For Peretz, the only positive aspect of the marriage, besides pleasing his mother, was that the father of his young wife, Sarah Lichtenfeld, was a well-known enlightenment figure, Gabriel Yehudah Lichtenfeld. This connection would turn out to be invaluable: his father-in-law arranged to publish Peretz's first book of Hebrew poems that included an embarrassing poem about a rape that was an "imitation of Heine, only in poorer taste."[12] However both Peretz and his wife were equally unhappy, and after bearing a son in 1874 named Lucian, they divorced. In 1877 Peretz married for a second time, this time fairly happily to Helena Ringelheim, with whom he had fallen in love after spotting her in her father's wine shop.

From 1877-1888, Peretz supported his family as a successful lawyer in Zamość. He was outwardly content, embracing Polish positivism, speaking Polish, and even shedding his traditional Jewish garb for modern Polish clothes. Later in his life, however, he asserted that his years in Zamość were filled with "spiritual misery," with him spending sleepless nights chain-smoking and reading.[13] Not yet a serious author, he nevertheless dabbled by writing poems in Yiddish and Hebrew, although he burned these efforts rather than show them to anyone. Peretz also evinced an interest in progressive concerns: fighting for women's rights, trying to open up an enlightenment style school, and offering evening classes for workers.

In 1888 Peretz published his poem, "Monish," and began to establish his literary reputation. The poem appeared in a journal edited by the most important Yiddish writer of the day, Sholem Aleichem (1859-1916), who Peretz had previously corresponded with (and humorously mistook for the "grandfather" of Yiddish literature Mendele Moycher Sforim [1836-1917]). Moreover, when Peretz first read Sholem Aleichem, it was in Polish translation rather than in Yiddish. Polish was an obvious literary language for Peretz, but he made a decision toward the beginning of his career that he would instead work in the Jewish languages of Yiddish and Hebrew.

In late 1888 or early 1889, to Peretz's complete shock, he was disbarred from the law, probably because of slurs made against him by a competing lawyer. He traveled to Petersburg to plead with the authorities to reinstate him, but without success. Suddenly, at 37 years of age, he found himself without a means of livelihood and with a son and a new wife to support. For Peretz, the only option for regaining control of his life and finances was to move permanently to the thriving urban metropolis of Warsaw.

At that time, Warsaw was the cultural center of Polish Jewish life, with a rich literary scene.[14] Numerous publishing houses, a motivated reading public, and a number of literary journals made it the perfect locale for Peretz's development as a writer. Moreover, moving to an urban center brought Peretz into even more contact with Western cultural trends that would influence his literary development. Although Warsaw was the location for his growth into a major Yiddish writer, he never recovered financially and he spent the rest of his life with a much lower income than what he had enjoyed for ten years as a lawyer.

Looking for work, in 1890 Peretz took a job doing a sociological and statistical survey of small town Jewish life for the wealthy convert to Christianity, Jan Bloch. Bloch was conducting the survey in an attempt to show the Tsarist government that the Jewish population were neither parasites nor draft dodgers. Arriving in Jewish towns in the Zamość environ, Peretz, who looked like an urban Polish intellectual with mustache and modern garb, was initially mistrusted by the Jews whose stories he was supposed to collect. Eventually his persistence and fluency in Yiddish paid off and the shtetl Jews shared their tales of horrific poverty.[15] For Peretz, the trip was an eye opener that challenged his love of rationalism and science discovered in the Zamość library and made him reconsider the efficacy of statistical accounts: "What will be the upshot of the statistics? Will statistics tell us how much suffering is needed—empty bellies and unused teeth; hunger so intense that the sight of a dry crust of bread will make the eyes bulge in their sockets, as if drawn out by pliers; indeed, actual death by starvation—to produce an unlicensed gin mill, a burglar, a horse thief?"[16] The visit to the poor underbelly of Jewish life was a shock to a middle-class boy who probably had never experienced such Jewish poverty firsthand.

Peretz turned the trip into a story collection, published in 1891 entitled *Bilder fun a provints-rayze* (Impressions of a Journey Through the Tomaszow Region).[17] The book marked the real beginning of Peretz's literary career. The sketches show "an intellectual affinity with ordinary traditional Jews" who manage to hold on to their dignity while undergoing terrible hardships.[18] They also draw a clear demarcation between Peretz, the urban intellectual, and the Jewish masses, while making it evident that he wanted to draw closer to them. The portraits show the tension that had, and would always, pull at him, between wanting to embrace traditional Jewish life and being a worldly intellectual. The trip also awoke in him a love of Jewish folk culture that would play a prominent role in all his later works.

Returning to Warsaw in 1891, he found the job that he held for the next 26 years of his life: overseeing the Jewish cemetery and working with families of the deceased to ascertain their financial needs. Peretz regularly complained that the job was suffocating, stifling, and soul destroying and that the managers persecuted him. His starting salary was only 500 rubles, versus the 3000 he had earned as a lawyer, and he and his family had to quickly adjust to their reduced straits by living in a small cramped apartment. Although he was perpetually broke, like other writers such as Franz Kafka, a full-time bureaucratic job with a steady income was surprisingly conducive for Peretz's writing. The 9-3 work day gave him a set schedule to structure his writing around; he had a regular (although tiny) pay; and the position also kept him in constant touch with the Jewish masses of Warsaw, who would visit his office when filling in their forms and would serve as a great inspiration for his stories. Peretz was a good worker, never late, and he received tiny but steady pay raises.[19] Frequently he would spend the summers in Switzerland, which would rejuvenate him for the following year of dull paper shuffling.

The tiny Peretz home was crammed with artwork and books and was often filled with visitors.[20] Over the years it became a salon, always open on Saturdays, where Yiddish authors met to chat, eat, sing Jewish folksongs, and tell stories.[21] According to Chone Shmeruk, Peretz's apartment gatherings were directly responsible for the ascension of Warsaw into a Yiddish literary center: "For if Peretz was right that, in 1890, no one knew in Warsaw 'who was the master and who the assistant, who the Rabbi and who the pupil,' it is clear that, in the course of the 1890s, Peretz's home on Ceglana now Pereca Street became the address of the master and rabbi of virtually the whole of Yiddish literature." Thus, according to Shmeruk, "It was thanks to the personality of Peretz that Warsaw became the centre of all centers of Yiddish literature."[22]

The same year he started his job, Peretz began editing the journal, *Di yidishe bibliotek* (The Jewish Library, 1891-95, five volumes). *Di yidishe bibliotek,* much to the annoyance of Sholem Aleichem, was a continuation of a journal that the great Yiddish storyteller had once edited but had gone bankrupt. The majority of the essays, stories, and poems were by Peretz himself under a range of pseudonyms and the literary scope was impressive, appealing to secular and religious readers alike. The journal finally closed for good in 1895, because of pressure from censors and because there was no money left to continue publication.

Between 1894 and 1896, Peretz also edited the *Yontev-bletlekh* (Holiday Papers, 1894-96), which made a huge mark on Yiddish literature. The editions contained tales framed by the motif of Jewish holidays. While seemingly simple accounts of traditional Jewish life, the stories would frequently hide subversive, socialist themes by cloaking radical ideas within traditional costumes. Many of the tales satirized traditional Jewish life, and the *Yontev-bletlekh* thus became immensely popular with Jewish progressives. Moreover, because the tales seemed traditional, they got past the Tsar's censor.

The *Yontev-bletlekh* solidly established Peretz as a radical Yiddish writer and turned him into a star amongst the Jewish workers of Warsaw. At this time he was also playing an ever more prominent role as a mentor to writers beginning their careers. Many young, cosmopolitan Jews then had no interest in Yiddish literature, much preferring German, French, Russian, or Polish texts. They were Westernizing at a rapid rate and assumed that Yiddish literature was a poor relation to world literature; that it was best left in the shtetl and had no place in intellectual city life. Peretz devoted his life to proving them wrong, and was largely successful, shaping a modern Yiddish literature that appealed to secular and religious, young and old, city and country Jews alike. In fact, according to Ruth R. Wisse, "With the exception of Theodor Herzl, founder of political Zionism, no Jewish writer had a more direct effect on modern Jewry than Isaac Leib (Yitskhok Leybush) Peretz . . . If Herzl pointed the way to a national Jewish homeland in Zion, Peretz represented the no less genuine determination of modern Jews to flourish as a minority in Poland, and perhaps elsewhere, with a language and a culture of their own."[23] With the writings of I. L. Peretz, a whole new generation discovered Yiddish literature. And not only that—many chose to be Yiddish authors based on Peretz's inspiration. In some senses, Peretz made it "cool" to be a Yiddish writer.

Numerous accounts of Peretz, the "powerful imp with the glowing eyes," categorize him as restless and highly gifted with a prodigious memory.[24] With a full head of bushy hair and a large, unruly mustache, he looked like Albert Einstein in his Princeton years. Peretz liked to have his hand in everything, not only because he was always curious, but according to his niece Rosa Peretz-Laks, because he felt no one else could do the job as well as him.[25] Keeping busy with work, socializing, and writing also diverted him from a tendency towards depression, since Peretz was someone who found relaxation far more challenging than activity. Passionate about his likes and dislikes, as he became more well known, he grew both more arrogant and more insecure, feeling cut to the quick if he did a public reading and few people showed up. He had numerous quirks, and could switch from kindness to coldness in the blink of an eye.[26] Yet when he committed himself to a young author he could make the difference between a failed and successful literary career, and as the years progressed, and his fame solidified, nearly every young Yiddish writer of importance made a pilgrimage to Peretz's apartment to meet the famous writer. Because of all the traffic, he even had a plaque put up outside his door stating when he would receive callers.[27]

Peretz's most profound and important friendship was not with his wife, but with the writer Y. Dinezon (1856-1919). Dinezon was a constant visitor and Peretz never made a move, literary or otherwise, without consulting him first. Dinezon, in return, virtually gave up his own literary career to devote his life to assisting the great writer Peretz.[28] It was a friendship that enabled Peretz to have an ever enthusiastic "yes man" to share literary and personal interests with, and the friendship supported him intellectually and emotionally.[29] The relationship, at least from Peretz's end, had no hint of a homosexual attachment, but Dinezon's extraordinary devotion did have the feel of unrequited love. When Peretz died, Dinezon fell into a massive depression, counting the days until he would happily "join" his friend in heaven.[30] Moreover, he requested and received permission to be buried next to him upon his own death. When Peretz wrote his Tannhäuser tale about healthy and unhealthy devotions, the two strongest models for the story were undoubtedly his mother and Dinezon.

✭ Peretz had two sons, Jacob, who died young, and Lucien, who lived an unhappy life and died shortly after Peretz in 1919. Like Peretz, Lucien was a restless soul, but he never found anything to channel his energies into and always felt overshadowed by his celebrity father. He tried to be a mathematician, dropped out of medical studies, held numerous jobs, had a broken marriage, and fathered a son, Yanek. Lucien never showed any interest in the writings of his father and even despised Yiddish and refused to speak it. He saw it as a dated, parochial language of the shtetl. Peretz's lifelong commitment to finding a balance between assimilation and Judaization failed two generations later when his only grandchild, Yanek, converted to Christianity. Like Heine and Herzl, Peretz had no forbears to continue his legacy.

Post-Prison Writings

In 1899, Peretz served his famous three-month prison term for "revolutionary" activities that caused him to reorient his writings. After being locked up, his work became less satirical and used figures and motifs from traditional life to present Jews who were struggling to find solid ground in a changing world. The archetype of this new heroic protagonist was the Hasidic rebbe. The new stories present religious Jews as ethically evolved individuals who have found a path for living a deep spiritual life.

What was it exactly about his stay as a political prisoner in the Warsaw Citadel that caused this turn in Peretz's writings? First, the shift was not as radical as it looks. Before his incarceration, Peretz often had a great interest in all things Jewish: choosing Yiddish over Polish, rediscovering the dignity of the poor Jew during his statistical survey, regularly scanning his friend's memories for Jewish folksongs. What was new was the decision to stop satirizing the Jewish community and instead imbue his works with a profound respect for Jewish culture.

Perhaps being locked up in prison awoke a nostalgic longing for his Zamość childhood at a time when he was surrounded by revolutionaries agitating for a new world. Or, the daily prison walks outdoors may have reminded him of rural life in the shtetl, leading to his desire to reincorporate the world of the provincial Jew. Maybe, as he interacted with deeply committed socialist prisoners, he realized that his own socialism was actually less important to him than his attachment to all things Jewish. Or perhaps his stay caused the pendulum to swing from rebellion against the world of his mother to a desire to be less the rebel and more the obedient son. The prison may also have scared him profoundly, making him realize how much he hated confinement and leaving him desirous not to put himself at risk again of being locked up.[31] Whatever the cause, the prison term diverted Peretz towards both his Hasidic tales, and the genre of his Tannhäuser work, the *Folkstimlekhe geshikhtn* (Tales in the Folk Style).

His job overseeing the Warsaw Jewish cemetery also must have played a part in his new direction. As the families of the dead trudged through his office to fill out forms requesting financial aid from the Jewish community, Peretz was constantly forced to admit the difficulties they faced. These daily confrontations with mourning families who had just lost their loved ones to sickness, poverty, and violence must have made him increasingly uncomfortable with portraying traditional Jews negatively in his stories.

Peretz's new tales also grew out of the popularization of folk culture among the Jewish intelligentsia. Urbanized Jews, such as Peretz, began to feel that in the process of leaving traditional Jewish life they had lost something of deep importance. It was a typical nostalgic gaze to the past that often goes hand in hand with an attempt to create a more progressive future. For them, Jewish life could be mined for materials in the same way that great Russian writers, such as Pushkin and Turgenev, had in the past mined Russian folk life.[32] Where the previous generation had rejected Jewish folk life as backwards and parochial, authors such as Peretz reoriented the viewpoint, seeing it as rich and ethical. This stance could even sit comfortably in conjunction with more progressive beliefs. Peretz thus did not see any contradiction between populating his tales with ultra orthodox Jews while at the same time agitating for women's rights. The way he handled this paradoxical stance was to give the traditional Jews untraditionally progressive ethics. For instance, in his famous tale, "Oyb nisht nokh hekher: A khasidishe dertseylung" (If Not Higher: A Hasidic Narrative, 1900), the rabbi's "miraculous" trait is not that he actually does miracles, as the father of Hasidism, the Bal Shem Tov, was reported to do, but rather that he unselfishly devotes his life on earth to helping others.

This balancing act between tradition and progress worked remarkably well, making Peretz's stories popular with a huge range of readers, who saw in them reflections of their own beliefs: a respect for Jewish life, an embrace of shtetl culture, a push for modernist ethics. His works succeeded also in large part because of the style in which they were written. They often had a lively and chatty narrator who brought the reader into the tale in a one-on-one conversational structure. Peretz, moreover, had learned from Heinrich Heine how to create an ironic narrative stance. As Ruth R. Wisse has written in *I. L. Peretz and the Making of Modern Jewish Culture*, Peretz was teaching the Jews how to navigate the modern world while holding onto their Jewishness.

Peretz had developed a great love for Jewish folk culture in all its manifestations during his work on the statistical survey, and this was cemented during his prison stay. His favorite way to spend an evening in Warsaw was to have his friends and family recount folktales, and he urged his young followers to collect folksongs and share them with him. Many of these would inspire his writing. As Peretz's critic and friend A. Mukdoni recounted, Peretz's apartment "was a veritable clearing-house for folklore of every kind."[33] It was Peretz who was in large measure responsible for the trend in modern Jewish writing that turned to folklore for literary inspiration.[34]

The vision that he offered in his reworked folk stories, including his version of Tannhäuser, was of a premodern, archetypal, Jewish reality. The name itself of the stories, *Folkstimlekhe geshikhtn*, or Tales in a Folk Style, reflects that they were reworked and stylized forms of folktales.[35] The tales read differently from Peretz's other works because they were (so he claimed) based on oral reproductions of stories recounted by shtetl Jews. A. Mukdoni recounts how Peretz described to his close friend and fellow Yiddish writer and ethnographer, Sholem Ansky, how he turned a "colorless, sketchy" folktale that Ansky had told him into a "colorful, detailed folk tale." He stated that "Peretz then told us that for years now he had followed this method of treating his folk tales. This type of story was of its very essence an oral one, not meant to be committed to writing. He could best preserve its viva voce characteristics by not fixing it in written form until he had shaped its oral version."[36]

This oral quality is evident in Peretz's version of Tannhäuser, where the unnamed narrator rambles on in a number of different directions as he picks up themes that become important to him in the act of telling the tale. It is a narrative style that continually diverts from the central plot and weaves secondary stories into the central one. By creating a novella that reads like an oral text, Peretz is Judaizing the narrative so that it mimics the oral folktale. He is thus transforming Wagner's German opera into a Jewish one both in the language—Yiddish—and in the style—the Jewish oral tale.

The *Folkstimlekhe geshikhtn* are about Jewish noblemen and women, viscounts, and rabbis in the postexilic Land of Israel dealing with sin and redemption within a Jewish context. Unlike Christian notions of sin, where people meet their fate in heaven or in hell, in the Jewish context, sin and redemption unfold during one's life. In the Peretz worldview, salvation or redemption is related to keeping one's soul pure by focusing on virtuous deeds and thoughts. The highest virtues are often the simplest, such as the devotion of a common man to working hard and earnestly, as in his story "Dray matones" (Three Gifts). These tales show Peretz's desire to place status not on material things, but on higher traits such as being good to others or studying for its own sake rather than as a means to show off one's knowledge. In Peretz's post-prison Hasidic tales and folktales, his characters sin when they forget the broader ethics and become caught up in their own egotistical needs.

At the same time that his *Folkstimlekhe geshikhtn* were turning to Jewish settings and characters, Peretz began to assert the decreased influence of world literature. As a young man in the library, world literature, in works from Alexander Dumas to Victor Hugo, had been his first, great literary love. Yet according to Ken Frieden, "From Peretz's universalistic literary beginnings . . . he gradually drifted toward a narrower Jewish cultural nationalism,"[37] which required in large part that he reorient his literary inspirations towards Jewish themes. This we see in both the Hasidic and folk tales. Eventually the desire to stay completely within a Jewish framework would lead Peretz to deny the influence of "foreign forms," including Heinrich Heine.[38] Nevertheless, his rendition of Tannhäuser was based on the "foreign form" of Wagner's opera.

Moreover, in 1908, at the Czernovitz conference where Jewish intellectuals gathered to discuss and argue the role of Yiddish, Peretz asserted that Yiddish literature really began with the writings of the great Hasidic rebbe, Nahman of Bratslav.[39] Peretz was thus rooting modern Jewish literature in a soil that was far more "Jewish" and less influenced by world writing than Maskilic literature. Furthermore, when Peretz went against the mood of the conference by asserting that Yiddish was a Jewish language, not the Jewish language, he sought to spread the Jewish cultural net far wider than mere language. Peretz was devoted to making both Yiddish and Hebrew literature home-grown from Jewish sources. This marked Peretz's increasing discomfort with assimilation (particularly as anti-Semitism was steadily increasing in Poland) as he sought to enable the Jews to develop a culture independent from the Polish one he himself had embraced as a young man. Assimilation as a path to acceptance into Polish society was not a sacrifice he believed that the Jews should any longer have to make.

For the final sixteen years of his life, Peretz wrote stories and experimental plays and was the central figure of the Jewish cultural revival in Poland. He served as a mentor and friend to a whole new generation of authors and continued to have a rich writing career. His memoirs came out a few years before his death and were mined by his readers for clues about the great man. While Peretz had always given to those in need, even when broke he now directed his philanthropic activities more and more towards helping to establish Jewish communal institutions such as food banks and orphanages.

Peretz died of a heart attack on April 3, 1915, with his final composition on his desk, a children's poem he was planning to read at an orphanage. A hundred thousand people were reported to have attended his funeral, and the name of Peretz still is used around the world for a variety of Jewish institutions.[40]

Tannhäuser

Peretz's adult ambivalence about being inspired by Western culture was played out dramatically in his version of Tannhäuser, where he takes Wagner's opera and Judaizes it to such a degree that the original is barely noticeable.[41] It was as if he was being pulled in two directions: inspired by a Western trope, Tannhäuser, yet desiring to negate that inspiration and conceal it. His version of Tannhäuser is thus, externally at least, a typical Peretz Jewish folktale delivered in an oral style that represents, according to David G. Roskies, "Peretz's most accomplished romance."[42] However, the real inspiration is not from Jewish culture, but from the emblematically Christian tale of a young prince seduced by a pagan goddess. Peretz's version of Tannhäuser gracefully juxtaposes the dual pulls of the Jewish and Western cultures that stimulated him throughout his life.

    It is strange, however, that Peretz, a man proudly Jewish, would turn to Wagner's opera as a literary source.[43] As a Jewish cultural nationalist, he had to undermine and deconstruct Wagner's original. Peretz takes *Tannhäuser* and transforms it into a paean to Judaic life and learning.

Mesires-nefesh

The setting of *Mesires-nefesh* (Self-Sacrifice) is Safed, the center of Jewish mysticism in the land of Israel during the post-exilic era of the Ottoman Empire. Safed was a cherished locale in the minds of the Hasidim because during the sixteenth century it had been a leading center for scholars and schools devoted to Jewish mysticism. For Peretz to set his work there was to locate it in an idyllic locale of the Jewish cultural memory. However, while the narrative unfolds in a positive location, life during this period was far from easy. Peretz makes sure to insert into the text numerous instances of anti-Jewish actions that had taken place in the years leading up to the story. For instance, he writes that the father of the woman the Jewish Tannhäuser will marry lost his entire family in anti-Jewish pogroms in Iraq. While the family lineage that is the basis for the tale is hardworking and devout, their background is of profound hardship. According to the text, it is a time when the Jews are undergoing "forced conversion" to Islam and facing "lashes and chains" (35). Yet, while the Jews as a group face horrendous violence, individuals are able to rise above the horrors and live a life of dignified learning. By infusing Jewish hatred into the story, the setting mimics the anti-Semitism in Poland at the start of the twentieth century, when Peretz was composing his story. The tale thus suggests that even as the Jews face external hardship, they can and should find a way to transcend it by rooting themselves in a strong faith and a commitment to Jewish learning.

The story is very complicated, and first describes the family background of the Jewish Tannhäuser's beloved, Miriam (Peretz's version of Wagner's Elizabeth). The parents and grandparents of the woman who will redeem Tannhäuser face an external world of anti-Jewish actions; however, their home life is pleasant. The grandfather of the Jewish Elizabeth, Miriam, is a wealthy jeweler, and the family resides "in a palace of his own, a palace whose windows were gleaming eyes looking out upon the Sea of Galilee. A magnificent garden encircled this palace, a garden with a most attractive variety of trees, with all kinds of fruit, with singing birds, fragrant herbs, and luxurious vegetation of great beauty and medicinal value." It is, as he writes, a "veritable earthly Garden of Eden" (30). Nine years after writing *Mesires-nefesh*, Peretz in his memoirs discussed how the garden in the story was based on a Zamość garden he loved to visit as a child.[44] By setting his story there, Peretz was nostalgically returning to a positive locale from his childhood (although, as he would recount in his *Memoirs*, his geography was completely wrong, especially locating Safed within sight of the Sea of Galilee).[45]

The parents of Miriam are Sarah and Reb Hiya. Reb Hiya always helps the poor and is a "spokesman" for the Jews. Once again, Peretz makes helping the needy a central aspect of being a good Jew. Hiya is also a virtuous figure because he constantly turns himself away from the outside world and focuses entirely on Jewish texts. For instance, "when he rode a camel across the desert, the camel-driver led the animal by the bridle, but Reb Hiya himself always kept a book in his hand and never lifted his eyes from its pages." Or, "When he voyaged in his ship, he had a private cabin, wherein he sat alone and occupied himself with religious studies" (32-33). This is a clear contrast with European notions that adventure is a positive undertaking filled with growth, excitement, and fun.[46] Peretz's vision of travel is one where the Jew refuses to participate in the outside world that wishes to hurt him and instead draws back into study. It is a push for a Judeo-centric focus, particularly in a time of intense anti-Semitism. However, while the Jewish character retreats from the broader reality, he nevertheless delves into secular study, finding "time to learn the seven secular sciences from old sheiks" (32-33). It is a virtuous life by being Jewish focused while open to secular studies.

When Miriam's mother Sarah is dying, she promises her husband, Hiya, that she will "exert herself in heaven to obtain for her only daughter a husband of worth, honor, and virtue" (36-37). Peretz, who believed in women's rights, created female characters very different from Wagner's Elizabeth, who must die to bring on her man's redemption. Here, both the mother-in-law and wife of the Jewish Tannhäuser hold the real power over life and death, and can either sway the heavens (as does Sarah) or outwit the heavens (as does her daughter Miriam). While the men can and do have influence over their own actions on earth, the women hold the key to the much more important powers of the heavens.

After Sarah dies, Reb Hiya decides to sell his belongings and turn his palace into a Yeshiva, where he will teach students to study Torah for its own sake rather than for material rewards or for vanity. For Reb Hiya, any learning that is undertaken merely to show off is forever stained. This mimics an Eastern philosophy of doing things purely for their own sake. This notion, which is propagated throughout the text, is opposed to materialism or a functional world view where one only does good deeds in order to receive rewards.

Reb Hiya is seeking the student who desires knowledge in a pure way. He thus listens to his students to discern who has a pure voice, because Hiya believes that it is "easier to recognize the true character of a human being by his voice" (43-44). Intentionally or not, by elevating the voice as the arbiter of character, Peretz is tapping into how Wagner revolutionized opera by having the arias reflect the personality of the singer. He is also playing with ideas from Hasidic culture, where individuals sought to create pure songs that reflected the heavenly orders.

Finally the narrative switches from a focus on the parents of Tannhäuser's future wife, Miriam, to the Jewish Tannhäuser himself, called Chananiah. Chananiah arrives at the Safed Yeshiva run by Miriam's father. He has a pure voice, so Hiya invites him to be his student. In response, Chananiah tells how he came to the Safed Yeshiva. According to Chananiah, his mother spoiled him and made him vain and arrogant, but when he gained a spot at a renowned Yeshiva in Jerusalem, his mother did not allow him to attend, "for she was reluctant to be separated from the light of her life. She wanted him at home near her" (52-53). This, of course, recalls when Peretz's own mother made him remain in Zamość for an arranged marriage, even though he had been accepted to a distant college.

For the young Chananiah the results of the mother's inability to let him go are disastrous, much as they were for Peretz. She decides to find him a tutor and unfortunately selects a teacher who is "one of those casuistic sages who do not study the Torah for its own sake or for the greater glory of God but who are primarily interested in showing off their knowledge and acumen at the expense of the Torah" (52-53). The influence of his pedantic teacher and over-indulgent mother leads Chananiah to use his knowledge to show off and to put others down for their ignorance. Eventually, Chananiah decides to repent his prideful ways after the Jerusalem Yeshiva head admonishes him that his "entire knowledge is essentially negative." As the narrator states, "He could destroy but not substitute something constructive" (56-57).

Both the mother and the pedantic teacher are forms of Wagner's Venus. Their seduction is egotistical knowledge, which, following cultural stereotypes, is apparently as enticing to a Jewish lad as physical sensuality is to a Western one. However, Chananiah never blames his mother for what she has done. He instead asserts that "an evil man led me off the right track and on to a well of bitter waters, poisonous waters, which I mistook for dew of heaven" (82-83). It is almost as if the adult Peretz can not fully recognize how a parent can hold a child back, because Peretz still loves and respects his mother, even while acknowledging on some level that their relationship was troubled.

Chananiah continues his story. He tells of a wicked ex-butcher who was seeking a husband for his virtuous daughter, Hannah, but rather than letting her marry a carpenter, "who wanted the daughter for her own sake, even without a penny's dowry," he has two servants seek out a renowned scholar (60-61). After searching everywhere, they discover a young penitent in "white linen, with a hempen rope about his loins, and carrying in his hand an ordinary staff made of the branch of an almond tree" (62-63).

Chananiah recounts how he was a guest at their wedding, and how after the bridegroom arose and gave a brilliant speech about the Torah, Chananiah became jealous that the bridegroom was being acclaimed for his knowledge. Chananiah reacted by spewing forth his own interpretation of Torah. This scene is a Jewish version of the singing contest that brings down Wagner's Tannhäuser. In reaction to this, the father goes crazy, thinking the intended bridegroom is being derided for his lesser knowledge. He ends up kicking out the bridegroom and having his daughter marry the carpenter (who she really loves). The scene reflects Peretz's own discomfort with arranged marriage and shows his belief in love and marriage "for its own sake." The interpolated tale also adds a more complex and interesting take on the origin of the blooming staff than is found in Wagner. Here the staff first resides with another penitent before it makes its way to Chananiah.

Chananiah leaves the wedding humiliated at his own actions and makes his way to the head of the Jerusalem Yeshiva. The leader of the Yeshiva is a Jewish version of the Pope in Wagner. He curses Chananiah for what he has done, telling him, "You can ruin an entire world. It is better that you forget your learning" (68-69). In this most Jewish of texts, the worst curse a man can face is to forget his learning. Chananiah has abused knowledge and language, and his fate is to lose both. The Jerusalem Yeshiva headmaster orders the repentant Chananiah to put on the bridegroom's old white penitent robes and to carry the staff, for when it blossoms again, then your "soul too will again burst into blossom and you will recollect everything." (72-73)

Chananiah wanders through the desert with a broken soul because he can no longer remember any Torah. In a dream, the head of the Jerusalem Yeshiva (that cursed him) tells him that Elijah has interceded and that he must now go to the Safed Yeshiva, where its leader will find a wife for him, adding that "on the eighth day after the wedding, you will awaken in the morning and you will find the staff at the head of your bed blossoming and sprouting almonds. Then your soul too will blossom and sprout . . . You will expound a portion of the divine law before Reb Hiya and your speech will be constructive and not destructive" (74-75). Redemption in the Jewish tale lies not with absolution from the Pope, but with the reclaiming of one's own relationship to Torah and Jewish learning.

The narrative then returns to the Yeshiva in Safed, where Chananiah has just explained his travels to Miriam's father, Reb Hiya. At the Yeshiva, Chananiah, who loves "Torah for its own sake," becomes an extremely studious and humble student. Soon Reb Hiya overhears two snakes discussing how one intends to fatally bite Chananiah on the eighth day after his wedding. There are thus a number of forces working to accelerate Chananiah's downfall, far more than are involved in Wagner's opera. The snakes are doing the bidding of the "powers above" who believe that the curse of the Yeshiva head is not strong enough to bring down Chananiah. For them, the only outcome is that Chananiah must die.

Although aware that he is marrying his daughter Miriam to a man who will die after the wedding, the father nevertheless allows her to wed. Soon thereafter, Hiya's deceased wife Sarah comes to him in a dream to "resolve his doubts" and assert that everything will be all right. Moreover, she tells him that he must trust in his daughter and "leave everything up to her." The father responds by empowering his daughter to choose her own mate and to pick her own destiny. Miriam chooses the ultimate sacrifice, since she believes that "self-sacrifice in the truest sense can be achieved only by a wife" (94-95). In Peretz's schema, for better or worse, it is women who are given the ability to perform the ultimate sacrifice.

Peretz is showing his modern readership that they also have the power to focus their energies on a noble cause. Moreover, having the sacrifice done by a young person teaches Peretz's readers that they are strong enough to fight for causes or people they believe in. And Miriam's power to decide her own destiny reflects Peretz's conviction that marriages should not be arranged and that women should be empowered (although one wonders if a husband would so readily sacrifice himself for his wife).

On the seventh day of the wedding ceremonies, the staff begins to blossom, allowing Chananiah to finally regain his learning and reveal the mysteries of Torah to Hiya. At the same time, the tale takes on a metafictional quality by stating, "These mysteries are recorded in the Book of Chananiah, which Reb Hiya published in a gilt-edged edition" (104-05). The narrative is thus proclaiming its basis in an external reality, since these events have even been documented in other texts. As in the Hasidic tales of the Bal Shem Tov, these miraculous events really happened.

Miriam dresses up like Chananiah to trick the snake into killing her instead. She dies and in heaven the hosts are appalled at the mistake and order her back to earth so that they can take the correct victim, her husband. She refuses, and only agrees to return to earth if they will not kill him. They agree, and she returns to her body and reunites with Chananiah. All is perfect. Miriam and Chananiah give birth to son who becomes a "great luminary" and they live happily ever after.

In Peretz's modernist reworking of a folktale, the ultimate power in the world resides not in the heavens, but on earth in the actions of brave humans who will not back down.[47] In a manner typical of Talmudic discourse, a powerful argument is the best means of effecting change. The influence of the supernatural world, a stock belief of Hasidism, is here shown to be less powerful than the individual's actions. It reflects Peretz's humanistic belief in individual responsibility. Moreover, according to Ruth R. Wisse, it symbolizes Peretz's notions about gender roles, by giving both men and women clear paths for inner redemption:

> The story thus inverts the biblical text where Eve, fallen prey to the snake's temptation, invites Adam to share in her sin. Miriam's selfless love redeems the false intelligence that uses learning as an instrument of power, and false sexuality that uses lust to corrupt. Miriam the wife is just such a hallowed Jewish mother as Peretz describes in his memoirs, and in placing her at the heroic center of his Jewish myth he is ascribing to her the ultimate value from which all others flow. Intellectual prowess, the male domain, depends for its moral confidence on the female's self-sacrificing love. This is what Peretz established as the hierarchy of Jewish values.[48]

The tale, however, does not end with the couple's triumph. There is a final concluding paragraph. In a style typical of a Hasidic folk narrative, the future of the
couple and of the snake, Achnai, are discussed: "The story of the great luminary
who was born of the union of Chananiah and Miriam and of the happiness that
came to Reb Hiya in his later years—this story we shall (God willing) relate on
another occasion. We merely want to add that the Achnai that let itself be fooled
was never again entrusted with any further missions and is indeed no longer seen
on earth" (108-09).

This is part of an incomplete cycle of stories that the narrator will in time
share with the readership. The concluding sentence about the snake's fate is mock
serious, pretending that the miraculous events of the story are real. By jarringly
focusing on the snake's fate rather than the couple's at the tale's end, the conclusion reminds us that this is a constructed narrative. (Closing with an additional
paragraph that diverts from the story's main focus was used throughout Peretz's
Tales in a Folk Style.) This humorous, modernist trick makes fun of the narrative,
the narrator, and the plot in one light-handed touch. It pushes the reader to read
the text as a stylized, self-aware, "tale in a folk style."

Mesires-nefesh "has the highest density of Hebrew-Aramaic words in all
of Peretz's oeuvre."[49] This helps give the text the flavor of premodern Palestine,
while the title is a Hebrew term and gives the story the aura of a sanctified text.
To further strengthen the sense that the work is part of the lineage of Jewish oral
narratives, Peretz lets the reader know that the characters themselves write in
Hebrew, which the narrator is "translating" into Yiddish for the contemporary
listener and reader of Eastern Europe. He writes, "In the course of his correspon-
dence with his relative, the headmaster of Babylon's School of Learning, whom
he used to consult both on learned matters and on family affairs, he once wrote
the following letter in flowery metaphorical Hebrew, a letter which loses much of
its sweetness when translated into a profane tongue."[50] The narrator gives the letter's text in awkward Yiddish. He is not only filtering the original tale through his
own story-telling style, and many generations after the event, but is also translating it, moving the account numerous steps away from the original occurrences.
This causes the reader to question the credibility of the text and the miracles
it describes. This use of a Yiddish account of events originally orally transmitted years before mirrors the *Sippurey Mayses* of the leader of Hasidism, the Baal
Sham Tov, which were "transcribed" into Yiddish after being orally transmitted.

Heine's Influence

✡Peretz Judaizes Wagner's version completely, setting it in a Jewish space (Safed in
the Land of Israel), making every character Jewish, and asserting Jewish cultural
beliefs. In fact, at first glance Peretz's rewrite seems so distant from Wagner's
German medieval-set original, the question arises concerning whether this is an
adaptation at all. And if it is, is it based on Heine's or Wagner's original?

● The similarities between Peretz's and Heine's use of Tannhäuser are much less overt than the ties between Peretz and Wagner. With Heine, what we find is Peretz using just a few elements of the Tannhäuser trope, such as Venus as the needy seducer or religious leaders asserting that Tannhäuser can not be redeemed. However, the differences are much more pronounced and suggest that while Peretz may have been influenced by Heine in the sense that he showed him that a Jewish writer could rework Tannhäuser, he was nevertheless not directly reworking Heine's poem. The crucial differences are:

The tone. Heine's piece is clearly a humorous satire of the original ballad. Peretz's novella, which ends with a mock serious statement, throughout employs a serious tone much closer to what we have in Wagner than in Heine.

The characters. In Heine, Tannhäuser's ruin is straightforward and the characters who influence it are minimal. In fact, the only characters he deals with are Venus and the Pope. In Peretz, as in Wagner, Tannhäuser interacts not only with Venus (for Peretz Venus becomes his mother and teacher) and the Pope (in Peretz as the Yeshiva heads and heavenly hosts), but also with a new, earthly love Elizabeth (Miriam).

The fall. In Heine there is only one fall—Tannhäuser's relationship with Venus. In Wagner and in Peretz, there is a second fall, a public humiliation: the singing contest in Wagner; the wedding speech in Peretz.

The budding staff. In Heine there is no budding staff. In Wagner and in Peretz, the plot completely turns on if and when the staff will blossom. These major variations make it clear that Peretz was basing his story on Wagner's version and not on Heine's.

The Evidence

Now let us consider why we should view Peretz as a reworking of Wagner's opera.

Historical Affinity

The most important question of course was whether Peretz was in fact aware of Wagner's *Tannhäuser*. Although the opera and many reworkings of it were circulating at the time, was there documentation that Peretz had seen it? A citation in Ruth R. Wisse's book on Peretz[51] led me to Nahman Sokolow's *Perzenlekhkeytn* in which the author states that he ran into Peretz at a performance of *Tannhäuser* in Warsaw.[52]

Plot

The similarities in plot are numerous. In both, the main story is about a young man seeking redemption from his fall. In Peretz's case, the fall comes about in the pursuit of knowledge, rather than from physical love as in Wagner. In each, redemption arrives by way of the protagonist's beloved. Both are set in a mythic past, as was typical in both Wagner's and Peretz's works of the time.

A woman leads to the downfall of both men. However, in Peretz's version, the sexual aspects are downplayed. As Sol Liptzin has noted, this is because "to a Jewish narrator writing for a Jewish audience, this entire problem, the conflict between asceticism or heavenly love and Venus or earthly love was largely devoid of meaning."[53] Instead, the paradigm of devotion shifts from earthly love to Torah love, and the woman causing the protagonist's troubles is not the sexual Venus, but his own mother. After all, she pushed him to become arrogant about his knowledge, set him up with a pedantic tutor, and did not let him attend the Yeshiva where he wanted to be a student. Peretz's story is of an overbearing Jewish mother and her weak coddled son (intentionally or not playing into one of the most negative and persistent Jewish stereotypes). The mother "seduces" her son with constant admiration and spoiling (like Venus with Tannhäuser in Wagner's opera) and makes him stagnate intellectually and morally (again like Venus with Tannhäuser).

To reflect a society where physical love is not generally discussed in literature, Peretz adapts Tannhäuser into a story of mother-son love gone awry. This theme also resonates with Peretz's relationship with his mother, which had led him to a stagnating and unhappy marriage and the sacrifice of a college education.[54]

In both versions, the young man finally breaks free of the seductress and seeks absolution from his sins. In Wagner's *Tannhäuser*, the Pope refuses to redeem him and instead curses him. Peretz offers a more layered description of the search for redemption by making the Pope three characters instead of one: the Jerusalem Yeshivah head who curses him, Reb Hiya who offers him guidance for his spiritual renewal, and the heavenly hosts who refuse to absolve him. In the Jewish schema, where Rabbis are no closer to God than the average person, the redemption cannot be granted, as in the confessional, but must be actively internalized through changed actions in the world.[55] By his own active pursuit of true knowledge, Chananiah gains what Wagner's Tannhäuser can not be granted from the Pope—a return to the true path.

A second role of women in both is to guide the men, either for bad (as with Wagner's Venus or the mother in Peretz's version), or for good (as with Wagner's Elizabeth and Peretz's Miriam). Where men can have an independent self that can focus on a variety of things (sex, learning, business), the women in both tales exist entirely in relationship to the male characters. The protagonists, Tannhäuser and Chananiah, are intellectually and morally weak and their personalities are under the influence of women. Their final redemption comes at the hands of the women they love. In the end, no men can sway the heavens in the way the women do.

In both works, the protagonist "falls" in a public setting. In Wagner, Tannhäuser humiliates himself at a singing contest with a song of pagan love, thus manifesting to the world at large that although he has left Venus' realm, he is still under her sway. In Peretz, the singing contest becomes a speech at a wedding party, where he is unable to control his vanity and launches into a nasty assault on the bridegroom's learning, lowly in comparison to his own brilliance. By transforming the fall into a wedding speech, Peretz is utilizing a typical Jewish public setting where the *badkhn*, or Jewish wedding singer, would perform a series of frequently funny and often sentimental songs. In this case, however, the fallen voice is not lusty or sexual, as in *Tannhäuser*, but pedantic, reflecting the utterly different focus of the works: in Wagner's Western worldview, love is a central motif in the individual search for redemption, in Peretz's Judaic worldview, learning is a key component of mature male identity. Moreover, both Wagner and Peretz create a positive local community within which Tannhäuser falls and wishes to redeem himself. For Wagner, the intention was to strengthen the German communal volk, for Peretz, to present a positive community of Jewish learning.

Both tales end with the staff blooming to show the protagonist's redemption, which has been brought about by the sacrifice of the woman they love. Wagner's Tannhäuser has renounced pagan love for Catholic, virtuous love, while Peretz's Chananiah has renounced boastful learning for true knowledge.

Symbolism

The most convincing proof of the connection is the use of the same central symbol—the flowering staff as a sign of redemption. The flowering staff is an image that shows up in Christian iconography, but as a sign of redemption it is tied directly in folkloric iconography with *Tannhäuser*. [56]

In Jewish iconography, the staff first appears in the Hebrew Bible, Numbers 17: 20. In this case, the Lord tells Moses to gather twelve staffs, one from each tribe, while putting Aaron's name on the "staff of Levi." He then states, "The staff of the man whom I choose shall sprout, and I will rid Myself of the incessant mutterings of the Israelites against you." [57] The blossoming staff is intended to show the rebellious tribes that Aaron will take on the mantle of high priest, and that the tribe of Levi will be elevated amongst them. In this case, the blossoming staff is a symbol of God's choice. The staff also appears in the 1602 *Ma'aseh bukh* (Story Book) collection of Jewish tales as the "staff of Judah." [58] It also appears in some other instances of Jewish iconography, but as an image of the soul's redemption it is only found in a few cases. [59] While Peretz would have known of the passage about Aaron's staff and possibly of the *Ma'aseh bukh*, the way he uses the symbol in *Mesires-nefesh* replicates much more directly Wagner's opera. In this case, the staff represents a soul that has been redeemed rather than that the individual is God's chosen one.

The fact that Peretz attended the opera that his story bears such an overwhelming resemblance to makes it clear that the blooming staff originated in large part with Wagner's *Tannhäuser*. It makes sense that the central visual icon of the opera, the budding staff, becomes a major motif in Peretz's work. After all, if he was basing his novella on an opera he saw once, it was likely that the visual aspects of the opera stuck in his memory more insistently than other things.[60]

These three proofs—historical affinity, plot, and the use of symbolism—together work to show the tie between the two and mark Peretz's *Mesires-nefesh* as a Judaized version of Richard Wagner's *Tannhäuser*.

Peretz's Adaptation

While being influenced by Wagner, Peretz clearly reworked the story to match his unique vision. Foremost, in the Peretz framework, paganism, so central in Wagner's portrayal of Tannhäuser's seduction by Venus, does not play any role whatsoever. Instead, the binary of paganism/Catholicism becomes gradations of Jewish devotion, be it sacrificing oneself for one's mate (the route of transcendence for women in Peretz) or sacrifice for learning (the means of male transcendence).[61] The other divergences include the fact that the plot in Peretz is much more sophisticated and complicated than in Wagner and the endings are different—Tannhäuser dies while Chananiah lives.

The simplicity of the plot in Wagner—there is only one narrative—reflects that this is an opera rather than a prose work, and the composer needs to keep the libretto reasonably basic so that the audience will not get lost. Peretz, free of the need to keep the plot linear, makes his story extremely complicated. It moves at a slow and meandering pace, typical of an oral tale. To accomplish this, Peretz employs a highly sophisticated narrative.[62] Where Wagner's *Tannhäuser* begins with the knight in the Venusberg, Peretz takes some time, and the introduction of many characters, for the story to arrive at the protagonist's tale. The plot thus begins a generation before the life of Chananiah, with the grandparents of Chananiah's wife Miriam. Their story establishes the "kingly stock" of the lineage from which Chananiah's son will generate. Interestingly, in *Mesires-nefesh*, the framing narrative is about Miriam, the wife. In contrast, in *Tannhäuser*, we get virtually nothing of Elizabeth's background. Miriam's heritage explains how she has become so good (she comes from kingly, virtuous stock and a line of extremely devoted and loving parents). She is thus humanized and much less archetypal than Wagner's Elizabeth.

Peretz's version teaches the readers how to be good parents, how to be good individuals, and how to be good Jews, while in Wagner's opera the extreme, yet often unexplained "black and white" actions of the characters negate a gradated analysis. In Peretz's novella, fall and redemption are described in a humanistic schema where they are influenced by family, culture, and religion. In contrast, in Wagner's opera, fall and redemption reflect singularly Christian notions of sin and virtue. Peretz adds the family dynamics and psychology that are missing in Wagner's spectacle-focused opera.

The works' endings are vastly different. Wagner's Tannhäuser dies yet has his soul redeemed by God; Chananiah lives and saves his own soul. As Sol Liptzin rightly notes, the shifted ending points to the differences between Jewish and Christian concepts of death and the afterlife:

> An early death is also foretold for Hananya [Chananiah] and yet, were this destiny fulfilled, the whole tale would not be meaningful from the viewpoint of Jewish tradition. The Christian's striving is to escape this world and its bonds. The greatest reward for the penitent is to be received, purged of sin, in the realm beyond death. The Jew, however, strives for knowledge in this world, so that he may live more fully here and now . . . Hananya must, therefore, be redeemed from ignorance and spiritual night, but not at the cost of death.[63]

Wagner's Tannhäuser can live "happily ever after" in heaven, while in *Mesires-nefesh*, matching Jewish concepts, the earthly realm is the only locale for this. In fact, the heavenly realm is often a comedic area in Jewish literature ranging from Peretz's 1894 "Bontshe Shvayg" (Bontshe the Silent) to Itzik Manger's 1939 *Dos Bukh fun gan-Eydn* (the Book of Paradise). As a setting, it often subverts the sanctity of Christianized readings of heaven. So Peretz must literally bring the conclusion "down to earth."[64]

Peretz's Intention

So what are we to make of Peretz's appropriation of one or even two of Wagner's operas? Peretz subverts the Romantic, Germanic work of a prominent anti-Semite and turns it so completely around that his story becomes an ode to the importance of Jewish learning and a well-lived Jewish life. Peretz's intention in transforming the original may have been to distance *Mesires-nefesh* from the opera of an anti-Semite, though on first reading it hardly seems a version of *Tannhäuser* at all but instead a neo-Romantic Jewish myth about learning for its own sake.

Did Peretz make his adaptation so loose as to distance it from Wagner or was it done unintentionally? The opera may have sparked some ideas, as did a myriad of other things, and may have been one of many catalysts for the story. However, if Peretz's appropriation was indirect to distance it from Wagner, how to explain the many similarities such as the blooming staff, the singing and speech event, and the mirrors in plot, which anyone familiar with both would notice? At a time when there were numerous versions of *Tannhäuser* being produced and published, Peretz must have known that some of the readers would make a connection between the two. So again we return to the question of what was the point of adapting a narrative from Wagner, who was for many Polish Jews a well-known anti-Semite?

Perhaps Peretz intentionally subverted Wagner, in essence to say, "Look, I, a Jewish writer, have taken the most German of myths and turned it into something that shows the merits of Jewish learning. In the act of literary adaptation I've used the anti-Semite's works against him to show the virtues of the Jewish in place of the German." However, the problem with this interpretation is that while Peretz took enough of *Tannhäuser* to draw a tie, he did not take enough to make it an outright subversion. If he had intended that to be the case, he would likely have made the parallels more obvious. The ties are too loose for this, and more than likely if it was an overt rewrite, it would have employed satiric elements, a commonplace tool in Jewish literary subversion.

I suggest that Peretz's rewrite lies somewhere in the middle, between an attempt to tie his work closely enough to the original to make it obvious that he was intentionally undermining it and a desire to distance himself from Wagner. I imagine his reasoning was something like the following: "The whole artistic terrain is a field that can be appropriated by the artist. As a writer, I have the freedom to pick and choose the motifs that work for me, be they from German or Jewish society." As a folklorist, what appealed to Peretz were the symbols and myths of folklore, such as the budding staff, and what mattered most was what he did with them: creating Judaically empowering literature. Wagner was an anti-Semite, but *Tannhäuser* was also a representation of German folklore. It is from this, and the archetypal motifs that it offers, that Peretz was inspired to write his story.

Peretz's decision to base a novella on Wagner's opus shows how the act of appropriating folklore can enable a distancing between the art and the artist. The folklore iconography of the blooming staff as redemptive is disassociated from its source in a German myth on Christian virtue, and becomes for Peretz something to appropriate into a Jewish context. Interestingly, where Heine, deeply attached to Germany, used the Tannhäuser myth to satirize Germany and thus to politicize the Romantic impulse, Peretz did the opposite by taking a politically relevant source—the work of an anti-Semite—to seemingly Romanticize it into a pure, depoliticized symbol of redemption.

The evolution of Tannhäuser has gone full circle in Peretz's story. From a medieval ballad about Christian redemption, down through Heine's subversion, followed by Wagner's reconstitution as a nationalistic tale, Peretz's story returns the tale to its original form as a story about redemption. However, in this case it is Jewish rather than Christian redemption.

Using a folk story narrative style (although occasionally in a tongue-in-cheek way) to tell a Judaized version of a German folk ballad, Peretz taps into the appeal of the original as a basis for exploring ideas of sin and redemption. The modern Jewish experience that Peretz was exploring in his life and work, and that he became a figurehead for, could be expressed most directly through the indirect means of a folk story. Furthermore, the return to folklore marks a political act typical of minority groups seeking a means to create a national vision around which they can all be unified. By creating a new Jewish folktale version of the German original, Peretz was taking part in Jewish culture building.

Moreover, Peretz's work, intentionally or not, challenges the idea that originality is the key factor in his construction of modern Jewish culture. Instead, he shows that rewriting another text can be an immensely creative act. His tale displays this by using a controversial source text: a trope employed to inspire German nationalism as the basis for a story about Jewish empowerment. The story shows Peretz's readership that they have many available choices for navigating the modern world.

In Safed, the Jews of his tale were facing horrible anti-Jewish violence, and this external reality is the largest variation between the creations of Peretz and Wagner. In Wagner's opera, Tannhäuser does not have to deal with any external political traumas, but instead has the power and freedom to embrace his own destiny without being influenced by external complications like race and religion. It is a level playing field for him, and the quest that he undergoes is a spiritual and individualistic one. Peretz alters this in a most radical way. For the Jew, there is no such level playing field. While he may seek out his own path, because he is Jewish the choice is inevitably influenced by how much political and personal freedom the broader world grants him. For Chananiah's father-in-law for example, life begins grimly with the loss of his entire family in anti-Jewish riots. The importance of this variation cannot be underestimated. It alters the whole story, and it makes sense that Hiya's path of redemption turns inwards to shield himself from the larger world, a world that has literally exterminated his own family.

The Jewish path for redemption is a cloistered one of learning and retreat from non-Jewish surroundings. The Jews of Eastern Europe in 1904, when Peretz wrote this, were facing new anti-Semitic terrors: the Kishinev pogrom had broken out the previous year and because of its level of violence it had a profound influence on Jewish life. Peretz's tale offers readers forms of retreat from the violent world that are both highly dignified and extremely Jewish. Instead of reacting to the terror through prayer, as was the premodern way, or by physically fighting back, as the great Hebrew poet Haim Bialik urged that same year in his famous poem Be'ir Hahareyga (In the City of Slaughter), Peretz offers a third alternative, as Hiya says to Chananiah, "stop only destroying: you need to build instead." [65] The best path to confront mass anti-Semitism is to build a strong Jewish culture, to make a dignified retreat into Jewish study, to find true love and be willing to sacrifice oneself for it, and to use the Torah as a guidepost for an ethical life. In Peretz's rendering, texts, be they his own tales or the Jewish ones that Chananiah turns to, are the real weapons for combating those who wish to destroy the Jews.

By taking the most typical and standard of German tropes, as put forth by the anti-Semitic Wagner, and making it into a motif to show how to live a good Jewish life during a time of political terror, Peretz taught his readers that any piece of culture can be transformed into a positive guidepost to empower them. In Peretz's other *Folkstimlikhe-geshikhtn* (Tales in a Folk Style), he showed his readership that Jewish folk culture had deep and authentic wells of creativity that they could tap. In *Mesires-nefesh*, rather than turning to Jewish indigenous culture, he instead mined the resources of Germanic volk culture. By so doing, he made all folk resources, be they Jewish or otherwise, tools to strengthen Jewish culture. Moreover, any hierarchy of culture, of German over Jewish, is leveled. *Mesires-nefesh* gives both the medium and the message: the medium of transforming Western cultural tropes for the Jewish good, the message of a man transforming himself by returning to Jewish culture. In Peretz's rendering, his hope is that the pen is indeed mightier than the sword.

Notes

1. For insights into prison life at the time, see Rosa Luxemburg's letters discussing her stay as a political prisoner in Warsaw in 1906, in *Rosa Luxemburg: Letters to Karl and Luise Kautsky from 1896 to 1918*, ed. Luise Kautsky, trans. Louis P. Lochner (New York: Robert McBride and Co., 1925), 116-21.

2. For discussions of Peretz's arrest and prison stay, see the Yiddish essay, G. Eisner, "Y. L. Peretz's Arrest in 1899," in the *Yivo-bleter* (1933), 5:353-61 and Mordechai Spektor, "In tseyntn pavilyon (fun mayne zikhroynes)," in *Tsum ondenk fun I. L. Peretz* (Odessa: Yidishe sektsye bam "gubnarobraz," 1920), 22-24. Also see Mordechai Spektor, *Mit Y. L. Peretz in festung* [With I. L. Peretz in Prison], (Odessa: Farlag literatur, 1919).

3. *Mesires-nefesh* can be found in I. L. Peretz's collection, *Folkstimlikhe geshikhten* [Tales in a Folk Style] (Poland: Vilner farlag, 1925), 155-200. There is also an English translation which is published in a split-page format with the Yiddish original on the left. See Sol Liptzin, ed. and trans., *Peretz* (New York: Yivo, 1947), 30-109.

4. Mordechai Spektor, *Mit Y. L. Peretz in festung* [With I. L. Peretz in Prison], (Odessa: Farlag literatur, 1919).

5. Ruth R. Wisse, "Introduction," in *The I. L. Peretz Reader*, ed. Ruth R. Wisse (New Haven: Yale University Press, 2002), x.

6. The biographical and bibliographical information on Peretz came from the following sources. The most thorough information is found in I. L. Peretz, *Mayne zikhroynes*, in *Ale Verk fun I. L. Peretz* [Collected Works], vol. 11 (New York: CYCO, 1948). The English translation, entitled *My Memoirs*, is found in I. L. Peretz, *I. L. Peretz Reader*, ed. Ruth R. Wisse, trans. Seymour Levitan. (New Haven: Yale University Press, 2002), 265-359. See also the encyclopedia entry, Eliyahu Shulman, "Yitskhok Leyb Peretz," in *Leksikon fun der nayer yidisher litarature*, vol. 7 (New York: CYCO, 1968), 231-84; Ruth R. Wisse, *I. L. Peretz and the Making of Modern Jewish Culture* (Seattle: University of Washington Press, 1991), 231-83; Ken Frieden, *Classic Yiddish Fiction: Abramovitsh, Sholem Aleichem, and Peretz* (Albany: SUNY Press, 1995), 225-309; Nachman Mayzel, *I. L. Peretz: zayn lebn un shafn* (New York: YKUF, 1945); Ruth R. Wisse, Introduction, in *The I. L. Peretz Reader* (New Haven: Yale University Press, 2002), x-xxx; David G. Roskies, *A Bridge of Longing: The Lost Art of Yiddish Storytelling* (Cambridge: Harvard University Press, 1995), 99-156.

7. For an interesting discussion of the perception, and reality, of cheder educations, see the chapter "Reinventing Heders" in Steve Zipperstein, *Imagining Russian Jewry: Memory, History, Identity* (Seattle: University of Washington Press, 1999).

8. *Mayne zikhroynes* are found in I. L. Peretz, *Ale Verk fun I. L. Peretz* [Collected Works], vol. 11 (New York: CYCO, 1948). The English translation, entitled *My Memoirs*, is found in I. L. Peretz, *I. L. Peretz Reader*, ed. Ruth R. Wisse, trans. Seymour Levitan (New Haven: Yale University Press, 2002), 265-359. Critical analysis of the Peretz's memoirs include Mikhail Krutikov, *Yiddish Fiction and the Crisis of Modernity, 1905-1914* (Stanford: Stanford University Press, 2001), 200-09, and David G. Roskies, "A shlisl tsu Peretz's zikhroynes" [A Key to Peretz's Memoirs], *Di Goldene Keyt* 99 (1979): 132-59.

9. Nachman Mayzel, *I. L. Peretz: zayn lebn un shafn* (New York: YKUF, 1945), 32.

10. I. L. Peretz, *My memoirs*, in *The I. L. Peretz Reader*, ed. Ruth R. Wisse, trans. Seymour Levitan (New Haven: Yale University Press, 2002), 344. For the Yiddish original see *Mayne zikhroynes* in I. L. Peretz, *Ale Verk fun I. L. Peretz* [Collected Works] (New York: CYCO, 1948), 11:112.

11. Ibid., English, 346; Yiddish, 113.

12. Ibid., English, 321; Yiddish, 76.

13. As quoted in Ken Frieden, *Classic Yiddish Fiction: Abramovitsh, Sholem Aleichem, and Peretz* (Albany: SUNY Press, 1995), 238 and also as recalled in Nachman Mayzel, *I. L. Peretz: zayn lebn un shafn* (New York: YKUF, 1945), 69.

14. For a comprehensive history of Jewish life in Warsaw, in which Peretz makes regular appearances, see Jacob Shatski, *Geshikhte fun yidn in Varshe*, vol. 3 (New York: Yivo, 1953).

15. Nachman Mayzel, *I. L. Peretz: zayn lebn un shafn* (New York: YKUF, 1945), 113.

16. "Impressions of a Journey through the Tomaszow Region" in I. L. Peretz, *The I. L. Peretz Reader*, ed. Ruth R. Wisse, trans. Milton Himmelfarb (New Haven: Yale University Press, 2002), 60. The first pieces from the Impressions came out in 1891 in *Di yidishe bibliotek*.

17. The translation can be found in I. L. Peretz, *The I. L. Peretz Reader*, ed. Ruth R. Wisse, trans. Milton Himmelfarb (New Haven: Yale University Press, 2002), 20-84.

18. Ruth R. Wisse, *I. L. Peretz and the Making of Modern Jewish Culture* (Seattle: University of Washington Press, 1991), 25.

19. Nachman Mayzel discusses his job and outlines his pay raises in *I. L. Peretz: zayn lebn un shafn* (New York: YKUF, 1945), 119-22.

20. Rosa Peretz-Laks, *Arum Peretzn (zikhroynes un batrakhtungen)* (Warsaw: Literarishe bleter, 1935), 7.

21. See Sholem Asch, "My First Meeting with Peretz," in *In This World and Next: Selected Writings of I. L. Peretz*, trans. Moshe Spiegel (New York: Thomas Yoseloff, 1958), 349-51.

22. Chone Shmeruk, "Aspects of the History of Warsaw as a Yiddish Literary Centre," in *Studies from Polin: From Shtetl to Socialism*, ed. Antony Polonsky (London: Littman Library for Jewish Civilization, 1990), 129.

23. Ruth R. Wisse, *I. L. Peretz and the Making of Modern Jewish Culture* (Seattle: University of Washington Press, 1991), xiii-xv.

24. David Frishman's obituary quote as recounted in A. A. Roback, "A Psychologist Evaluates Peretz," in *In This World and Next: Selected Writings of I. L. Peretz*, trans. Moshe Spiegel (New York: Thomas Yoseloff, 1958), 362. Nachman Mayzel describes him in a similar manner in *I. L. Peretz: zayn lebn un shafn* (New York: YKUF, 1945), 102-03.

25. As recalled in Rosa Peretz-Laks, *Arum Peretzn (zikhroynes un batrakhtungen)* (Warsaw: Literarishe bleter, 1935), 4. This memoir offers an honest portrait of Peretz, warts and all, in the latter part of his life.

26. Ibid., 19-21.

27. The Yiddish modernist writer, Lamed Shapiro, humorously discusses the first time he "called" on the famous writer, and how intimidating this was to him, in *Der shrayber geyt in kheyder* (Los Angeles: Farlag Aleyn, 1945), 8. The anecdote is translated in Lamed Shapiro, *The Cross and Other Jewish Stories by Lamed Shapiro*, ed. Leah Garrett (New Haven: Yale University Press, 2007), xi-xii. Sholem Asch also wrote an essay about being a young writer visiting Peretz, entitled "My First Meeting with Peretz," in *In This World and Next: Selected Writings of I. L. Peretz*, trans. Moshe Spiegel (New York: Thomas Yoseloff, 1958), 343-51.

28. See A. Mukdoni, "How I. L. Peretz Wrote His Folk Tales" in *In This World and Next: Selected Writings of I. L. Peretz*, trans. Moshe Spiegel (New York: Thomas Yoseloff, 1958), 352.

29. As recalled by Rosa Peretz-Laks in *Arum Peretzn (zikhroynes un batrakhtungen)* (Warsaw: Literarishe bleter, 1935), 8-10.

30. Ibid., 68.

31. See Mordechai Spektor, "In tseyntn pavilyon (fun mayne zikhroynes)," in *Tsum ondenk fun I. L. Peretz* (Odessa: Yidishe sektsye bam "gubnarobraz") (1920), 22-24. This account of the prison stay describes how awful it was for Peretz to be in jail, how he yearned to escape outdoors, and he cried with joy when he was released.

32. Nachman Mayzel, *I. L. Peretz: zayn lebn un shafn* (New York: YKUF, 1945), 171.

33. A. Mukdoni, "How I. L. Peretz Wrote His Folk Tales," in *In This World and Next: Selected Writings of I. L. Peretz*, trans. Moshe Spiegel (New York: Thomas Yoseloff, 1958), 354.

34. Dan Miron, *The Image of the Shtetl and Other Studies of Modern Jewish Literary Imagination* (Syracuse: Syracuse University Press, 2000), 80.

35. The brief essay "Vos iz taytsh folkstimlekh?" [What does folkstimlekh mean?] asserts that labeling the tales *Folkstimlekhe geshikhtn* is meant to suggest a stylized, rewritten folktale because "geshikhtn" connotes histories or stories that have a previous incarnation. In *Yidishe sprakh* 33 (1974): 51-52.

36. A. Mukdoni, "How I. L. Peretz Wrote His Folk Tales" in *In This World and Next: Selected Writings of I. L. Peretz*, trans. Moshe Spiegel (New York: Thomas Yoseloff, 1958), 359.

37. Ken Frieden, *Classic Yiddish Fiction: Abramovitsh, Sholem Aleichem, and Peretz* (Albany: SUNY Press, 1995), 242, 255.

38. Ibid., 251.

39. Peretz's statements to the Congress, entitled "Oyf der Tshernovitzer sprakh konferentz," can be found in *Ale Verk fun Y. L. Peretz* (New York: CYCO, 1948), 10-11:293-96.

40. Ruth R. Wisse, *I. L. Peretz and the Making of Modern Jewish Culture* (Seattle: University of Washington Press, 1991), 108.

41. In June, 1984, "Levels of Devotion" was performed as an opera at the Jewish Theological Seminary in New York. Raymond Scheindlin wrote the opera version of Peretz's story as "Miriam and the Angel of Death." For an extremely positive review of the performance by Ben W. Belfer, see *The Journal of Synaggogue Music* (June 1984): 3-7.

42. David G. Roskies, *A Bridge of Longing: The Lost Art of Yiddish Storytelling* (Cambridge: Harvard University Press, 1995), 127.

43. The only detailed comparison of *Mesires-nefesh* and Wagner's *Tannhäuser* is found in Sol Litzin's introduction to the volume that he edited and translated, *Peretz* (New York: Yivo, 1947), 23-29. Parenthetical page citations below refer to this version.

44. I. L. Peretz, *My memoirs*, in *The I. L. Peretz Reader*, ed. Ruth R. Wisse, trans. Seymour Levitan (New Haven: Yale University Press, 2002), 335.

45. Ibid., 333.

46. For a detailed discussion of the differences between Jewish and Christian notions of travel and adventure, see my book: Leah Garrett, *Journeys beyond the Pale: Yiddish Travel Writing in the Modern World* (Madison: University of Wisconsin Press, 2003).

47. David G. Roskies shows how the ending mimics a story for the Babylonian Talmud, Shabbat 156b, which describes how Rabbi Akiba's daughter outwits snakes who intend to bite her in her bridal chamber. See David G. Roskies, *A Bridge of Longing: The Lost Art of Yiddish Storytelling* (Cambridge: Harvard University Press, 1995), 132.

48. Ruth R. Wisse, *I. L. Peretz and the Making of Modern Jewish Culture* (Seattle: University of Washington Press, 1991), 90.

49. David G. Roskies, *A Bridge of Longing: The Lost Art of Yiddish Storytelling* (Cambridge: Harvard University Press, 1995), 127-28.

50. I. L. Peretz, "Self-sacrifice," in *Peretz*, ed. and trans. Sol Liptzin (New York: Yivo, 1947), 38.

51. Ruth R. Wisse, *I. L Peretz and the Making of Modern Jewish Culture* (Seattle: University of Washington Press, 1991), 122-23, n. 21.

52. Nahum Sokolow, *Perzenlekhkeytz* [Personalities] (Buenos Aires: Tsentral Farband fun Poylishe yidn in Argentine, 1948), 171.

53. Sol Liptzin, Introduction, in *Peretz*, ed. and trans. Sol Liptzin (New York: Yivo, 1947), 25.

54. Peretz also explored the Venus theme in his early tale, "Venus and Shulamith" (1889). In this story, he has a Yeshiva student explain to his incredulous friend about the mythological Greek goddess Venus. The friend responds to the explanation by dissecting it from a traditional Jewish perspective and contrasting the negative Venus with the positive Jewish Shulamith. See I. L. Peretz, "Venus un shulamis," in *Di yidishe folksbibliotek* (1889), 2:142-47. The translation is in Seth Wolitz, "Venus and Shulamith," in *I. L. Peretz Reader*, ed. Ruth R. Wisse (New Haven: Yale University Press, 2002), 88-93.

55. One cannot help but think of Peretz himself in this role as Pope, having the young Jewish writers of Warsaw come to him to gain admittance to the literary elite.

56. For a consideration of the budding staff in Christian iconography see George Ferguson, *Signs and Symbols in Christian Art* (Oxford: Oxford University Press, 1961), 73, 127. For a general study of the budding staff see James George Frazer, *The Golden Bough: A Study in Magic and Religion*, vol. 1, and in particular chapter 68 (New York: Macmillan, 1960).

57. From the JPS translation of the Jewish Bible: *Tanakh A New Translation of the Holy Scriptures According to the Traditional Hebrew Text* (New York: Jewish Publication Society, 1985), 237.

58. The story, "Reb Judah Hasid and the Apostate" is not included in the Yiddish reprint, *Mayse-bukh*, ed. Shmuel Rozshanski (Buenos Aires: YIVO,1969), but can be found in the English translation entitled, *Ma'aseh Book: Book of Jewish Tales and Legends*, trans. Moses Gaster (Philadelphia: Jewish Publication Society, 1934), 2:380-83. The story can also be found in the Judeo-German 1929 edition, adapted from the 1723

Amsterdam edition of the *Mayse-bukh*, entitled, *Maasse-Buch: Buch der Sagen und Legenden aus Talmud and nebst Volkserzahlungen in judisch-deutscher Sprache*, ed. Bertha Pappenheim (Frankfurt, 1929), 190-93. Dov Sadan, in his essay, "Mateh Aharon vetse'etsa'au," documents the evolution of the flowering staff motif in the Mayse bukh and its relationship to how the staff blooms in *Tannhäuser*, in his book, *Ben she'ilah le-kinyan* (Tel Aviv: Tel Aviv University, 1968), 171-208.

59. See Rella Kushelevsky, "Ha-mateh haporeah-iyyun be'ikkaron hamkhonen shel hasidrah hatematit," *Jerusalem Studies in Jewish Folklore* 13/14 (1991-92): 205-28.

60. His niece Rosa noted that Peretz had "no musical ear," which may help explain why he makes the visual aspects of his appropriation central, as recalled in Rosa Peretz-Laks, *Arum Peretzn (zikhroynes un batrakhtungen)* (Warsaw: Literarishe bleter, 1935), 14.

61. David G. Roskies, *A Bridge of Longing: The Lost Art of Yiddish Storytelling* (Cambridge: Harvard University Press, 1995), 128.

62. Yudel Mark discusses Peretz's narrative strategies in his essay, "The Language of Y. L. Peretz," *Yivo Annual of Jewish Social Science* 4 (1945): 64-79.

63. Sol Liptzin, Introduction, in *Peretz*, ed. and trans. Sol Liptzin (New York: Yivo, 1947), 26-27.

64. Miriam's attempt at self sacrifice also mimics the plot of Wagner's opera, *The Flying Dutchman*, which climaxes with a woman, Senta, offering her life for her beloved Dutchman. Her sacrifice proves her loyalty and devotion to him. After throwing herself off a cliff into the ocean, she rises and ascends towards heaven in the arms of the Dutchman. Through her sacrifice, the Dutchman is redeemed from his endless wandering, and the two are together forever in heaven. Peretz may well have been conflating these two operas, taking the theme of self-sacrifice from the *Flying Dutchman* and the themes of self-sacrifice, sin, and redemption, from *Tannhäuser*.

65. Ruth R. Wisse points out that Peretz was uncomfortable with the ideology propagated in Bialik's poem and reacted to it by doing a translation of the original into Yiddish that was so "weak" that Sholem Aleichem "accused him of intentionally sabotaging the text." See Ruth Wisse, *I. L. Peretz and the Making of Modern Jewish Culture* (Seattle: University of Washington Press, 1991), 61.

Conclusion

The Transformed Knight

The medieval knight Tannhäuser has been on a remarkable journey in the course of this book, during which he has come into contact with, and been transformed by, three of the most important figures in the construction of Jewish culture in modern Europe. While he himself has changed, he has also been a tool for change that has been used to transform those with whom he comes into contact. Heine, Herzl, and Peretz all used the knight to further their cultural work, whether to challenge the prevalent rhetoric of German nationalism, to strengthen Jewish cohesiveness, or to offer a lesson on survival for the Jewish community.

Heinrich Heine changed the knight from a hero desperately wanting to escape his sins to a bored thrill seeker looking for adventure. Where the original Tannhäuser was temporally located in medieval times and seeking future redemption, Heine turned the timeline on its head by transplanting him into the claustrophobic present with no way to move forward. Heine's poem ends with Tannhäuser living a stagnant life with the house-frau Venus, unable to seek out new adventures like his medieval counterpart. In "Der Tannhäuser," Heine levels an attack on a contemporary Germany, which is stuck in the past and censoring future-looking artists such as himself. The present-day Germany that the knight travels over, before returning to a permanent home in the Venusberg, is caught in a time warp of decay and ruin, unable to move culturally forward.

In transplanting the medieval knight into current-day Germany, Heine overshadows the present with this symbol of the past and therein infects all locations of the poem with a medieval stagnation. In both the form and the content of his work, Heine thus levels an attack on Germany and its most cherished tropes.

In Richard Wagner's opera *Tannhäuser und der Sängerkrieg auf der Wartburg* (Tannhäuser and the Song Contest on the Wartburg), the knight transforms again. Now he embodies a lost soul who is torn between epochs: the black-and-white medieval past, where redemption can obliterate and remove one's sins, and the grey present, where the search for salvation is filled with pitfalls and no clear answers. Yet even in the midst of the chaos of his search, Tannhäuser is a hero precisely because he takes control of his own destiny and actively seeks answers. He is a model of keeping faith in a greater reward who, in the end, dies in order to receive the light of pure love from his counterpart, the equally torn soul, Elisabeth.

Wagner was unable to find a way to rectify the two compulsive drives of his modern hero: the desire for a purified redemption, and the urge for sensual experiences. In his opera, the shallow cad from Heine's poem becomes a man torn between the past where stability prevailed, the present where everything is uncertain, and a future of eternal salvation through death. However, by having the closing music of the opera bring together the conservative beat of the Wartburg with the chaotic sounds of the Venusberg, Wagner offers a musical joining together of the two spheres. In art the sides can merge, while in the life of the soul they are severed. In contrast, Heine's critique is leveled against the Germans who are seeking to transplant the ideals of the heroic medieval past into the current time, but are thwarted by the stifling energy of the present. Thus, in his poem the hero lives for eternity in the Venusberg instead of dying for his Christian redemption.

In both works, the knight must either be in the pagan or the Christian sphere, with both spaces cut off completely from the present world; however, Wagner offers the possibility that music can rectify the two sides. Heine's modern-day knight is too cynical to seek Christian redemption, and instead finds nothing but a moribund culture. Where Wagner's opera shows that the arts can help the modern man in his quest for a fulfilling and holistically unified life, Heine has lost hope in the redemptive possibilities of German art.

In I. L. Peretz's Yiddish novella, *Mesires-nefesh* (Levels of Devotion), the knight transforms so completely as to be barely recognizable; everything—his clothes, name, languages, lands he travels through, relationships—is utterly Judaized. And it is in Peretz's work alone that Tannhäuser's legacy continues into the future rather than dying with him, as in Wagner, or being locked away forever from time, as in Heine's poem. In Peretz's work, the final words of the tale are: "The story of the great luminary who was born of the union of Chananiah and Miriam and of the happiness that came to Reb Hiya in his later years-this story we shall (God willing) relate on another occasion. We merely want to add that the Achnai that let itself be fooled was never again entrusted with any further missions and is indeed no longer seen on earth." Peretz has given his Jewish knight, Chananiah, a happy ending. He lives, his beloved lives, and they have a son who is a "great luminary." Not only that, but they have outwitted the evil snake who is now permanently banished from earth. Peretz has thus restored the tale back into a remarkable legend, like the medieval original, where miracles still happen.

Peretz offers his Jewish readership, who have just suffered the communal trauma of the Kishinev pogrom, a legend with which to salve their wounds. The knight has shown them the virtue of a life devoted to Jewish learning and is a hero for the troubled times, while the narrative's construction, emulating in form and content myriad aspects of the Jewish oral tale, shows the richness of Jewish folklore. Where Wagner's adventurer is riddled with angst, Peretz's is redeemed on earth by figuring out the correct path. Yet, Peretz's hero is also temporally located in the distant past. He lacks the uncertainty of the modern era, although his troubles are no less profound, since they ultimately stem from the pogroms that wiped out many in his community. Both Wagner and Heine used the knight to shed light on contemporary Germany while Peretz did something completely different.

His hero is located entirely in the past, although his descendents stretch into the future. This is a means for Peretz to show his readership that they can reach back into Jewish traditions to help them in the difficult present. This is the opposite of the fissure between past and present that is so apparent in Wagner and Heine, where there is no possible future. With Peretz we have a continuum where the past needs to flow into the future and where Jews are not cut off from time but instead locate themselves in its flow. Rather than searching for new ways to deal with anti-Jewish violence, they need to remember the means of resistance that have always worked and that have banished evil, as Chananiah and Miriam's actions exiled the snake.

Theodor Herzl's relationship with the story of the knight is of a very different type than we have with Heine, Wagner, and Peretz, who were inspired to create art. Herzl, in contrast, used the opera as one instrument among many as he sought to clarify his political program. He was not rewriting the tale but instead tapping into its emotional potential to inspire himself, and the Jewish masses, to transform their world view and to embrace Jewish nationalism.

Heine, Wagner, Herzl, and Peretz, like Tannhäuser in his later incarnations, were master-singers. Yet, all used different forms of discourse when reworking the Tannhäuser legend: poetry, opera, political prose, and fiction. The differences between the genres played a role in the type of story that they told. Heine used the same traditional medieval ballad rhyme scheme as the 1515 version: four lines per stanza with the final word of the second and forth line frequently rhyming. In both form and content, Heine created a dissonance between his version of the ballad and the original and established a satiric discord between his parody and the original. In content, the contrast between the iconic knight's previous heroism and current debasement satirizes the figure.

Wagner perhaps had the richest palate to work with, since the opera form could potentially bring together words, music, and the visual. It is from this tapestry that he stitched together a production where the music expressed the unity between paganism and Christianity, and conservatism and rebellious sensualism, while Tannhäuser's words and the visual layout of Wartburg and Venusberg showed the gap between the spheres.

Relationship with the Preceding Version

The most important contrast between Heine, Wagner, Herzl, and Peretz was their relationship to the incarnation of the legend that inspired them. Heine's poem was a rewrite of the medieval ballad as it was published in 1806 in *Des Knaben Wunderhorn* (The Wondrous Horn of the Boy). Wagner's opera was directly tied to Heine's subversive poem, but also grew out of other sources such as Ludwig Tieck's "The Faithful Eckart and Tannenhäuser" (Der getreue Eckart und der Tannenhäuser) and E. T. A. Hoffmann's piece about a Wartburg singing contest entitled *The Singers' Contest* (Der Kampf der Sänger). Both Herzl and Peretz were responding to Wagner's opera.

In other words, each adaptation was written and should be read or viewed with the original somewhere in the background. And in each case the artist was seeking to reappropriate the trope to express not only his perspective but to draw a light on how it contrasted with the previous form of the meme. For Heine's parodic representation, this meant that his poem seeks to subvert the staid original and undermine a culture that holds it in high esteem. Wagner's serious opera is tied directly to the medieval one, although he aims to rework and better it in order to captivate a contemporary audience. Moreover, Wagner's opera can also be read as attempting a rejuvenation of a trope that Heine destroyed in his poem. Although we will never know the full extent of Heine's influence, since Wagner chose to hide it, Heine's poem was clearly of central importance in the creation of his opus. And perhaps by distancing his opera from Heine's poem, Wagner hoped to also publically minimize Heine's influence on him, in particular the ugly fact that his other opera, *The Flying Dutchman*, also was based on a Heine poem. (Wagner only reluctantly admitted in 1843 that *The Flying Dutchman* was in large part inspired by Heine's poem of the same name.)

Theodor Herzl and I. L. Peretz, in contrast, were responding to the opera of a prominent anti-Semite. How they chose to deal with this demarcates their very different understandings of Jewish society. Herzl was comfortable using Wagner for his own ends, as is most evident when Herzl opened the Second Zionist Congress to the overture of *Tannhäuser*.

Peretz gave no public reference to Wagner's role, simply taking for his own use the motifs and content of the opera. Where Herzl believed the Jews would have to leave Europe to build a Jewish Europe in exile, for Peretz the Jews needed to have a strong life *in* Europe. They could do this by Judaizing the broader world, much as Peretz did in appropriating the Tannhäuser meme. Intentionally or not, in both cases the joke was on Wagner: the anti-Semite's art was transformed to inspire the Jewish masses to save themselves. Moreover, where Wagner assails the "babble" of the Jews in *Judaism in Music*, I. L. Peretz Judaizes the knight's speech by turning his voice from German into Yiddish. Peretz's novella makes the derided language of the Jews a medium of high art and therein uses Wagner's opera to elevate Jewish discourse and weaken its derision.

When Peretz transforms Wagner's opera into a morality tale for his audience, much as Wagner did, he restores the dignity of the legend by imparting the story in a serious tone and presenting a world where miracles are still possible. Both Peretz and Wagner set the story in medieval times, although in Peretz's case it is a Jewish locale where the Pope is replaced by a Yeshivah head. Peretz has his tale unfold in the same time period to teach a different set of lessons: that the past was also plagued by pogroms but that the Jews nevertheless survived and even thrived, as they will now, and that Jewish history is cyclical and bad times are followed by good and vice versa. The only way to thus weather time is to hold onto Jewish values, for those alone can still bring minor miracles. They are the real bulwark against the vagaries of history.

Personal Responses

On a personal level, Heine, Herzl, and Peretz all were at a stage in their lives where they could relate to the theme of an individual seeking transformation and rebirth. The knight Tannhäuser has awakened to the darker, erotic underworld and can never return to his former naïveté. This idea resonated with attempts they were each making to change their art after having recently become "awakened" to some type of individual or communal Jewish trauma. In Heinrich Heine's case, it was the censoring of his works by the Prussians. For Theodor Herzl, the Dreyfus affair and the election of Karl Lueger were the final straws proving the permanency of anti-Semitism and the bankruptcy of assimilation as a solution. For I. L. Peretz, his job overseeing the Jewish cemetery which brought him into daily contact with the poor and their troubles, combined with the aftermath of Kishinev, led him to appropriate and Judaize folklore to strengthen his culture.

For all four artists, Tannhäuser is a figure who is a rebel against the norms of society and this must have spoken to them on a personal level. For Heine, in an artistic dry spell in Paris, perennially broke, too pessimistic to find comfort in any single ideological position, and censored by the authorities, the knight of the medieval ballad who follows his own path and is in the end proven right must have been a comfort in his distress. For Wagner, poor and in exile in a city he hated while writing groundbreaking operas which many were reluctant to appreciate, the knight's search to find an authentic path showed him to be a kindred soul. For Herzl, who was considering propagating an idea that could make him an object of derision in assimilationist circles, the knight's quest for redemption at all costs must have been emotionally soothing. And finally, for Peretz, seeking to be a successful writer while in a terribly depressing job where he was underpaid and underused as compared with his previous work as a lawyer, the knight's attempts to transcend his base needs for the greater good must have been comforting as he sought to transcend the mire of daily life in order to create a viable culture for the Jews of Eastern Europe.

Venus

For all four men, the figure of Venus enabled them to reflect on their own relationships with women. Wagner had frequent affairs and struggled throughout his life with his sexual urges that he desired to sublimate in order to live a
virtuous life. Heine and Herzl both believed themselves to be caught in intense
and troubled relationships and they likely found in the story of Tannhäuser and
Venus a mirror to their own inability to break free of their wives. For Peretz in
Eastern Europe, to speak to his readership in terms that they would not reject, he
transformed Venus into a cloying mother whose actions were similar to his own
mother forcing him into an unhappy first marriage. The four men's understanding of the Venus character reflects on their understandings of gender relations.

Paris

Heine, Wagner and Herzl all came to Tannhäuser while in Paris. Being at a distance from Germany brought each to return to the homeland through one of
its most popular legends, and each embedded his view of Paris in the use of the
meme. Wagner thus made the German landscape positive and exemplified by the
Wartburg castle—even though he also was critiquing it in the conservative castle
music. Heine, in contrast, made the German landscape completely negative.

Heine's subversive poem was like a letter of break-up to the home he had
held a conflicted yet deep love for but which had rejected him. His strategic assertion that Venus was based on a Parisian suggested that he was seeking to view
France as an alternate homeland. Wagner, who discovered Tannhäuser through
Heine in Paris, created a mythical foundation story in which he wrote the opera upon returning to Germany and escaping corrupt France. Where Heine thus
sought to assert the centrality of Paris in creating his poem, Wagner wanted to
distance his ties to France and raise the importance of Germany as a catalyst.
Wagner thus returned to the noble past in his opera as a means to fight the vapid
excess of current day Paris, while Heine's used a modernist perspective to de-
construct the idealized medieval world. And Herzl, homesick in Paris, found in
Wagner's opera one tool among many to help him sort out his Zionist mandate.

Christianity, Sin, and Redemption

The Christian aspects of the ballad were understood and dealt with in different
ways by each of the four. The 1515 ballad presents conflicted views of Christianity. On the one hand it evinces anticlerical tendencies in its presentation of a
misguided and mistaken Pope, while it also elevates Mother Mary as a force of
salvation for the troubled knight. Whether or not the portrayal of the Pope was
intended originally to be negative, both Heine and Wagner understood it to be
so and reacted to that in their works.

Heine, who dabbled in St. Simonianism, which sought to juxtapose a sensual worldview over the modern times, and who mistrusted organized Christianity since he felt it suppressed the vitality of the pagan urges, draws the Pope as a ridiculous and weak figure. Moreover, as a Jew who had experienced his fair share of anti-Semitism, it must have appealed to him to work with a ballad that seems to overtly criticize Christianity, or at least its clerical aspects.

Wagner shows very contradictory views of Christianity in his opera. On the one hand the Pope is mistaken in not giving Tannhäuser his absolution. Yet, on the other, Elisabeth is a positive Christian heroine who returns those around her to the true path (even if she is still conflicted about her own urges). Wagner's mixed views of the subject were manifested in his remarks, both asserting and denying that the opera is a Christian morality tale.

Peretz's tale shares some of Wagner's messages about organized religion, although in this case it is Judaism instead of Christianity. In his novella, Yeshivah heads are as fallible as Wagner's Pope. However, in the Jewish context, where the leaders of the community are no closer to God than the average woman or man, the fallibility is far less remarkable than with a Pope who is closer to God. In all three cases, however, as with the 1515 ballad, the trip to Rome (or in Peretz's case to the Jerusalem Yeshivah), is not rendered but only recounted after the events. Thus it is how Tannhäuser interprets the meeting that is as crucial as what has occurred.

In all cases the concept of redemption shifts. Heine's cynicism has obliterated all absolute notions about sin and salvation. Here, paganism is embodied by a weak housewife desperate to keep her man, while Christianity is symbolized by a Pope with no power. There is no possibility for redemption because in the free-wheeling contemporary world, real sinning has become boring rather than intoxicating. For Wagner, redemption follows the traditional Christian schema of sin and absolution, culminating in Tannhäuser's redemption and death. This is perhaps a lesson for the German volk that they should embrace self sacrifice for the greater good. And for Peretz, redemption becomes Judaized. What matters is living a life devoted to Jewish learning and ethics. By so doing, one can be "saved" on earth, as occurs with Chananiah. In Wagner's opera, the knight's life ends with a return to Christ, while in Peretz's novella, Chananiah's life moves forward with a return to positive Judaism.

Lessons for Cultural and Jewish Studies

The evolution of the Tannhäuser meme has shed light on how cultural products move between societies. For the Jewish people, their portrayal as the "people of the book" is, in fact, true. Often without recourse to political power and its institutions, in much of European Jewish society before the late nineteenth century social life was institutionalized in Jewish discourse, and those who produced books often became akin to statesmen. The circulation of knowledge in the Jewish world thus had unique aspects tied to the exclusion of Jews from the centers of power. A writer was not merely an author, as we see in Christian European society, but was also imbued with political status and power by his or her ability to use discourse for Jewish culture building.

For the politically disenfranchised Jews of Europe, living in lands where they were a minority population who were discriminated against, appropriating the symbols and ideas of the majority culture was one way to infuse themselves with powerful means of group resistance. It enabled them to build their own culture on their own terms by claiming the goods of the majority society through acts of Judaization. This in turn subverted the original message of the non-Jewish trope. From the Golden Age of Hebrew poetry in tenth- and eleventh-century Spain, where the poems fused together the subjects of Jewish life with the cadences of Arabic poetry, to the 1541 Yiddish *Bovo-Bukh*, which was an adaptation of an Italian romance, Jews have always subverted, rewritten, and reworked the literature, art, and symbolism of the broader world as a way to enrich the Jewish environ. When Wagner was reworking the Tannhäuser meme, he did so as a member of the nation that held power and was free to partake of its cultural assets. For a Jew, in contrast, during that time period, he or she often created art from a more tenuous position. For the Jewish audience, the transformation of the European trope into a Jewish one legitimizes it and makes it accessible, while at the same time it "de-Europeanizes" the original meme. Thus, the dominant culture is transferred into the home space of Jewish life. It is a subtle but powerful means of raising Jewish culture while minimizing the power of the broader world.

In constructing a viable Jewish culture in Poland, Peretz has no interest in fusing together elements of both the Jewish and Christian worlds. Although he embraced Polish nationalism as a youth, by the time he wrote *Mesires-nefesh*, Peretz had given up on the idea that assimilation into Poland would strengthen Jewish life and ease its suffering. In contrast Heine and Herzl were attempting to create a dual Jewish-German identity and found in Tannhäuser a lesson on how they could bring together both sets of identifications. These different ways of using the meme reflect the variations in identity between Eastern and Western European Jews.

The Role of Wagner

It is certainly both evocative and confusing that Wagner's opera played a role in Jewish culture building. With Peretz's novella, however, it is easy to accept this because of the manner in which he twisted and overturned Wagner's intentions to strengthen the volk, instead reworking Wagner's opera to inspire the Jewish masses. In the case of Peretz, the relationship between his version and Wagner's original ties his novella into a long tradition of Jewish writers and thinkers using the building blocks of the broader world to create a viable and strong society.

In the relationship between Herzl and Wagner, however, the ties are more troubling and can lead to the mistaken and insidious suggestion that both Zionism and Nazism were somehow rooted in Wagner's art. As previously discussed, this was suggested (and later recanted) by the well-known British Social theorist, Jacqueline Rose in her 2005 book *The Question of Zion*, when she wrote that Herzl and Hitler attended the same performance of *Tannhäuser* in France. And although Paris is the great city of coincidental meetings, J. D. Salinger did bump into Hemingway at the Ritz Hotel bar, and James Joyce and Marcel Proust did once share a taxi cab, the Hitler-Herzl encounter is entirely fictional. By placing the two at the same opera, Herzl's, Wagner's, and Hitler's visions of nationalism are conflated. This idea, moreover, ignores the rich interplay between Jewish and mainstream culture because it posits that the nexus between Jewish and non-Jewish and particularly German culture is so fraught with danger that one can only see the contact as one of the Jew being destroyed by, or even worse, infected by the anti-Semitic mainstream culture. Rather, this story of Tannhäuser shows us quite the opposite. The site of interaction is instead remarkably fluid with creative appropriations of the mainstream cultural narratives.

Tannhäuser Today

The evolution of the Tannhäuser meme underscores the importance of studying societies in the context of the surrounding historical and social environment, rather than in isolation. Culture is produced and developed through interactive moments and Jews have always intermingled with and been influenced by the environments where they live. The use made of Tannhäuser by the Jews herein discussed has been as a tool to subvert, to sabotage, to inspire and to empower. Tannhäuser has been so successfully replicated in Jewish life because its motif of sin and redemption is open to being translated into different contexts: a secular quest, the Jewish struggle for national unity, the individual's search for knowledge. The relationship between the Jewish and German uses of the Tannhäuser myth shows how cultural definitions of nationhood are fluid rather than static, even when nationalists such as Wagner assert that they are not.

This long history of a two-way dialogue between the Jewish and non-Jewish worlds is evident in the evolution of the Tannhäuser meme. Heinrich Heine's poem directly influenced Wagner, while Wagner's opera directly influenced Theodor Herzl and I. L. Peretz. In each case, the meme was transformed to express the variations in culture, standpoint, time period, and language of each of the participants and in each case the simple ballad of 1515 took on rich and resonant new aspects. By ignoring this type of cultural interplay Jewish thinkers are unfairly denied their heritage—by claiming connections to Nazism, or by discounting the way they reworked someone as problematic as Wagner to build their visions of a viable Jewish society.

It is uncomfortable, certainly, to see how Wagner played a role in these Jewish cultural heroes' lives and works; writing about the role of Wagner in Jewish life may lead to more people buying copies of his works and thereby putting money in the coffers of his family estate, some of whom still have troubling ideas about Jewish life in Germany. This is particularly problematic since, of the four men on whom this book has focused, only Wagner has direct descendents today.

Yet in the end what is most interesting and inspiring is not that Heine, Herzl and Peretz used the Tannhäuser myth, but what they did with it. Beginning with Heine, we have a German Jewish poet using a German myth to satirize the culture that produced it. For Peretz, the opera was transformed into a manifesto on being Judaically empowered, both intellectually and spiritually. For Herzl, Wagner's opera became another tool to discover how to boldly nationalize the Jews by means of spectacle and a potential model for ideas on Jewish self-sacrifice and redemption. This creative repositioning, where the iconic German knight becomes reworked to express Jewish visions, bespeaks the manner in which Jewish thinkers and writers have always used the cultural products of the broader society to strengthen and refashion the Jewish milieu, even when they were generated by people as problematic as Richard Wagner.

Concluding Remarks

This is not to assert that Wagner needs to be played in Israel. Israeli political life is extremely complicated, particularly because Israel has such a high proportion of Holocaust survivors. For some of them, Wagner's operas can still open raw wounds. In this case, perhaps the survivors' trauma needs to be weighed against the positive tradition of Jewish appropriations of mainstream symbols. Perhaps at a later point in time, when the Holocaust is not so fresh to those who have personally survived it, the subject should be revisited in Israel.[1]

Whether or not the debate takes place now or in ten years, this historical conversation between Heine, Wagner, Herzl, and Peretz should be considered, as well as all debates about the uses made of art in the Jewish world and whether some art is taboo. If the discussion is not kept open, regardless of whatever conclusions are reached, then the myths discussed during the course of this book, from Hitler's supposed destruction of Heine's grave, to Wagner's creation of the opera in Germany rather than it being inspired by Heine, to the equation of Zionism with Nazism, will trump the reality.

And finally, it is hoped that Israeli orchestras in the future will not be afraid to appropriate and perhaps even subvert Wagner to reflect their own vision, much as these central Jewish thinkers have done. This would be a powerful assertion that Jewish culture is not to be relegated to a relational, marginal position where it is too weak to withstand the dominant culture. And the next time that Daniel Barenboim or others want to try Wagner in Israel, instead of giving the audience selections from *Tristan und Isolde*, perhaps they should slip in a stave or two of *Tannhäuser*.

Notes

1.   In opposition to this idea is Israeli intellectual Na'ama Sheffi, whose writings chart out how opposition to Wagner in Israel is complicated by profound levels of insecurity on how best to commemorate Holocaust remembrance. She argues that "having given Holocaust survivors a special place in Israeli society, how can we then brazenly wait for their deaths in order to discuss more freely the difficult experiences that they carried around with them all their lives?" This quote is from her essay, "Wagner's Emblematic Role: The Case of Holocaust Commemoration in Israel," trans. Martha Grenzeback, in *Richard Wagner for the New Millennium*, ed. Matthew Bribitzer-Stull, Alex Lubet, and Gottfried Wagner (New York: Palgrave Macmillan, 2007), 168. Her book on the subject is *The Ring of Myths: the Israelis, Wagner, and the Nazis* (Sussex: Sussex Academic Press, 2001).

Discussion Questions

1. What does the legacy of Tannhäuser in Jewish culture tell us about the relationship between Jewish and German life during the modern era?

2. What was plot of the original folktale Tannhäuser?

3. What are three reasons why the story of Tannhäuser appealed to Heine, Herzl, and Peretz?

4. Why was the Tannhäuser motif so popular with German nationalists?

5. How did Heinrich Heine adopt and adapt the Tannhäuser folktale?

6. What were three of Heine's intentions for making such a subversive version of the folktale?

7. Where did Richard Wagner claim that he got his inspiration for his opera *Tannhäuser*? What was the true story?

8. When viewing and appreciating a piece of art, should it be considered independently from the artist, even when he or she is a prominent anti-Semite, as is the case with Richard Wagner?

9. How and why did Theodor Herzl find Wagner's opera to be so inspiring?

10. How did Peretz adapt the story of Tannhäuser so that it became Judaized? What were three reasons why he made such major changes to the story?

11. How did Heine, Wagner, and Peretz deal with the motif of "fall and redemption" in the Tannhäuser story? How was Peretz's version more infused with Judaic notions?

12. Why are folktales a good tool for looking at the manner in which a culture views itself and others?

13. What was Venus like in the Tannhäuser versions of Heine, Wagner, and Peretz? What did she symbolize in each of these works?

14. Are there ways that Heine and Herzl, as German Jews, responded differently to adapting Tannhäuser than did Peretz, a Polish Jew?

15. Discuss whether you believe it is appropriate for Wagner's operas to be played in Israel. Give three reasons for and three reasons against performing his work there.

Index

58-59, 125-26; use of Christian motifs
and iconography in, 60; Venus in, 58,
59-60; why he created his opera, 4;
Wolfram in, 58

Tannhäuser: Poet and Legend (Thomas),
10n1

"Tannhäuser im Exil. Zu Heines Legende
Der Tannhäuser" (Zinke), 38n40

Theodor Herzl (Stewart), 93n29, 93n35

Theodor Herzl: A Biography (Bein), 93n29

*Theodor Herzl: From Assimilation to
Zionism* (Kornberg), 75, 91n6, 91n12,
91n14, 93n29

Thomas, J. W., 10n1

Tieck, Ludwig, 9, 25, 31, 49, 128

Timms, Edward, 74, 91n7

"To the Gentile Poet" (Leyb), 5

Toulmin, Stephen, 92n29

*Tragedy of Knighthood, The: Origins of the
Tannhäuser Legend* (Clifton-Everest),
10n1, 10n3

Travel Pictures II (Heinrich Heine), 21

van Geldern, Peira (mother of Heine), 14

Varnhagen, Rachel, 17

"Venus in Exile: *Tannhäuser* Between
Romanticism and Young Germany"
(Borchmeyer), 64n9

"Venus un shulamis" (Venus and Shulamith) (I. L. Peretz), 123n53

"Vermachtnis" (Bequest) (H. Heine), 34

Vienna, 72, 74

Vitlin, Joseph, 5

von Bülow, Hans, 60

von Westernhagen, Curt, 66n47, 68n92

"Vos iz taytsh folkstimlekh?" (What Does
Folkstimlekh Mean?), 122n35

Wagner, Cosima (second wife of Wagner),
46, 49, 60

Wagner, Johanna (mother of Wagner), 42

Wagner, Minna (first wife of Wagner),
40, 42

Wagner, Richard, 12, 22, 64n10, 68n92;
anti-Semitism of, 43-47, 76, 86;
banning of his music in Palestine, 1;
biographies of, 64n10; early life and
work of, 42-43; influence of on opera,
43, 108; stealing of Heine's ideas, 32;
view of Paris, 40; view of the Prussian
government, 41; and the Wartburg
castle, 40-42

Wagner: A Biography (von Westernhagen), 66n47, 68n93

"Wagner Lives: Issues in Autobiography"
(Deathridge), 64n10

"Wagner and the Third Reich: Myths and
Realities" (Potter), 6-7n1

"Wagner's Emblematic Role: The Case of
Holocaust Commemoration in Israel"
(Sheffi), 135n1

"Wagner's Most Medieval Opera" (McFarland), 66n59

Warsaw, 100

"We Shall Not Go to Canossa" (T. Herzl),
84-85

Weiner, Marc, 46, 47

Werner, Michael, 37n32

"Who Did Heine Think He Was?" (Sammons), 37n23

Wilde, Oscar, 50

Wisse, Ruth R., 102, 104, 111, 113, 124n64

Wissenschaft movement, 18

Wittgenstein, Ludwig, 74

Wittgenstein's Vienna (Janik and Toulmin), 92n29

*Yiddish Fiction and the Crisis of Moder-
nity, 1905-1914* (Krutikov), 121n9

Yiddish literature, 102

"Y. L. Peretz's Arrest in 1899" (Eisner),
120n2

Yontev-bletlekh (Holiday Papers), 101

Young Germans movement, 23, 41, 42, 57